MARATHON, CROSS COUNTRY
AND ROAD RUNNING

2.2.

MARATHON, CROSS COUNTRY AND ROAD RUNNING

Cliff Temple

STANLEY PAUL
London

First published 1990

5 7 9 10 8 6 4

First published in the United Kingdom by
Stanley Paul
Random House, 20 Vauxhall Bridge Road, London SW1V 2SA

Random House Australia (Pty) Limited
20 Alfred Street, Milsons Point, Sydney,
New South Wales 2061, Australia

Random House New Zealand Limited
18 Poland Road, Glenfield,
Auckland 10, New Zealand

Random House South Africa (Pty) Limited
PO Box 337, Bergvlei, South Africa

Random House UK Limited Reg. No. 954009

Set in 10/12pt Century Old Style Roman by
Tek Art Ltd, Croydon, Surrey

Printed and bound in Great Britain by
Mackays of Chatham PLC, Chatham, Kent

A CIP catalogue record for this book
is available from the British Library

ISBN 0 09 174331 1

CONTENTS

FOREWORD

When the original version of my book *Cross Country and Road Running* was published in 1980, no-one could have guessed that we were just a short way from a remarkable participatory explosion in distance running.

An activity which had long been considered by some people as just an esoteric offshoot of track and field athletics became, in the succeeding years, much, much bigger than athletics itself. There are probably fewer pole-vaulters in the entire UK, for instance, than the number of runners who now take part in an average modest-sized town centre road race on a Sunday morning.

Within a year of publication of *Cross Country and Road Running* it had become clear that there was a rapidly growing demand for a separate book specifically covering marathon preparation. The result was its complementary volume, *Challenge of the Marathon*, published in 1981.

Throughout the eighties, both these books were regularly revised, but distance running probably changed more dramatically and more rapidly during that short period than it had done in the rest of the twentieth century.

So with the 1990s approaching I decided to start again, and merge *Cross Country and Road Running* and *Challenge of the Marathon* into one completely revised volume. There were already slight overlaps anyway, but by producing a new version, retaining some of the most pertinent sections of the originals, updating others, and introducing completely fresh material, I hope to have arrived at an acceptably comprehensive formula to help you through your preparations for Cross Country, Road and Marathon Running. We may need to revise it again for the 21st century, but I hope this will prove sufficient until then!

Cliff Temple,
Hythe, Kent
March 1990

PROLOGUE

The first smell is usually liniment, wafting through the corridor of the changing rooms as you try to find a spare peg or a corner in one of the crowded dressing rooms to put down your bag. You hear snatches of conversation above the chatter of preparing athletes. . . .

'Only managed 72 miles last week. . . .'

'Had this twinge in my knee after 17 miles of the London Marathon. . . .'

'Building up for the Hog's Back race . . . doing a flat-out 15 miler on Sunday morning with Bernie. . . .'

At that moment you feel you are the least trained, most ill-prepared entrant in today's race. Visions of darkness falling and of officials out with torches looking for you flash across your mind. The hour or so before a race is usually your least confident. You'd pull out now, but you've come all this way. . . .

You collect your number. 'There's a map of the course over there,' says the official at the numbers table. You drift over to look at the map, a photocopied Ordnance Survey with coloured arrows added in felt-tipped pen. If you are going to be in the lead, you'll need to know the way. But you aren't. On the other hand, when darkness is falling. . . .

You don't need a map to find the toilets. Then, outside, time for a glance at the multi-coloured running shoes being sold from the back of someone's car. 'Haven't got your size with me, but if I take your name and address. . . .'

A jog. Have you eaten too late? Too early? Are you tired? Have you trained too much this week? Too little? Funny how negative things keep floating to the surface of your mind when you've been through this dozens of times before. It's only a road race, isn't it?

Two laps, 5 miles each. If it gets too hard, you can always drop out after one lap and get out of the changing rooms before the rest come back and ask how you got on. But you've come all this way. . . .

A shaky line forms for the start. Must be 500 here. Serious faces at the front: lean, tight-skinned, hungry-looking runners. Never seen *that* sort of shoes before. At the back of the assembly, the banter. Talking, laughing – probably all be facing the wrong way when the gun goes.

'Hold it, lads . . . just one picture for the local paper. Now here's the mayor to start you off.'

At the third attempt the gun fires. Doesn't seem too bad. A mile gone, lots of runners in front of you, but lots behind you too. 3 miles: overtaking a few, being overtaken by a few. The figures you pass are the young, inexperienced runners who started too fast. The ones coming past are the older runners, slower to start, but whose pace probably won't fluctuate by more than a few seconds a mile all the way, and who will keep overtaking relentlessly until the finish.

Halfway. Inside 40 minutes anyway, feeling okay. The possibility of dropping out seems ludicrous now. You instinctively speed up slightly as you pass the knot of spectators, then tell yourself to ease back into what was a comfortable pace.

7, 8, 9 miles. You're going to finish. You try to pick it up a little on the final mile, and as you cross the line you feel a weight being lifted from your chest and a momentary urge to be sick over the timekeeper's clipboard. Swallow hard.

Your legs feel suddenly numb and sweat trickles into your eyes, as you try to find your tracksuit among the abandoned garments by the side of the road. Wonder who won?

Tracksuit on. You jog another half-mile back down the course. Just coming in is the voice who 'only managed 72 miles last week'. Behind him comes the '17 mile knee twinge in the London', just getting the better of 'flat-out 15 miler with Bernie on Sunday'.

You're glad you came all this way.

A clearing in the wood. Leaves scrunch underfoot but there is a stillness in the air. In the distance voices can be heard. 'Come on, get up with them!'

Footsteps, laboured breathing, then suddenly a lanky boy in a red vest and blue shorts runs across the clearing and disappears down the path opposite. For a few seconds silence descends again. Then another boy, stockier, in a yellow and green vest, follows the first across the clearing and down the path.

Two more, together, both in blue, appear; then suddenly the whole pack. There must be well over 150, running two and three abreast, winding through the wood like a multi-coloured streamer, and not one of them older than fifteen.

Coaches in tracksuits and mothers in headscarves pop out from behind trees, yelling at the puffing youngsters, and then disappear again in search of the shortest cut back to the finish.

The streamer slowly fades into one or two stragglers. Then a tiny lad in a vest three sizes too big for him appears, walking and holding his side. He sees you, and starts running again. 'Stitch,' he gasps, half defensively, half apologetically.

'Never mind,' you say. 'Keep at it.'

Going up the second hill, all she can see is a winding file of muddy legs in front of her and then, as she comes over the top of the climb, she can spot the leader in the distance, already 200 perhaps 300 yards ahead. It's probably that Jane whatsername who won the Southern title, she thinks; that girl with the loud mother. Like to see her lose for once but she seems to win everything.

Half a mile further on, and some of the girls around her are almost walking. Not her, though. She'll keep running until the end, despite the mud and the hills. Last year she was 264th in this race, and she wants to do better this time. That's what she's been training for, isn't it? Her Dad said she could have a new tracksuit if she got into the first 200. She thinks her Dad will probably get her the new tracksuit anyway if she really wants it, but she'd like to earn it properly.

Good old Dad. He drives her all over the country to different races, and he's never seen her win anything. Yet. But he'll be there at the finish, like he always is, holding her tracksuit and training shoes, and he'll say what he always says: 'All right, dear? Never mind, you'll beat them all next time.'

Coming up to the finish now . . . she can see the crowds, and she is aware that the runners around her are trying to sprint, which is almost impossible on this mud. Several go past her, but then wilt again and one girl actually stops and walks within sight of the finish. Voices are screaming encouragement from both sides. It's all right for *them* to say, 'Sprint now!' *They* haven't got to run.

Across the line, she takes a metal disc. An official shouts at her to keep moving and she follows the file of gasping athletes down the roped-off funnel, her hands on the shoulders of the girl in front for support. She feels the hands of the girl behind on her shoulders, but she is too tired to turn and look. Hope no one falls over, or we'll all go down, she thinks.

At the other end of the funnel she sees Jane whatsername posing for a photographer, already back in her tracksuit and looking as though she's been out for an afternoon stroll. Jane's mother is talking in a loud voice to no one in particular about there being 'no opposition'.

She glances down at her own muddy legs, then remembers to look at the disc she is still clutching in her right hand. It is stamped 176.

Then, alongside her, a voice. 'All right, dear? Never mind, you'll beat them all next time.'

The flags aren't really needed, because the crowd, three or four deep in places, lines the course, straining for the first view of the runners. They started 12 minutes ago to the muffled explosion of that maroon, which sent over 2000 runners sprinting into their 9 mile journey. They'll be slowing by now, but the English National Cross Country Championship always has a spectacular, colourful and fast start.

There is a buzz among those spectators who can actually look round the clump of bushes not 60 yards away, and some shouts, getting nearer. Then this huge mass of humanity, squeezing into every available inch, comes pouring round the corner, filling the gap between the rows of spectators with a sea of colour punctuated by the fleshy streaks of arms and legs, all pumping furiously.

In the lead, it's . . . no, it's . . . well, at least twenty of them. Familiar faces, most of them winners in their own patch with giant local reputations but fighting today for a place in the first ten, or even hundred. They came in cars and coaches and special trains with their wives and girlfriends, parents and club officials, who know only too well that Saturdays in winter are spent waiting for muddy runners to appear around clumps of bushes.

How many thousands and thousands and thousands of training miles have gone into the preparation for this frenzied 9? In Bury and Exeter, Hastings and Tamworth, Sunderland and Shanklin, the training has been faithfully logged. On sunny Sunday mornings and bleak Monday nights, along slippery footpaths or partially lit back streets, these men have woven their own route to this moment, when all of them would come together on common ground and brush elbows in getting round three long laps.

A mass of runners, still passing. Surely the leaders will be round again in a minute, and yet we haven't seen the last man through. The faces tell you little of the real story. How many of these runners are having the race of their lives, far in excess of anything they could have hoped, and are at this moment living an experience which they will be recounting to their clubmates on the long Sunday morning runs for years to come? How many are enduring a private hell, wondering why, today of all days, their legs will not respond, leaving them so frustratingly far down on their norm?

How many of these runners will be having their final race today, retiring tonight in disgust, and perhaps making a comeback next week? How many will be so encouraged by the little figure stamped on the cold metal disc they will take as they cross the finishing line that their running careers will henceforth be given greater momentum, as they decide to devote even more of their life to pursuing a gold medal, or something less definable?

So this was the English National Cross Country Championship. It started at three o'clock and it will be over for many of them by four. They ran thousands of miles individually before today, yet more than one life will have been altered by the 9 miles they have just run together.

The Olympic Stadium. Every seat filled. The runners have been gone over 2 hours now. There were sixty-five starters, but we hear they're down to forty-nine now. No progress reports for 25 minutes, though. We've seen the relays, seen the 1500 metres and the 5000 metres finals in the stadium while they have been out there on the road.

The announcer says the leader is now within a kilometre of the stadium. We can hear the cheering outside, as the thousands of people who could not get tickets at least see part of one of the classic Olympic events. The accompanying motorcyclists will leave him when they get up to the stadium gates and he will be alone for 50 metres through the tunnel, 50 metres in which he will hear only his own echoing footsteps. He will be momentarily isolated from a world in which 80,000 pairs of eyes in the stadium and 200 million viewers watching television are staring at the other end of the tunnel, waiting and wondering.

The noise as he emerges from that tunnel envelops him like a blanket. Some know instantly who he is; others will have to search for his number in their programmes. But his plan to break from the field when he did has worked. He was near exhaustion until his entrance to the world's greatest sporting arena gave him a new lease of life, a massive burst of adrenalin which will see him safely around the final lap of the track he had left just over 2 hours earlier at the start of his 26 mile journey.

His sweat-soaked vest is stuck to his skinny body, his hair plastered to his head, but the thousands of miles he has run since he was that scraggy boy, trailing in the cross country race in a vest three sizes too big for him, have paid off in the best possible way. He crosses the line and he is among the immortals: the Olympic marathon champion.

1

THE BOOM IN RUNNING

To run, says *The Concise Oxford Dictionary*, is to 'progress by advancing each foot alternately, never having both feet on the ground at once'. Even the dryness of the definition cannot fully submerge the exhilaration of the activity. Never having both feet on the ground at once. Just reading the words stimulates your legs into imaginary action – the echo of runs remembered and anticipation of runs to come.

For running is as old as man himself. And while it was certainly an effective means of getting away from anything hostile, or simply for getting from A to B, the opportunities it provides for sporting competition were appreciated by the Ancient Greeks. There have always been challenges and races and, while modern competitive athletics may have its roots only as far back as the nineteenth century, the interest in finding out who was the fastest runner in the town or the country goes much further back than that. Now we can discover the fastest runners in the world too.

Since the inaugural modern Olympic Games, held at Athens in 1896, the swiftest runner has become a universal hero. A Greek shepherd named Spiridon Louis was greeted with almost hysterical acclaim in Athens when he won that first marathon race and with it Greece's first Olympic title.

In the years that followed names like Paavo Nurmi, Emil Zatopek, Lasse Viren and Said Aouita have transcended the political and language barriers and become famous worldwide for an ability to run just that little bit faster than their contemporaries. And as time passes other names will become similarly well known simply because of the speed with which they can 'progress by advancing each foot alternately, never having both feet on the ground at once'.

But while the keenest students of the sport engage in endless hours of inconclusive argument about the stars of past and present, and whether the 1952 triple Olympic champion Emil Zatopek would have beaten the versatile Aouita, breaker of so many world records, a whole basic attitude has altered, grown and developed during the 1980s.

The birth of the London Marathon, first held in 1981 and guided by its race director Chris Brasher to become the biggest marathon in the world, played a crucial role in stimulating and sustaining the running boom. Now, in the 1990s, the general enthusiasm to participate in marathons may not be quite at the same level as half a dozen years ago, but the demand for entry to the London Marathon each April remains much greater than the number of available places. In 1990, some 72,000 applications were received for the 33,500 places on offer.

Support for marathons other than London has eased, but running itself is still flourishing. While it may have been marathons which initially attracted the attention of the new runner, a subsequent widening of competitive opportunities to include half-marathons and 10km events diverted many runners and attracted thousands more who realized they would never have time to prepare properly for the marathon's 42km.

In the same year as the first London Marathon, 1981, another massive running event was inaugurated on Tyneside. It was known as the Great North Run, and was the brainchild of local running hero Brendan Foster. This half-marathon, which started in the centre of Newcastle and finished on the coast at South Shields, quickly grew to rival the London Marathon in terms of support and participation; the 25,000 places now offered each year are practically snapped up overnight.

Elsewhere, the whole base of competitive opportunity for the runner of any standard has expanded and broadened dramatically in the past few years, with the consequent upsurge of activity among a population firmly reassured that you do not have to be a fast runner to enjoy running.

The signs are all around us. That man in the tracksuit puffing down the road last night. Not exactly flying, was he? But he'll be there again tonight. That group of girls jogging in the local park: laughing, giggling, but jogging and enjoying it. All those boys you saw competing in a cross country race on the common last Saturday afternoon. There were hundreds of all shapes and sizes, and some of them obviously finding it harder work than others. But did it really matter that some took 15 minutes to run the course, and others took 25 minutes? Not at all.

For now at last there is a new realization among the many thousands of runners the world over who are not destined to win an Olympic gold medal or to break a world record. Their role in running need not be confined merely to sitting in open-mouthed amazement at the exploits of that fraction of 1 per cent who are simply more gifted or more dedicated to the pursuit of excellence. To reach the heights is an admirable achievement certainly, but it is not the *only* achievement available to those who run.

In the past decade, a definite and glorious backlash has been growing against that often expressed view that 'winning is everything, second place is nothing, silver medals are for losers, and who cares who was runner-up anyway'.

As a dogma for those whose livelihoods depended upon success, such as highly pressurized US college coaches, who may not have invented it but certainly help to preserve it, the win-at-all-costs attitude may even have worked to a certain degree. Or, if the results did not come, then the attitude could at least serve as a sign to their employers that the failure was not for want of motivation.

But for the rest of us whose limited running ability meant that no one was scrambling to sign us up for their athletics club or track scholarship, to hear this view persistently repeated during the 1960s by the coaches, the spectators and the stars themselves was like being constantly hit on the head with a hammer. You reached the stage where you almost felt a fraud just pulling on a pair of running shoes if you could not break 4 minutes for the mile, and you tended to go out training late at night, after dark, in case someone saw you and word got round that you were getting ideas above your station.

It was not just an athletics inferiority complex, self-generated by those of us who had difficulty breaking 5 minutes for the mile, let alone 4. It was simply that we *were* athletically inferior, and we knew it. Or if we did not, there was generally someone around with a lot of badges on their tracksuit and a loud voice to make sure that we soon did. (I wonder what happened to them all? I suppose they just became so wonderful that one day they floated away on a cloud.)

But during the seventies an almost revolutionary idea that success in competition was not really vital as long as you took part and enjoyed it gained popularity. And although it did not emanate entirely from the USA – the land of win, win, win – it gathered a lot of its momentum there.

The growing concern about the spiralling heart-attack fatalities of the 1960s certainly contributed to this popularity, particularly as the medical authorities were blaming obesity, lack of exercise and too much soft living as some of the prime causes. Jogging and running became new discoveries in a nation which was used to driving everywhere. A boom started.

At first everyone was jogging, because it was a simple, cheap and effective way of retaining (or regaining) health, losing weight and physically stretching yourself. Before that, stretching was something a lot of Americans did mainly in bed.

Then the victory of Frank Shorter in the 1972 Olympic marathon at Munich, and the success of a book entitled *Aerobics* by Dr Kenneth Cooper, which gave measurable values to different levels of gentle exercise, became two big boosting influences. Shorter's win, unexpected as it was, earned a lot of coast-to-coast television time, and suddenly all the joggers following the advice in Cooper's best-selling book became Frank Shorter striding to victory.

An over-simplification, perhaps, but road race fields began to increase, providing as they did an incentive beyond jogging, a thermometer for those who needed a target at which to aim. Marathons became particularly popular, however long they took to complete. Finishing was the goal, never mind the time.

The benefits of exercise were enough to sell running. The word of mouth praise it was suddenly receiving for the consequent weight loss, the regained vitality, the new awareness, the lowered pulse and blood pressure, and 'getting a fresh start in life' sold it more effectively than any Madison Avenue campaign could have done. The same people who had cried win, win, win, were now muffled by the commotion over a re-discovered exercise, and instead they looked down at their own paunches, felt their own galloping pulses, and started jogging themselves.

No longer did it matter about winning. As long as you were running you were doing something positive to aid your health, and increasing your chances of living longer. The day that running took off was the day that losing became respectable.

The running boom was at its most marked in the USA, but elsewhere similar growth was taking place. 'Fun runs' were becoming popular the world over. The fun run is a kind of halfway house for the jogger who wants to try something with a little more of a challenge, but does not yet feel ready to tackle organized athletics events. People of all ages and abilities run a relatively short course (perhaps 1½ miles) in what is strictly speaking a run and not a race. Certificates are awarded for finishing, not for winning, which reinforces the concept of taking part regardless of ability.

The most prestigious of these is the *Sunday Times* National Fun Run, held each September in Hyde Park, and which pre-dates even the London Marathon. It was first held in 1978, and within six years its total annual entry had risen from 12,000 to 30,000, as runners and joggers of all standards took part in its series of age group events, all held over the same flat, grassland 4km course.

With a mild element of competition, but the chief emphasis on participation, the National Fun Run, itself based on a Paris event called the Cross du Figaro, soon became the role model for many other similar events in Britain.

The effect of this upsurge of interest in jogging and fun runs has also shown itself in the mushrooming numbers of competitors taking part in hundreds of inter-club and open-road and cross-country events staged every weekend throughout Britain. And if there is one main competitive celebration of cross-country running which has in itself reflected the growth of the sport, it must be the English National Men's Championships, staged each February.

In the main event, the Senior 9 mile race, the most humble club runner can find himself lining up and jostling elbows with the top internationals in the country over the first mile in what is always a colourful and spectacular start. You can even feel the ground tremble beneath your feet as the swarm of runners passes by.

To appreciate the growth of cross country, consider these figures. In 1974 there were 968 finishers in the race, a splendid total in itself. Just five years later, in 1979, there were 1555 finishers. And in 1988 there were 2136 finishers. Compared to marathon fields that may not seem such a dramatic growth, but potentially, it could be many times larger because each club can field only nine runners at the most, and some clubs have literally hundreds of runners from which to choose their nine-man team. So, whichever way you look at it, cross country is growing.

Brendan Foster, who has experienced the whole running spectrum from the level of the sixties 'scrubber' who was afraid to race because he was running so badly in training, up to becoming an Olympic medallist and record breaker in 1976, summed up the changing attitude after winning the English National Cross Country title in 1977: 'If winning is everything, then I will be the only bloke here today who is pleased, and the 1500 runners I beat will all have to go home miserable. But I bet there are some runners today who may have improved from 1300th last year to 1250th this year, and they are probably even more delighted than I am. It's wrong to think that every race has only one winner. Running is about improving yourself, and if you ran faster or finished higher than last time, then you're a winner, no matter how many others finished in front of you.'

If changing attitudes are partly responsible for the increase in popularity, what, apart from the health aspect, are the particular attractions of road running and cross country themselves? Both after all are strenuous physical activities and, although they also include team scoring events, unlike soccer and rugby you cannot pass the blame for your own poor performance on to your team-mates. The individual stands alone.

The first attraction must be its simplicity. You do not have to book a court, or find an opponent or a team-mate before you can practise. You just run. And the longer and more often you run, the stronger you become and the more likely to do well in a branch of athletics which, after all, tests simply your strength and ability to run a long way, and not your technical skill or your capability at using specialist equipment.

Improvement is directly related to the amount of time and effort you put into training, and if you have not trained you will have no one but yourself to blame. This aspect was the one which always appealed to me most when I was at school, where the main sports we played were rugby, cricket and athletics. I was hopeless at rugby because without my glasses I found it difficult to differentiate between my team-mates and opponents, and from time to time made some splendid runs in the wrong direction!

Cricket was too slow and too much of a team game inasmuch as I never felt there was enough I could do on my own to influence the result.

Running was quite different, however, and with a pair of spiked shoes on my feet I was a total disaster! In my first ever cross country race, as a thirteen-year-old, I ran in a 2 mile event for my school against Shaftesbury Harriers at a horribly muddy place called Brook Farm at Totteridge in North London, and was left so far behind that I got lost because the officials did not believe there could be anyone else still out on the course, and so collected in all the marker flags.

Yet even then the attraction of a sport for which you could train, alone, any time, anywhere, and in which the results depended upon your perseverance, was as strong then as it remains now, thirty years later. Unlike gymnastics or ice skating, you do not have to rely on someone else's opinion of your ability. Unlike soccer or rugby you do not have to rely on your team-mates. Unlike boxing you do not have to rely on meeting the right opponent at the right time, and being seen by the right person. Instead, I found that by reading a couple of books from the library at Wembley, where I then lived, and undertaking a few training sessions on my own around the local King Edward's Park I could actually become a better runner.

Not a world beater, not a record breaker, but a better runner. At school the boys who used to romp away with every race still did so, unchallenged by me and probably totally unaware that I was making even a tiny dent in their vast lead every week. (I once worked out that if I continued to improve at the same rate as I did in the first week of my training, then we would all be forty-eight years old before I caught them!) But if I did not appear to be troubling the outstanding runners, I did seem to be making progress over those unfortunates who were about my own natural athletic standard – and most of whom were recognizable by having only one leg or weighing 18 stone.

There was an inner pleasure in lining up for each successive race knowing that I was slightly fitter than last week and perhaps ready to beat someone else whom I had never beaten before. The fact that they were not spending their evenings training, while I was, seemed irrelevant; they had the same chance to do so. And later, as the opposition began to include a higher percentage of those runners who did train instead of relying on their natural ability, so the aim was to do more training more often than they did, and so close the gap that way.

It had such a satisfying simplicity about it, and such an open-ended future. In running everything depends on the individual, and looking back now I can honestly say that the only reason I did not break the world 10,000 metres record was not because I did not have contacts in the right places, or that a particular official did not like me; it was just that I wasn't good enough. And that really is the best, most satisfying reason.

In running, everyone can reach their own natural peak. It does not matter whether you live in Penzance or the Outer Hebrides, Birmingham or London. The only criterion as to whether you can break the world record or win a gold medal is whether you can run fast enough. Running is a great leveller. Social background, income, political beliefs and rank are all forgotten when you line up for a race. Instead, training and determination take over, and in the Army Championships a private can outrun a field marshal.

Even the actual process of training for distance running can be reduced to very basic practical terms. You can change into your running kit, go out of your front door, run for as long as you want to, and end up at your front door again. A 20-minute run can take 20 minutes, an hour's run can take an hour. That may not be ideal, because most physiotherapists insist you should spend some time on mobility exercises before you run to try to avoid possible injury. In fact, I wonder how many runners actually do, because the feeling of most is probably that they would rather use the time for an extra 2 or 3 miles' running, and take the risk of injury.

Not the ideal attitude, perhaps, but it does highlight why road running is such a popular participant sport and method of training. Although, like all amateur sports, the demand on one's limited spare time is regular, in running it can be reduced to the bare minimum. Home by 6 o'clock, out running by 6.15 p.m., back by 7.15 p.m., showered and dressed not long after 7.30 p.m., with another 8 miles or so to put in the diary. Those who participate in other sports, or even some other branches of athletics, may have to travel to a ground or stadium, then wait for others to arrive, and travel home afterwards, often tripling the total time that they actually spend on training.

To go out and run at a steady pace is not merely a preparation for races. In itself it can be relaxing and therapeutic, easing away the stresses and tensions of the day, with its benefits for racing being only by-products for some people. But in sufficient quantity, and with reasonable regularity, it will enable the average healthy man or woman to get comfortably through a road or cross country race, as it does for many thousands of runners throughout Britain every week.

And it is these athletes, who are content to run at a comfortable pace over a range of distances from 2 to 20 miles or more at a time, who form the vast majority of the running population of Britain. They train and race at a constant level in clubs, and are perfectly happy to do so with no dreams of Olympic glory.

Many of them seldom race on the track, for two main reasons. Firstly, there are adequate road races available in most parts of the country all year round, as well as cross country races throughout the winter, and these cater for all standards of runner. Being longer and slower in overall pace than track races, they are more attractive to the steady speed athlete, who would rather run in the middle of a half-marathon field at a top speed of seven or eight minutes a mile, than run very little faster in a 5000 metre track race, and probably be lapped by the winner two or three times.

Secondly, to do well in track races normally involves the inclusion of speed work as an extra or alternative training session – a type of running which is often unacceptably uncomfortable to some recreational club runners. They prefer to stick with their programme of enjoyable steady running in which they just get pleasantly tired.

The world of distance running can count the vast majority of active athletes in this country among its participants. The rewards of racing can be an all-expenses-paid trip to the other side of the world to race internationally, or just a shared mug of tea and a piece of home-made cake after a local road race. But, whatever your motivation and your ambition, the joy of running is that the choice, the target and the means are always yours and yours alone.

2

TYPES OF TRAINING

· The three related areas of distance running covered in this book – road running, marathons and cross country – all deserve their own more detailed analysis, and this follows a little later.

But they also share a common denominator in that the basic types of training used in preparation for competition are the same. Running is an uncomplicated activity, although the forms of training can be adjusted in their volume and detail according to the target to be attempted.

So before we come on to examine the precise differences in the worlds of road running, marathons and cross country, let's familiarize ourselves with the types of training necessary for them all.

Assessing your Needs

Like a building, any training programme needs good, solid foundations. It is no use trying to run substantial distances fast until you can run the same distances slowly first, and even the most ambitious international starts a year's training cycle with a large amount of steady paced running. This method of training was popularized by the New Zealand coach Arthur Lydiard, a former marathon runner who coached Peter Snell and Murray Halberg to Olympic track gold medals in the early 1960s, and whose views on the importance of 'conditioning' for all middle- and long-distance runners are now subscribed to, either directly or indirectly, by the majority of the world's leading runners.

Lydiard by no means invented the system, but refined it and held that the key to success was a basic conditioning programme of 100 miles a week of steady running through the winter, followed by a transitional period which brought in hill training, and then moved on to track work. Even for 800 metres runners like Snell, Lydiard prescribed this programme on the basis that speed was inborn but that additional strength obtained through conditioning gave athletes the ability to sustain their top speed for longer, and with less effort.

But the eventual success of any training programme depends on striking the right balance with perhaps a dozen or more variables, including stamina running, speed running, the correct racing programme, diet, and sufficient rest. Every single athlete is a special case, and no two are ever exactly alike in their background, ability and mental approach. If two athletes undertake identical training, they may still both improve, but the chances are that at least one of them will not be training to optimum effect.

This never-ending search to find the training programme which is exactly suited to the athlete and his current condition is one which involves the coach and athlete in a lot of thought, study and, it must be admitted, occasional guesswork. But the aim is to cut the guesswork to the absolute minimum.

For the serious athlete, it can sometimes be like playing a fruit machine – trying to get three oranges in a line. You may get the first and third, but miss the second; you may have stamina and be free of injury, but be short on speed. You may have the second and third, but lose the first; your speed is good, you are injury free, but you lack stamina. And so on, until finally the day comes when you do manage to get all the oranges in a line and hit the jackpot. Except, of course, that there are probably nearer to twelve oranges than three, and that makes it even more difficult. The Olympic champion is the athlete who, on the day, has more oranges in line than anyone else: his speed, stamina and confidence are all good, his racing programme has been right, he is rested, injury-free and has no dietary problems or illness. And the final most elusive orange of all is a little thing called luck, which even the best prepared athletes need on the big day, whether it is in an Olympic stadium or at the local cross country championships.

You cannot legislate for luck, nor is it possible to state conclusively in a book that 'this is the exact training programme that *you* need'. No one will ever be able to write a book like that, containing the ultimate answer for every athlete, which in itself points to the very fascination of running: 'Have I got the formula exactly right this time?' or 'How many oranges will I get in a line this weekend?'

For, even if two runners have the same personal best time for 10km on the road, they could need completely different training programmes to improve their performance in the most efficient and effective way.

If, for example, you have run 10km in 40 minutes on regular weekly training of around 40 miles a week, and you step your mileage up to 60, then the chances are quite good that you will eventually improve your time for 10km. But a closer examination of your training might reveal that you would also benefit from some speedwork once a week, to compete in some shorter races occasionally, or to undertake some hill running. You might have an uneconomical style for road running, and you might be over-striding or under-striding. It might turn out that instead of easing down, you are running a flat-out 10km time trial the night before a race (as I heard of one runner doing) to make sure you can get the distance!

Any of these aspects, and more, could be adjusted to improve your 10km time while still retaining your 40 miles a week. And if you made the adjustments, and also picked up your training level to 60 miles a week, then the improvement should be considerable. The most successful runners do not just go out and run haphazardly. They evolve, through thought, study and self-criticism, the best possible training programme to suit them.

This chapter examines in general some of the types of training in common use by distance runners the world over. But I stress now that this book is not, and could never be, because of the complex nature of preparing for competition, designed to be more than the basic materials and examples with which you can build, the planks of wood from which *you* must finally make the table which either stands up or collapses.

The other point to make here is that the spectrum of running is enormous, and to generalize too much can be dangerous and misleading. Thus I trust that coaches and parents of the youngest runners will appreciate that in this chapter I am concerning myself specifically with the more senior and experienced runners and, while the broad policies and types of training apply similarly across the board, the details of mileages and times are not designed for the less experienced or younger runner. Instead, a separate section aimed specifically at less experienced and younger runners is included later in the book.

What Happens Inside?

Running is a simple process. Oxygen is breathed in from the air, absorbed into the blood through the lungs, and taken by the blood to the muscles to assist them to perform the activity required of them, which in this case is to run. That is a greatly simplified version of what actually happens, but the limitations on running are very much governed by the ability of the body to carry out the oxygen transportation process efficiently and continuously.

Through regular training, though, it is possible to increase that ability considerably and thus raise the level of athletic performance. For example, nearly 6 litres of air can be processed in a single breath by even an averagely trained distance runner, while an untrained person would probably manage less than 5 litres. A trained runner also has more red blood cells and in each cell more haemoglobin (an iron-containing protein which provides the colour and the bulk of the contents of the cells, and is responsible for the transport of oxygen) than an untrained person. He can thus absorb and move more oxygen from the lungs to the muscle tissues.

As a result of training, the heart, which is itself a muscle, enlarges and strengthens to the point where it can pump a much greater volume of blood with more efficiency. The runner's resting pulse rate becomes correspondingly slower the fitter he gets, as the heart needs to beat less often to move the same amount of blood at rest. An average healthy non-runner might have a resting pulse rate of 72–74 beats per minute, whereas a well-trained runner may have a resting pulse of only 40, or even lower. Some people are born with a relatively low pulse rate, and these are often the lucky individuals who have a 'natural' talent for winning races at school.

But, unless they undertake some form of training themselves, the day will come when the regularly training runner will surpass their natural ability. It may take years, but the runner with only modest talent can continually improve his condition and his ability to shift oxygen around the body while a rival with natural ability but a reluctance to train will remain at a constant level.

The training effect, achieved through regular running, is simply a form of adaptation made by the body to be able to cope with the work asked of it. The adaptation is a response to the stress imposed by running, and once a certain level of fitness is achieved, the 'stress' has to be increased by graduating the amount of intensity of training, to keep the body constantly adapting to a higher degree of fitness.

All the time, the volume of air that can be taken in and processed through the lungs, and the rate at which it happens, the oxygen-carrying capacity of the blood, and the ability of the circulatory system to transport oxygenated blood to the muscle tissues are being greatly increased. Muscles become stronger and more efficient. Stamina increases. Body fat, which hinders the processes, is being burned up and reduced to a minimum. On every training run you are becoming a fitter, stronger, better-prepared athlete.

During a 20 mile run, for example, massive amounts of blood are moved around the body, the pulse is kept at a reasonably high and steady level (thus providing the type of 'stress' to which the cardiovascular system will adapt and strengthen for the future) and greater capillarization occurs, allowing the blood more routes to get oxygen to the muscles.

Sometimes in short, fast training runs, or in certain sections of a relatively short road or cross-country race, particularly going uphill, you will be in a situation where the blood just cannot get enough oxygen to the muscles because the demands being made are too high. In that situation, a state of 'oxygen debt' is said to exist, and the muscles begin to accumulate lactic acid, the waste product of the exercise and which can only be tolerated without loss of pace for a short while. As the lactic acid level increases, so the muscles become painfully hindered in their movement until an easing off is essential to allow the oxygen supply to catch up with the demand and repay the debt. Track races up to 800 metres are run at top level almost entirely in this anaerobic ('without oxygen') state, and the ambitious 800 metres runner has no choice but to adapt to running anaerobically and tolerating enormous oxygen debts in the closing stages of the race without losing too much speed.

As the distance of an event increases, the balance between anaerobic and aerobic ("with oxygen") running tips more and more towards the type of running in which the supply of oxygen is equal to the demand, until one reaches the marathon, which is considered to be a 99 per cent aerobic event. In other words, unlike the 800 metres it is not a lack of oxygen in the muscles which slows the runner in the closing stages of a marathon but rather the sheer fatigue of running continuously for several hours.

Obviously, the more the runner has to run anaerobically in his or her chosen event, then the greater proportion of their time will be spent in training anaerobically. In other words, they will deliberately put themselves into oxygen debt a number of times in training sessions, and by doing so their body will adapt to the situation and allow them a greater tolerance of such discomfort in the future. During a session of hard 10 × 400 metres runs on the track, for example, the athlete has the chance to experience severe oxygen debt ten times, with suitable recovery (and repayment of the debt) in between.

Mentally, as well as physically, it is nevertheless a severe form of training, and one not to be repeated too often. But then training is very much a rehearsal of the race. It would be of little value, for instance, to run a great distance at a very slow speed and then expect that on the race day you will subsequently be able to run 800 metres very fast.

By the same token, a marathon runner who did little but endless repetition sprints of 200 metres would not be improving their preparation for an event which is over 200 times longer.

The human body is deaf, dumb and blind. You can talk to it, write letters to it, or even draw it diagrams, but the only way it can really understand what you want it to do in races is if you take it carefully, patiently and regularly through the motions in training.

LSD

The form of training which has become known as LSD has nothing to do with pre-decimal money, nor drugs. Instead, LSD stands for Long Slow Distance, and became known as such after the publication of a successful book in 1969 written by the American author Joe Henderson. A prolific writer on the subject of running, and a long-time competitor of self-admitted modest ability, Henderson entitled his work *Long Slow Distance – The Humane Way to Train.*

He did not claim to have invented LSD, which involves running steadily for long periods at a pace of 7–8 minutes a mile or slower in order to gain strength and endurance. But some might say he re-invented it at a time when there had been an over-emphasis on speed. At least he gave reassurance to those who had discovered by themselves, as Henderson did, that they seemed to gain far more, both mentally and physically, from relaxed aerobic running than from constant sessions of speedwork.

Now, more than twenty years later, Henderson says he wishes he had left the word 'train' out of the original title, because some people have misconstrued his aim as trying to promote LSD as the best method of training for *racing*. He readily admits that in itself it is not, and that instead the right proportion of distance running as a base, and speedwork as a tune-up, is more effective for racing.

What he *was* promoting was simply an enjoyable way of running, and he later admitted:

> 'When I wrote in 1969 about casual, gentle, light-hearted running, it wasn't intended for people who view their running the opposite way. I never said everyone would like it. I never meant to imply that it was *the* method, only *a* method – an alternative for those who were sick of the idea that running had to hurt all the time, which was a fairly common attitude then.'

Henderson explained that his own interest in switching to LSD was:

> '. . . finding an immediate way to make training a little less painful. My racing times had sunk to terrible levels, and my lower legs ached

continuously. With the Boston Marathon as a convenient goal eight months away, I decided to make training comfortable enough to enjoy and run races long enough to yield satisfaction – no matter how long they took. I had neither enjoyment nor satisfaction just then, and LSD looked like a handy route for achieving both.

Undiluted LSD has worked in sometimes strange ways, but it hasn't produced a bad trip at all. Anything that gives a 4 minute 27 seconds mile (compared to a 4 minute 44 seconds in my last race before the change), and a 2 hour 49 minutes marathon (I couldn't have run one before the change), and is fun too, can't be bad. I'm anxious to get out and run, which is saying a lot at 6.15 in the morning. What a nice change it is padding softly and slowly along the side roads, either involved in conversation or in solitary thoughts unconnected with how, and why, I'll take another step. Racing, in these circumstances, is threatening to become an unnecessary incidental – except as a social event.'

It is important to understand the background and value of LSD running because it has been misrepresented in the past, and whether distance runners agree with Henderson's views or not, it forms a substantial part of nearly all their training programmes. You might be a twelve-year-old running 3 miles on a Sunday morning, or a senior international marathoner covering 28 or 30 miles at a time, but you cannot be a distance runner without running distance.

The choice which faces the newer runner, though, is whether to settle for a training programme made up exclusively of LSD, which can be less painful and more relaxing than any other type of running, or whether to include alternative elements of faster work. LSD builds an excellent stamina base, strengthens the cardiovascular system, lowers the resting pulse rate, develops muscular endurance, keeps down weight and can even help ward off possible heart disease in the older runner. It also enables the runner to get comfortably, and often very successfully, through distance races, although obviously the longer the race the more running will be needed in preparation.

But on its own it is never likely to allow the runner to reach his or her fullest potential at distances below, or perhaps even including, the marathon. I won't say that it will prevent the gaining of success, because success is relative, and I am sure that it would be possible for runners of a certain standard even to win races of reasonable magnitude on the basis of just LSD running. But winning a race does not necessarily equate to reaching full potential.

Serious athletes really need to include some other, faster types of running in their training, to place the kind of stress on their system which will allow the body to adapt to the feel of a fast race. This applied stress is absent from a programme that is totally orientated to LSD – a fact which the ambitious runner would regard as a drawback and which many others would say was a positive recommendation.

Fartlek

One method of providing the change of pace missing from LSD without undertaking too great a commitment to formal speed training is to introduce what is known as *fartlek* into the programme. This is a form of running which can be relaxing and enjoyable, but also as physically taxing and beneficial as you wish to make it, according to how the mood takes you.

The word is Swedish, and means 'speedplay'. The concept was developed over forty years ago by the Swedish Olympic coach Gosta Holmer at a time when Swedish runners like Gunder Haegg and Arne Andersson were dominating world middle-distance running. There was naturally a lot of interest in their training methods, which had originally been evolved to beat the Swedes' great rivals, the Finns, and Holmer's original fartlek routine went like this:

1 Easy running for 5 to 10 minutes (as a warm-up).
2 Steady, hard speed for ¾ mile to 1¼ miles.
3 Rapid walking for about 5 minutes.
4 Easy running, interspersed with wind sprints of 50–60 yards, and repeated until a little tired.
5 Easy running with three or four 'swift steps' now and then (trying to simulate the sudden speeding up to avoid being overtaken by another runner!).
6 Full speed uphill for 175–200 yards.
7 Immediately, fast pace for 1 minute.
8 The whole routine was then repeated until the total time prescribed had elapsed. 'But every athlete must remember that he must not feel tired, but rather stimulated by the training,' Holmer wrote.
   'Always finish by running on the track from one to five laps, depending upon what distance you run in competition.'

Holmer submitted that the benefits of this type of training were as follows:

> 'Fartlek brings us back to the games of our childhood where nature decided that we should expose our inner organs to much effort, so that our bodies will develop. A child plays while sitting, walks some steps, runs to its mother, walks or runs back to the playground, makes a longer excursion to get a toy etc. To keep its balance, a child prefers running to walking. The swift, but short, runs dominate, and develop the inner organs.
> The runner gets to learn his ability. He doesn't tie himself up on a

certain task (such as a run of two English miles on the track, or three separate 220 yards sprints at a certain pace) but he is forced to explore. It is not the fixed courses that make a Professor out of a student, but the student's spirit of exploration, his studies of other explorers and his friends with them. It is the same thing with an athlete. Fartlek is such a field of investigation. Fartlek is rich in contests. Richer for the athlete with a creative power and the ability of deciding where there is a limit for his strength. That is to say, the ability to decide for himself when the training is no longer improving him, but destroying him instead.'

If Holmer's exact schedule for fartlek running and his parallels with childhood behaviour have been rather clouded by the mists of time, the spirit of it remains. Because its very nature allows such a range of components, it is impossible to say emphatically that it now consists of *this*. But generally speaking it involves alternate fast and slow running of any distances over a course that has not been specifically predetermined.

Natural markers, like trees or pillar boxes, can act as starting and finishing lines for hard efforts. The session is usually for a duration of time such as 20 minutes or 45 minutes, rather than a particular distance, and the runner alternately sprints, jogs and sustains racing or steady speed for as long as he wishes. Obviously the beneficial effects depend very much on the mental attitude of the individual, and it would be easy to jog for an hour, sprinting just 50 metres in the middle, and then writing down '60 minutes fartlek' in your training diary. Its value would be rather limited. But in the same time it might be possible to insert any number of hard bursts of 200, 300, 600, 800 metres or more, with recovery jogs as long or as short as you felt you needed in between.

For instance, you might run through a park and decide to run hard from 'the main gate as far as that little old lady sitting on the bench over there'. As long as the little old lady doesn't think you are about to mug her and start jogging off rapidly in the opposite direction, such natural markers are ideal.

The basis of fartlek is to alleviate some of the physical hardship by introducing an air of mental relaxation into your training; to make it more interesting, you could possibly decide to increase your pace considerably from the time you first met a man with a dog until such time as you met another man with another dog! As long as you don't cheat and start the session outside Cruft's, it can be a valuable exercise, especially if the first dog is an Alsatian which looks ready to bite you.

This might seem a flippant example, and in some respects it is, but you can translate it into serious racing terms: a rival suddenly decides to put in a hard burst, and you have to go with him. You don't know how long he will sustain that burst, but you have to be ready for it to last a long while. In the same way, you don't know whether the next man-and-dog duo are just around the next corner or still at home debating whether or not to go out for a walk.

These faster sections of running raise the pulse in the same way as a racing effort, they lengthen the stride, and help to break up the monotony of the week's training. Twice a week is probably the maximum that it should be used in preference to more formal sessions unless you have an iron will in forcing yourself to the limit, but it is a refreshing alternative when you are feeling jaded or stale.

Interval training

Another classic method of race preparation is interval training, and although to some runners this instantly conjures up a picture of toiling round a track, that is certainly not the only place it can be done. But it is a more rigidly controlled form of training than fartlek running, and calls on the athlete to run a predetermined number of times over a given distance, with a specific recovery, or 'interval', between each run.

It was this type of training which was favoured by Roger Bannister in his preparations to become the first 4 minute miler in 1954, although it should be added that a scarcity of time from his medical studies precluded him from adopting anything more time consuming than a diet of specifically high quality track work.

Its value is in pushing the pulse rate up to around 180–200 beats a minute, near the maximum, during the run itself, and allowing it to drop down to nearer 120 during the recovery period, before pushing it up again with the next hard run. Obviously it is primarily a form of training for the runner who is basically fit to begin with rather than for someone who is trying to get fit.

The variations possible are enormous. How many runs altogether? Over what distance? At what speed? With what recovery?

For instance, a runner might start off the season by running 12 × 400 metres in 75 seconds, with a 2 minute walk recovery. If he can handle that comfortably, he might increase the volume in later sessions to 15, and then 20, runs of 400 metres in 75 seconds. Or he might stick with the total of 12 and then try to run each one faster than 75 seconds. Or he might just cut the recovery time down to 1½ minutes' walk. Or change the recovery from a walk to a jog. The combinations are endless.

Another variation is the 'up the clock' or 'pyramid' session, in which the individual runs become longer each time. The athlete runs 100 metres hard, followed by a 100 metres jog, then 200 metres hard and 200 metres jog, followed by 300 metres hard, and so on. He increases the distance up to a given limit – say 600 metres – and then starts reducing them, with 500 metres, 400 metres, down to 100 metres again. The possible combinations in interval running are endless, and although the pyramid session may seem complicated, it keeps the athlete's mind constantly occupied in working out where each successive run and recovery will start and finish on the track. It also gives a wide variation of pace in one session.

'Interval' distances can be anything from as short as 50 metres to 1200 metres, a mile, or even more. Lasse Viren, the Finnish Olympic 5000 and 10,000 metres winner, has used a 5000 metres track training session in which he alternately sprinted and eased for 50 metres sections, which, particularly on the later laps, is a very hard exercise. It contained more violent pace changes than he would ever be likely to meet in any race, and the total time it took, 13 minutes 32 seconds, was not a great deal slower than he would run with more even pacing in a top class race.

Interval training on the track also helps to develop pace judgement, both for those runners who include some track races as part of their training for road and cross country races, and for those who simply like to have a clear idea of the pace they are running when there is no other way of accurately assessing distance.

If a regular interval session on the track is being used as an integral part of a long-term build-up for a particular race, then it is a good idea to have at least one specific session which, carried out every two or three weeks, can give you a guide to your progress. You might, for instance, choose a session of 15 × 400 metres with a 2 minutes' walking recovery. Then, if you have no coach to assist you, you should try to find someone to time each run, note it down for you and time the recovery.

It is possible to do it all yourself, but running with a stopwatch in your hand can be slightly distracting and does not always give you the most accurate record of your run. You may anticipate the start, or the finish, of the run and whether that would give you a faster or slower time is irrelevant; the point is that it is inaccurate. Also you may find that, as occasionally happens, you have inadvertently stopped the watch during the hard effort and run yourself flat out only to discover that you apparently took just 8.6 seconds for that 400 metres!

Accuracy is of paramount importance in what could be your only timed runs of the week. And, if you accidentally slice off an odd $\frac{1}{10}$ of a second here and there, it will only make it more difficult to improve next week, while the value of the timed session as a progress pointer will have been negated.

The same misleading effect occurs if you allow yourself to stray away from your pre-set recovery time. 2 minutes may actually seem a long time after the first couple of runs, and you may be tempted to cut 10 or 15 seconds off the recovery. But by the sixth or seventh run you will be glad of every second, and by the eleventh or twelfth you may even be tempted to re-tie your shoes just as the recovery time is up, to delay the next hard effort. But it really is in your own interest to stick rigidly to your pattern, even if you wonder 'What difference will another 15 seconds' rest make?'. Quite apart from strengthening your self-discipline, which is a vital part of any successful runner's make-up, to shorten or extend the recovery period means that you cannot make an accurate comparison next time you do the same session.

We are talking about the use of interval running in that sense not only as a training method, but also as a kind of thermometer to check progress. But, of course, not every type of interval training needs to be timed at all. While some runners prefer the rigid framework of a track session, others are happier using paths, stretches of parkland, or any other suitable area. If the actual running is carried out with the same intensity, then it doesn't matter whether the distance actually covered is a nice round figure, like 400 metres, or something obscure like 369⅞ metres. The object remains the same: to raise the pulse as high as possible, let it drop in recovery, then repeat the exercise to bring about the adaptations of training the body to cope with physical stress.

During the winter even those fortunate enough to live near a track may find it impossible to use because of lack of floodlighting or, if it is a cinder track, because of the condition of the surface. For them, and for anyone who prefers not to use the track anyway, it is important to discover local facilities and areas which, with a little imagination, lend themselves to interval running.

For instance, I have solved the problem of winter interval work with my own group of athletes in Folkestone by taking them on to the Leas, which for more than 100 years has been a popular cliff-top promenade overlooking the English Channel. In the summer it is usually crowded with holidaymakers and visitors, but on winter Thursday nights we have it to ourselves, and it forms an ideal training site. It is wide, traffic-free, and slopes gently for about ¾ mile.

At somewhat irregular distances all along the Leas, ranging from around 50 metres to 100 metres, there are lamp-posts which not only provide our 'floodlighting', but are also the markers for the interval session we do there. The athletes start at one end of the Leas, sprint past the first two lamp-posts, turn and jog back past just one lamp-post, then turn again and sprint another two lamp-posts, and so on. That way, they gradually make their way along the Leas, always sprinting up the slight slope and jogging back down it, until they reach the end of the path. Then they turn and stride back down to the starting point and repeat the whole session two or three times.

Eventually the athletes have, in effect, run hard efforts on anything up to thirty-six repetitions at distances varying each time between 100 and 200 metres, with an average recovery jog of around 80–100 metres. Performed on a track, even with the flat ground, it would be a hard session both mentally and physically but, because we are using a natural setting, with the distances varying slightly on every run, the runners say that it never seems as hard as track training.

Not everyone, of course, has such an ideal facility on their doorsteps, though I hasten to add that it also has its drawbacks. The wind blowing off the Channel in winter can sometimes be bitter, and one night the temperature dropped well below freezing point during an interval session, turning the path into a skating rink. But, wherever you choose to run, remember that while *all* training is preparation for racing, some types are, in themselves, more like a dress rehearsal for the real thing than others.

Interval running, and to a lesser extent fartlek, gives you the chance to run to the limit, and experience the fatigue and the oxygen debt you will meet in races. Not just once, but ten or twelve or twenty times in a session. And, each time you force yourself to experience that limit, the more your body will be adapting to the stresses of needing more oxygen urgently in the muscles and coping with the other demands being made of it. For that reason, the ambitious cross country and road racer should include such a session at least once a week in his or her training programme.

Mentally, it is sometimes a hard task to keep putting your body on the rack in this way. But, if you understand the value, and indeed the need and the place in the training plan for such a session, then you will be less likely to drop it from your schedule each week and substitute instead a few more miles of steady running. Some aspects of training cannot be replaced.

Resistance training

Those who think that this section is about blowing up bridges will be disappointed, because the resistance in this case is that felt by your own body as it tries to run up, over or through some form of difficult terrain or substance which has been chosen to force it to work that much harder.

The most obvious form is hill running, in which the athlete has to increase his work rate considerably to maintain even a steady pace, and some specific alterations to the running action have to be made to assist with the added work load. The athlete runs more on the toes and leans slightly into the hill; the knees have to come up higher and the arms have to drive harder. What is virtually a sprinter's action has to be adopted and, if the hill is long enough, some form of oxygen debt will be incurred; certainly the pulse will be raised considerably.

But strength and power will be gained from the exercise and, although a cross country or road runner may rarely be called upon in a race to run *flat out* up a hill, he or she will nevertheless have to race up hills at some stage, and this form of training can develop good technique and economy in doing so. In training the aim should be to reach the top of the hill as tired as possible; in racing it is to reach the top of the hill as fresh as possible. The first, repeated often enough, can lead to the second.

Unless it is unavoidable, a session in which the athlete charges up a hill with all guns blazing, stops on reaching the top and then turns to jog meekly down again, is not the most beneficial. Physiologically, of course, it will have a solid training effect, raising and lowering the pulse as it does, and developing muscular power. But it also builds in an unhelpful mental reflex if repeated time after time, week after week, that 'when I reach the top of this hill I can stop or ease off'.

Unfortunately, in races there is no such respite. You reach the top and have to carry on running. Thus, a hill 'circuit' in which the athlete runs over the top and then continues the pace for another 50–100 metres, perhaps turning left or right, before jogging back down on a separate route, is ideal. Certainly it is essential if a group of athletes are training together, because inevitably they will become strung out and would probably end up with the descending and ascending athletes running into each other, unless the hill is wide.

In this respect, natural 'bowls' and paths in woods or parkland can be used to work out a challenging, yet mentally stimulating, circuit. Although the total distance may only be estimated, the runner can occasionally try to cover as many circuits as possible within a given time limit, although he should resist the temptation to turn every hill session into such a time trial.

Even if the use of a circuit is impractical, as it may well be on a midwinter evening, and the athlete has to resort to running up and down the same hill, at least every possible session should incorporate running on beyond the top of the hill.

One precaution with hill work, particularly if it is being used as a transitional stage from a period of long, steady running, is to include only a modest amount of uphill running at first and gradually build it up on each session. To rush into a great volume of hill work all at once is to invite shin soreness and strained Achilles tendons, which need time to adapt to being fully stretched again. The mobility exercises outlined later in the chapter are of particular value before hill training.

Incidentally, although running uphill produces undoubted benefits, I have also found some value in an occasional session of 10×150–200 metres down a gentle slope on grass. This session, which can be performed in bare feet if the surface is suitable, flatters the speed but it increases the cadence of the stride and can be quite exhilarating and mentally refreshing at a time of year when so much of the training can seem like pure slog. But it must be down a slope, not a hill, and on grass rather than road, which causes too much jarring in the ankles, knees and lower back.

Most runners have hills near them, although several of the athletes in my own group live on the pancake-flat Romney Marsh and often train in sweat-shirts emblazoned 'Romney Marsh Mountain Rescue Team' as an ironic reminder that they do not. What they do have in their vicinity, though, is the sea and the sand of the south coast, and both can be used effectively for resistance work.

On beaches which do not drop away too sharply it is possible to run hard through waves at ankle to knee height for stretches of 100–200 metres, which is far more tiring than on dry land, especially when repeated a considerable number of times in a session. On every single stride the knees have to come up high, and there is a drag resistance on the feet as they go in and out of the water. The arms have to pump extra hard to help the leg drive, and the abdominal muscles particularly benefit. Take any lazy strides and you are likely to fall flat on your face in the sea!

A drier form of resistance training is sandhill running, which gained particular popularity when the 1960 Olympic 1500 metres champion Herb Elliott of Australia attributed a great deal of his success to running in sand dunes. The principle is the same: instead of reaching the required level of stress by running fast or long, the athlete quickly reaches a fatigued state sufficient for the training effect to occur by the resistance of running in loose sand, particularly up hills. A popular training camp for athletes at Merthyr Mawr, in South Wales, has access to particularly challenging sand dunes which were blown in from the sea 300 years ago. One is known as the Big Dipper which, with its 1 in 3 gradient, is thought to be the highest in Europe.

Again the effort needed to run up such dunes involves exaggerated knee lift and aggressive arm drive if you are to make any progress in the shifting sand. But sand can be effective if you have dunes within reasonable reach, and can become used to running on them regularly over a long period. But an athlete with little or no sand experience must be careful not to overdo dune running at the first opportunity he gets to run on sandhills. The heels sink much deeper into the loose surface than he will be used to, and like any form of uphill running there is a danger that the Achilles tendons will become over-stretched unless they can adapt gradually to the extra range of movement.

Weight training is another form of resistance training popular in athletics generally. But, while it has its place for sprinters and at the shorter end of the middle-distance scale, my own opinion is that cross country and road runners will gain more specific benefits from actually running than from lifting weights. Few leading distance runners use weights, preferring to use the time instead to increase their training mileage, and this is a valid point. If runners wish to include weight training in their programme (and there are a number of good publications on the subject) then it should only be as an addition to their running programme, and not as a substitute for part of it.

Altitude

For those athletes bordering on international level, altitude training is another aspect of preparation for competition which they may wish to consider. Its particular problems and benefits came into focus during the mid-sixties as the world prepared for the 1968 Olympic Games, which had been controversially awarded to 7200 feet high Mexico City.

At such heights the natural air pressure is reduced, which allows improvement in performance at the short, explosive events like the sprints and jumps. But the lower concentration of oxygen in the air makes things very difficult for the endurance event competitors who normally live at sea level and who, without sufficient acclimatization, cannot get enough oxygen circulating to the muscles, causing an inevitable drop-off in performance. Such runners might be able to perform a series of repetition runs at a relatively short distance, say 200 metres, and apparently be running really well, although an abnormally long recovery between efforts might be needed. But, when the same athletes came to run a distance which involved a more sustained effort, they would find it much more difficult than usual, until acclimatization had taken place. Normally this may take up to a fortnight even to begin to occur noticeably, and so not surprisingly athletes who were born or had lived for most of their lives at altitudes of 5000 feet and above did particularly well at the 1968 Olympics, being able to cope with the difficulties much better than even acclimatized lowlanders.

But what has carried over from the research done at the time is the realization that a sea-level competitor who returns from a prolonged period spent at altitude has a supercharge of red blood cells produced naturally by the body as a means of dealing with the inadequate oxygen supply. Having these extra blood cells at sea level means that more oxygen than normal can be transported to the muscles, and a temporary improvement in performance may follow. Consequently, some leading athletes now spend considerable periods of time training at altitude in preparation for a major event, deliberately to increase their oxygen carrying capacity, even though the event itself is being held at sea level.

As this seems such a good way of using nature to improve performance, why does not every top runner subscribe to altitude training?

The answer is that it does not suit everyone. Some athletes find that even at a relatively modest altitude of 5000 feet they suffer headaches, nose bleeding and nausea. Others find that it just does not seem to benefit them sufficiently to justify the expense and disruption of living at altitude in Switzerland, Kenya, the USA or wherever. Also, there is still a lot of research to be done, particularly concerning the ideal length of time to come down from altitude before competition.

A short period of re-adjustment at sea level is needed, but after two or three weeks the benefits begin to diminish, so good timing is critical, as some members of the 1972 British Olympic team which trained at altitude in St Moritz before those Games discovered. A number of athletes who stayed at altitude for what was thought to be the correct amount of time before their events went down to Munich and performed rather disappointingly. But in meetings held in the immediate post-Games period the same athletes set lifetime bests, indicating that they had undergone insufficient re-adjustment before the Games.

But one female athlete, Sheila Carey, who had become bored with staying at altitude and left St Moritz for Munich before the recommended time, ran well in excess of all reasonable expectations at the Games and set a UK 1500 metres record which stood for seven years.

Thus, as each athlete may take a different shoe size, so each one may need a different period of adjustment at sea level before achieving their optimum performance, which could be seven to fourteen days or even longer after 'coming down'. Consequently, in considering whether altitude training can help you in a certain race, you have to be fairly sure of your own particular requirements before committing yourself. Instead of helping your performance, it could actually hinder it, so some form of experimentation, using a minor event, is preferable to taking the risk of ending up, as one of those frustrated 1972 Olympians remarked, 'throwing away four years of hard work'.

It is also thought that for athletes who do respond to altitude training well, the more frequently time can be spent there, the more benefit will accrue. However, as most runners have jobs, families and other considerations, it takes a particularly ambitious and single-minded athlete to live for regular extended periods away from home, often in a foreign country and with an unfamiliar diet, simply trying to boost their total number of red blood cells.

For what has to be set against the physical benefits are what can be the inestimable negative effects of boredom and change of routine. Sitting around waiting for your next training session for weeks on end, while hoping that your blood cells are duly multiplying, is scarcely the most fascinating of pastimes. The ability to cope mentally plays a big part in the success of altitude training.

Of course, circumstances can be favourably adjusted. Members of the athlete's family or close friends could possibly go to altitude too, employment could be found locally, and so on. But it all involves a major upheaval, not to mention an expensive one, because British athletes would inevitably have to go abroad.

Altitudes of at least 5000, and up to 8000, feet are generally considered to be the most beneficial for distance running purposes, so even jogging on the spot at the top of Ben Nevis (4406 feet) while taking deep breaths, won't help a great deal.

In the USA the 1972 Olympic marathon champion Frank Shorter found the ideal situation, having moved with his wife to Boulder, Colorado (5350 feet) in 1975, first as a lawyer and then operating his own business, selling running gear. He said:

> 'I've lived at altitude since 1967, and it's worked for me. It's simply harder to run up here – there's more of a training effect, or return for a given effort. Besides, you tend to train best where you're happiest, and if you like the mountains, you'll probably do well there.'

The place is almost perfect. Apart from the altitude of Boulder itself, nearby Flagstaff Mountain rises to 7200 feet, the weather is generally good and, even if it is not, then Boulder's University of Colorado offers indoor training facilities. More and more of the world's top distance runners have moved to Boulder, which has become a major world centre for training.

But, while there is no doubt that altitude training can, and has, produced excellent results for some runners, the difference between training at altitude away from your home environment and creating your own home environment at altitude, as Shorter did, are among the many aspects of this type of training which the athlete must consider thoroughly before it is judged as being the universal answer it may at first appear.

And one very important point must never be overlooked: training, even at altitude, still has to be hard, correctly planned, regularly executed, and allied to the right racing programme as effectively as at sea level to produce the results on the day that matters.

'Blood packing'

The practice of blood packing, blood boosting or, as it is sometimes misleadingly called, blood doping, has increasingly become a spectre over international sport in recent years, posing as it does an enormous ethical problem. I include it here by no means as a recommendation (indeed I believe that to tamper with bodily processes in such a way can be exceedingly dangerous), but simply to complete the picture.

Blood packing involves a manipulation of the level of a runner's red blood cells which can in certain circumstances give him the same supercharged effect it is possible to achieve through training at altitude. Several Finnish runners have admitted using the system to improve performances, including the 1980 Olympic 10,000m silver and 5000m bronze medallist Kaarlo Maaninka and the 1972 Olympic steeplechase finalist Mikko Ala-Leppilampi. More recently some leading Italian distance runners, including the 1984 Olympic 10,000m champion Alberto Cova, were accused of using the system to achieve competitive success, although they vigorously denied such accusations. An American gold-medal winning cycling team at the 1984 Olympics did, however, own up to having used the process, which was subsequently formally banned by both the International Olympic Committee and the IAAF. Enforcing the ban may be far more difficult.

The method involves withdrawing up to two litres of blood from an athlete two or three months before a major event, then freezing and storing the red cell content which is vital for oxygen transportation. Just before the major competition, when the body has made up the deficit by natural means, the previously withdrawn red cells are re-injected, giving the athlete an additional supply of oxygen-carrying cells. Unlike drug-taking, the process breaks no doping control rules, since the athlete is merely receiving his own blood.

The first clinical reports of blood packing came in 1971, when a well-respected 33-year-old Swedish physiologist, Bjorn Ekblom, conducted tests in the interests of research at the Institute of Stockholm.

> 'We took seven students from our school and let them run on our treadmill to get an indication of their capacity' he reported at the time. 'Then we drew 27 ounces of blood (approximately equal to 20 per cent of a human's entire quantity). On the test next day, we saw a clear decrease in capacity. Then, day by day, as new blood was produced in their bodies, the values went up. After 14 days, all were at their maximum again. Then, one month after the experiment began, we gave them back their own blood. The effect was stunning. Our test people increased their capacity by 20 per cent. The best was 23 per cent.
>
> 'It's easy to see the significance this could have on long distance runners and cyclists. I have even been offered $20,000 for my exact method. Now, when I reflect on my laboratory tests, I feel scared. Even if I appeal to the sense of justice of all leaders and doctors in the world, I'm not sure someone will not make use of the results, say in the Olympics. And what will become of sport then?'

Ekblom's concern, expressed 20 years ago, proved sadly prophetic. One Finnish athlete, however, had reason to wish he had never dabbled. Martti Vainio, who was disqualified from the silver medal position in the 10,000m at the 1984 Olympic Games following a positive doping test for steroids, was mystified as to how the banned steroids (which he admitted he had used, but months before the Games) came to be in his system so long afterwards. Only later did he realize that through blood packing as well, in a double bid to cheat his way to Olympic success, he had allowed the withdrawal of his blood at a time when he had been taking steroids. Months later, when the blood was restored, so were the traces of steroids. A bitter justice.

The health risks of blood packing have also been highlighted in recent years. Physiologists have warned of a possible thickening of the blood to a point where the heart cannot properly pump it, and of the risk of reintroducing infection which might have existed when the blood was withdrawn. The shadow of AIDS also falls across any processes involving blood transfusions.

Above all, though, the ethical problem remains. Can blood packing, using a runner's own blood, really be considered a form of cheating while altitude training, which achieves the same result but takes a great deal longer, is considered legitimate? The answer, surely, must be that altitude training is improvement by natural processes, but blood packing is not.

Exercises

Most distance runners tend to be greatly lacking in mobility, which can cause an unnecessarily restricted running action and sometimes even lead to injury. A few extra minutes before each training session spent on some simple exercises, such as those outlined below, can improve running style by 'unlocking' the muscles, and help to prevent injury by ensuring that the body really is ready to run. Trying to run hard with insufficient preparation is to ask the muscles to perform without giving them a chance to warm up, and that is when the muscle fibres rebel and tear. It is like asking someone to be at their brightest, most cheerful and creative just moments after being rudely awakened.

But if the muscles are gently stretched by exercises to at least the maximum level to which they will work in running, and slightly beyond, then there is little chance of running causing the over-stretching of cold, contracted, reluctant muscles.

Astride stretch

Stand with left leg forward, the knee bent, and the right leg back with the right knee just resting on the ground. With the hands on the left knee, keeping the right knee on the ground, lean right forward and hold for 15 seconds. Repeat with the opposite leg and then do the whole exercise again. Particular benefit to hip, hamstring and groin.

Quarter-squat

Bend the knees slightly and hold quarter-squat position for 20 seconds. Repeat three times. This stretches the quadriceps (front of the upper leg) and relaxes the hamstrings (rear of the upper leg).

Wall push-up

Stand facing a wall, about 3 feet away from it. Lean on it with straight arms, and then bend the arms to lean as far into the wall as you can, while keeping the feet flat on the ground. Hold for 20 seconds and then push away from wall. Repeat six times. Particular benefit to calves and Achilles tendons.

Kerb stretch

Stand on the edge of a kerb or step, facing inwards, with the heels 2–3 inches over the edge. Gently lower the heels about ½ inch at first, and then raise again. Repeat ten times each day, gradually increasing the amount of stretch. Particular benefit to Achilles tendons.

Bent leg sit-up

Lie on your back on the ground, with the knees well bent and the hands behind your head. Perform ten sit-ups, while trying to keep the feet on the ground. Particular benefit to abdomen and back.

Training diary

Every runner, whether a first-year colt, a top international, a seasoned veteran, or a keep-fit jogger, should keep a running diary in which they can record their daily training. The degree of detail could vary from a single figure indicating the number of miles covered that day to a complete breakdown of the length of the run, course, time taken, weather, what you wore, who you ran with, how you felt, and so forth.

By committing your running to paper, you provide the opportunity to look back in some years' time to compare your progress and training. If you want to recapture the form of a previous season, you can always look back to see what training you were doing in the months before your peak. You can keep a record of your fastest times on each training course you use regularly, and in each race. You can note your weight as it rose and fell, and your resting pulse rate (best taken first thing each morning) as it too rose and fell over the years when your fitness increased and declined, as everyone's does from time to time.

In short, with the expenditure of just a few moments of effort every day, you can put between the covers the definitive You, recording one aspect of your daily life more accurately than a photograph album.

An ordinary diary will do, though the more information you want to record the bigger it will have to be. Several specifically designed runner's diaries are now on the market, but another alternative is an ordinary large loose-leaf file into which can be inserted the result sheets of races in which you have competed as well as the training sheets.

Some runners cannot be bothered with such things as diaries, but I still find some kind of fascination in being able to look back and read what training I was doing thirty years ago.

Rest

What, you may wonder, is a section on rest doing in a chapter specifically dealing with different types of training methods? It is here because I believe that rest plays just as important and constructive a part in the preparation of a runner as any of the other aspects discussed earlier. Yet it is something to which few pay much attention, other than just to accept that to rest the day before a race will probably result in a better performance than carrying out another hard training session.

Others actually resent resting, feeling that to do so is to throw away valuable time which could otherwise be used to put in yet more miles. But, if that was the case, the best runner would be the one who trained non-stop for 24-hours a day . . . obviously impossible, so once again it is a question of striking the right balance.

In the short term, hard training, either in quantity or quality, is destructive. It tears down muscle tissues, accumulates waste products in the blood, can cause dehydration which in turn can upset the balance of electrolytes required for functioning of nerves and muscles, and reduces both the amount of energy-giving glycogen in the muscles and the level of blood sugar.

Nature repairs the damage, but it takes time. On each occasion that the body is subjected to hard training, it is eventually set back up again a little stronger than before. But if it is constantly being hammered by hard training without the process of repair ever being completed, it may eventually break down altogether. It is like a house being damaged by a storm. If the builders get to work they can make the house better prepared to face another storm. But if the next storm arrives before they have finished the job, and then another and another, the original damage may be made much worse.

For the runner, sleeping and eating regularly and well helps promote the recuperation, or repair. Alternating 'hard' and 'easy' training sessions also assists, for the demands of modern distance running tend to crowd out the possibility of complete recovery after every session. What has to be avoided is reaching the extreme level of fatigue in which susceptibility to injury or illness is greatly increased.

As Gosta Holmer said of fartlek training, 'the athlete has to decide for himself when the training is no longer improving him, but destroying him instead'.

But relaxing activities, like taking a sauna, a massage, yoga or easy swimming can help the regeneration process by stimulating the circulation without aggravating the temporary damage caused by the running training.

Time and again there have been examples of athletes who have been almost fanatical in their training and whose careers were interrupted by the inevitable breakdown injury brought on by overloading their systems. After an enforced rest, which they usually hated and resented, they often came back to competition on the minimum of training and produced superb performances. Not all of them realized that the performance probably resulted from their original training plus the rest working together. Instead they spent a very long time anguishing over what they could actually have achieved 'if the injury hadn't halted my training'.

The American writer and medical researcher Ned Frederick once wrote that too many runners treat their bodies as just another obstacle to overcome in their quest for success, and told a particularly significant story in explaining the theory that hard work plus rest equals success.

Two climbers reached the peak of a famous mountain together, but when they came down they had different tales about their exploit. One spoke of 'conquering the mountain'. The other put it more humbly: 'The mountain and I together attained the heights.' In the same way, it is not the athlete *against* his body. It is the athlete *and* his body against his rivals.

3

WHAT TO WEAR

Another attraction of running is that it need involve no great cost in equipment. There are no expensive helmets, bats, gloves, pads, face masks or racquets which are mandatory to buy before heading down the road. You can run in a T-shirt, shorts and plimsolls if you like.

There are, of course, manufacturers who would love to sell you a costly, fleecy-lined tracksuit, but to be honest your body won't really know whether it's encased in a £100 designer tracksuit or an old rugby jersey – only whether it is cold or not. Nevertheless, most runners like to feel smart in training and competition, so it is worth considering here the possible pitfalls in buying running kit.

We will begin with the equipment on which, if economy is a necessity, you should try to skimp least.

Shoes

When you consider that your running shoes are the only contact between your feet and the ground for nearly a thousand strides a mile, it is quite surprising that some runners are content to spend the absolute minimum amount of time shopping for them. If they rub or distort your feet on one stride, then they will do so on every stride, and that adds up to many thousands of miserable strides, perhaps millions, during the lifetime of the average running shoe. It also means a lot of rubbing and a lot of distortion, which in turn can lead to blisters and injury. It is obviously illogical to spend many hours training and only 5 minutes in deciding on a pair of shoes which may injure you and undo a lot of the good work you have put in.

There is now a very wide range of shoes on the market, both in make and model, and each different shoe is probably just right for someone.

But which is perfect for *you*? Unless you spend some time looking, examining and comparing, you may never find out. Two athletes may have the same length of feet, but one might have broad feet and the other narrow feet. In that case, the same model of shoe will not suit both, unless it is one of those now being made in different width fittings, or in a special ladies' version.

While you might get away with ill-fitting shoes for everyday wear, running shoes need to be just right, as you will know halfway through a long run if they do not fit properly. 'The last pair of running shoes I bought fitted like a glove,' said one runner. 'Next time I'm going to get some that fit like shoes.'

In Chapter 5 I discuss the type of grip needed for cross country running, so this section is confined to road shoes of the type the majority of runners probably wear for 90 per cent or more of their total running activity. But a lot of the points apply equally to selection of racing spikes.

The first essential whenever you are buying a pair of running shoes is that you should try both of them on, properly laced and tied. Only then can you tell what they really feel like on your feet. Sitting on a chair in the shop, trying on just one without even fully lacing it tells you very little about where the shoes could possibly rub or restrict your feet on a long run. Obviously you may not be able to go out and run a couple of miles down the road in them before you buy them, but you can walk or even jog around the shop in them first.

If they seem at all tight, try half a size larger until you are satisfied. There are now a good many sports shops set up by active runners who understand your needs and can offer sound advice from their own experience. Ask them what shoes *they* wear, and why. But there are also a larger number of general sports shops where the assistants serving you may only be interested in getting a quick sale before their tea break. If the shop is 'waiting for your size to come in', don't settle for the wrong size in the right shoe, or the right size in the wrong shoe. Either hold off buying them until your size does come in, look for another suitable model of shoe, or go somewhere else.

If the shoe feels tight in one place (say, over the arch) or has too much room somewhere else (perhaps in the toes), then forget that particular model altogether because the chances are that no size will fit you properly.

Don't be embarrassed if you have to try on a dozen pairs of shoes and then don't want to buy any of them. Remember that the onus is on the shop to find shoes suitable for your feet, not the other way round. I once bought a pair of strikingly gold-coloured lightweight road shoes, even though they were 1½ sizes too big for me, because the shop did not have any smaller ones in stock. I still don't know why I did it, but every day for two months I'd try them on in case my feet had unexpectedly grown. Then, when I realized they weren't going to, I had to sell them for about half what I paid for them. A fruitless, expensive, illogical exercise.

So don't be overwhelmed or distracted by the colour or flashiness of the shoes. A pair of vivid purple, green and orange shoes may be a wow at the club and help people to spot you easily in a fog, but if they give you blisters after 2 miles you are much better off without them. Don't be like the athlete who tried on two pairs of road shoes, one of which fitted and one of which didn't, and then bought the pair which didn't 'because the colour goes better with my new tracksuit'.

Above all, never forget that you are trying to find shoes which have virtually to become part of your feet for many miles of running. If the shoes you buy are going to try to alter nature by cramping and distorting your feet, there can only be trouble ahead.

Examine all aspects of the shoes closely, and particularly the thickness of the heel. The distance runner lands heavily on the heel on practically every stride taken, and it has to be substantial enough to cushion the shock of around 80 per cent of the body weight landing on an unyielding surface like pavement or road. Many shoes have a heel wedge – an extra layer of rubber between the midsole and sole – but the overall thickness of the heel must not be so great that the weight is thrown too far forward, making it feel as though you are constantly running downhill.

To have too thick a heel also reduces the force exerted by the Achilles tendon on each stride. So a happy medium is usually the answer; personally I prefer shoes with a heel about ¾ inch thick.

The heel counter is the reinforced section curving around the ankle and often covered with suede, which stabilizes the heel on landing. But the heel tab above it is a controversial aspect on many running shoes. It is the hump which rises on the back of the shoe, above the heel counter, and exists ostensibly to protect the Achilles tendon, and also to assist in pulling on the shoe. Some physiotherapists, however, insist that a rigid heel tab can itself cause Achilles tendon problems by digging into the vulnerable base of the tendon on every stride. Built-in arch supports are another point of debate. Theoretically, they should help, but evidence from the USA has suggested that, although they may feel comfortable, they actually offer no bio-mechanical assistance for most runners. Remember that the manufacturers are turning out millions of pairs of running shoes made on lasts which are designed to represent the average foot. In fact, relatively few people actually have an 'average' foot. Most feet are as different as our fingerprints, and one estimation is that arch-supports actually suit no more than ten per cent of the buyers of running shoes, and the rest are better off without them. In the USA the trend is towards orthotics, which are plastic shoe inserts, often custom-made, to correct any foot problems.

The sole of a running shoe needs the best of both worlds. It must be reasonably well cushioned to protect the forefoot against too much shock, but flexible enough to allow natural foot movement, particularly at the point of maximum bend, where the toe pushes off from the ground on each stride.

The toe-box, at the front of the shoe, should provide sufficient height and width to prevent the toes being cramped even when the feet expand, as they do when hot. It is actually better to buy running shoes in late afternoon rather than the morning, because your feet are slightly bigger at that time of day. Allow ¼ inch of room in front of the toes, especially if you have Morton's Foot, a condition in which the second toe is longer than the big toe. Running in shoes which are too tight, particularly going downhill, is like kicking a brick wall.

The eyelets for lacing should be reinforced with several thicknesses of material; anything less could result in the fabric being torn. There are several types of lacing. By far the most common is the U-throat, on the top of the foot, but the laces should be taken out and re-threaded every week or so to help spread the wear on the laces themselves. Although not an expensive item, a lace always seems to break at an inconvenient time, such as just before a race or when your available training time is very limited. Because the laces often become snagged on the material eyelets of the uppers, the lacing nearer the toes becomes slacker, and you end up each time just tightening up the two or three eyelets at the top of the shoes, and so the shoe is not fastened most efficiently.

A second type of lacing is speed lacing, where the laces pass through plastic or metal rings, and are easy to tighten all the way down. They can also be adjusted better for those runners with a high instep.

Spare laces should be taken everywhere by the runner, and fitted as soon as possible after a lace has snapped. Sometimes, in the absence of spares, it is possible, indeed necessary, to manage by missing out a couple of eyelets and using the short broken lace. But in that case a new lace should still be inserted afterwards. I have known some runners repair their shoes that way in an emergency, and then carry on running with the make-do lace still in place for months. Then they wonder how they had come to be injured, despite the fact that the unequal lacing in their shoes had been forcing them to run out of balance.

Padding around the ankle, the cushioned rim featured by some shoes, helps to prevent those blisters which are often caused in cheaper shoes by having little more than the thickness of the shoe material (and sometimes an irritating seam) around the ankle.

'Breaking in' is an important process, even for shoes that fit well. They need to adapt to the exact movements of the joints in your feet, and the best way is to wear them around the house for a few days, and perhaps jog a mile or so in them, before using them for training or racing – and even then start off using them only for shorter distances. Never wear brand new shoes in a race or on a long training run.

Surprisingly perhaps, experienced international athletes still, from time to time, find out the hard way that you cannot get away with wearing brand new shoes for a marathon. Usually they have been track runners moving up in distance, and who had suffered no damage previously when wearing new shoes in a 10,000-metre track race, or even a 10-mile road event. But the marathon, you will not need reminding, is different.

One culprit in this is the development of the road running shoe itself. The nylon which, since the late sixties, has almost completely replaced the heavier, less pliable leather in the manufacture of shoe uppers and certainly breaks in more quickly, is lighter in weight and dries more easily. But even nylon shoes have to be stitched together in places, and if they are made on a last which does not resemble your feet, then they will probably be engaged in some form of disagreement with your feet on every one of those 25,000–30,000 strides.

If you live in an area where you cannot easily get to a sports shop with a range of different shoes, ask as many other runners as you can which shoes they wear, and what they think of them. Don't just believe the advertising blurb; of course the manufacturers are going to tell you that every one of their shoes is just what you've been waiting for. If you have to order by post, send an outline of your foot with your order, because sizes differ slightly between manufacturers, and it may save you having to return the shoes later if they don't fit. But if they still don't fit, don't be afraid to send them back. It is better to wait an extra few days for the right-sized shoes than to run for six months in the wrong ones.

The weight of shoes is again a matter of personal preference. Very light road racing shoes (often made on the same type of last as spiked track racing shoes) are available, but to attempt to cover high training mileages in such shoes would probably lead to injury. They are simply not substantial enough to protect the feet from the constant pounding every day, and there is a growing feeling in the USA, as a result of the considerable research undertaken during the running boom of the last decade, that the lightest shoes are probably only of benefit to the fastest ten per cent of marathon runners.

The American podiatrist Dr Steven Subotnick has expressed the opinion that unless you are going to run a marathon at a speed faster than 5½-minutes-a-mile pace (2 hours 24 minutes pace), then you should be content to wear a good training shoe rather than a light racing model because otherwise, as your running form deteriorates in the last 10 miles of a slower marathon, your joints, muscles and skeleton have to absorb more stress and need greater shock absorption in the shoes.

Figures presented to the American College of Sports Medicine have demonstrated that the amount of extra energy expended by marathon runners wearing training shoes instead of the lighter shoes was only three per cent, whereas the heavier shoes in turn offered twenty-five per cent more shock absorption.

Protecting the legs from the considerable shock is one of the main functions of running shoes anyway, together with motion control (to stop the foot rolling too much inwards or outwards) and traction. For a time, in the quest for maximum shock absorption, some road shoes became too soft in the sole which resulted in a number of leg injuries, which they were trying to prevent. Now the designs are reaching a happy medium.

I am constantly being asked which model of shoes is the best, but unlike the date of the Battle of Hastings, there is no precise answer. If there were, all the other shoe companies would go out of business. Different shoes suit different feet, and the only real solution is to jump in – with both feet! – and try to find which particular model is most suited to you. But don't forget that those shoes should carry you for thousands of miles, so it is worth spending more than 5 minutes in finding them.

Socks

Socks cut down the friction between the foot and the inside of the shoe, reducing the chance of blistering, and help to absorb shock and moisture; again cotton is far better than nylon in this respect. The socks should be clean, with no inner seams to cause irritation, and no darns. If a running sock has a hole in it, throw it away!

Some runners prefer to run without socks, finding it cooler, especially in road races. Vaseline rubbed over the toes can cut down the friction which causes blisters, and sticking plaster applied before you run to any parts of the feet normally vulnerable to blisters can also help to keep down any trouble spots. Some runners put pieces of sponge in between their heels (a prime blister area) and the back of their shoe before a long race.

Tracksuits

The purpose of the tracksuit is to provide warmth both before and after running and, while many of the smartest tracksuits on the market are nylon or other man-made materials, they do not absorb moisture as well as cotton. Therefore at least a T-shirt or fleecy-lined cotton 'sloppshirt' is advisable between your running kit and tracksuit. Hooded sloppshirts, although more expensive, are another good way of keeping in essential warmth, particularly after a race, when you are cooling down rapidly.

All pockets on tracksuits should have zips, because if you try to run with a key or pound coin in your pocket it may jump out without your noticing it, and you could have to walk a long way back afterwards looking for it.

Tracksuit trousers with flared legs were obviously designed by someone who had never run more than 100 yards in their life, and may be fine for standing around in, but not so good for actually running in – especially in a high wind! The straight or tapered leg, with or without side zip, is far more practical.

Sometimes on cold days wearing two tracksuits may be necessary and, even if you do run round feeling like a Michelin man, the important thing is to keep warm. And, if you actually train in a tracksuit, always have another one to put on afterwards, unless you are showering or bathing straight away.

Keeping the body temperature as level as possible is the aim. Before you start running, you may need several layers to keep warm. As you start running, your body temperature rises and you can then discard some layers without discomfort. But, almost as soon as you stop, you begin to get cold and the extra layers have to go back on to maintain the temperature and prevent chills or muscle stiffness.

Rain suits

These suits are also known as wetsuits, and that is what they usually end up as, either inside or out. They consist of a light-weight showerproof jacket and trousers which are big enough to go over several tracksuits if necessary. They prevent you from absorbing too much rain into your tracksuit, and are very useful on many occasions – especially going shopping! But their disadvantage can be that, if you warm up for too long in them, they can become like mini Turkish baths and you end up almost as damp as you would have done in the rain.

However, a rain suit is still an essential part of every runner's kit, and it takes up very little space when folded up in your bag. It is often also overlooked for its value in keeping off the type of driving wind which blows right through many layers of cotton, wool and nylon.

Shorts

The difference between men's and women's shorts has narrowed considerably in recent years, with many female distance runners now adopting the same style of brief, loose and airy men's shorts. They should be secure at the waist, but not too tight, and allow a full range of movement. An increasing number of shorts now include a built-in brief, but some runners prefer to wear their own, and cut out this section from the shorts where appropriate.

The knee-length cycling shorts now worn by many track sprinters are much less suitable for the distance runner, and while the complete one-piece body suits may alleviate the discomfort of tight elastic around the waist, they can instead present problems in last minute pre-race dashes to the toilet, or (especially for women) in the case of a mid-race dash to a nearby bush!

The ladies briefs, in towelling or Lycra, are still favoured by most female track runners, but are now less in favour for long distance races.

Vests

Before deciding on which vest to wear in a race, it's necessary to check whether it is an event such as a team or individual championship where the wearing of club colours is mandatory. With the growth of commercial advertising appearing on vests, which are now increasingly monitored by officials to ensure that their content and lettering size are within the rules, there is greater emphasis than ever on wearing correct colours.

You do not need to have finished among the prize winners to be disqualified for not wearing the right vest and you could even affect your team result. While some runners dismiss this pernickety checking as petty officialdom, the best advice is that you won't go far wrong simply wearing your official club vest for racing.

Cotton vests are still the most comfortable, and far more absorbent than nylon, although the latter dries more quickly.

Recognising that on hot days, a dark coloured club vest uncomfortably absorbs more of the sun's rays than light colours, the AAA have introduced a rule which allows clubs to nominate an alternative light-coloured club vest (including white with a club badge) for events of 10km and above. The Women's AAA, meanwhile, permits the use of specialist-type vests with part mesh (of which they must approve) being worn in middle and long distance races, as long as they are 'designed and worn so as not to be objectionable, even if wet', a stipulation which exists in the rules of both men's and women's associations as a general rule for all competitive kit.

On hot days that mesh section of a vest allows heat to escape from the body and a cooling breeze to reach more of the skin surface. For a while totally-mesh vests (based on the string vest) were worn by most top runners, but the sawing effect of the sweat-soaked mesh across the chest sometimes created a painful grazing of the nipples, known as 'jogger's nipple'.

Heavily-built runners in tight vests still suffer from this condition on occasions, and the most effective pre-race preventive routine is either to smear petroleum jelly, such as Vaseline, over the nipples, or to cover them with Elastoplast. The small effort involved may be well rewarded.

Vests (and shorts) should always be well road-tested for comfort, and potential chafing points identified before they are worn in any long distance race. Smearing Vaseline under the armpits, crotch and thighs will also help reduce the chance of the painful chafing which sweat-soaked kit can cause during a long race or training run.

Bras

Even women who normally choose not to wear a bra are well advised to do so when running, because research has shown that the muscles and ligaments in the breasts can easily become damaged if they are not sufficiently supported. They will begin to sag and they will not regain their shape.

The choice of a bra is a personal decision, which a woman can make only through trial and error. There are now a number of specifically designed sports bras on the market, which most average-busted women would find suitable for running. The bra should have no seams across the cups, as they might rub or irritate the nipples and there should be a broad band around the base under the cups to ensure it does not ride up during exercise.

Some large breasted women still find the problem of a bouncing chest somewhat embarrassing. Apart from wearing a loose-fitting top so as not to draw too much attention to themselves, the bounce has been effectively controlled by some women through wearing a second bra on top of the first.

Bra straps are often a problem because they tend to slip down, or simply show and look untidy. Most specialist sports bras are joined at the back by a central panel which prevents the straps slipping off, while some women have successfully adapted their own favourite bras by snipping the straps at the back and re-sewing them in a crossover style.

4

THE WORLD OF ROAD RUNNING

Q. Why did the chicken cross the road?
A. To get the bend in its favour.

'Mummy!' cried the little girl, rushing indoors from the front garden. 'There are a lot of men outside taking their trousers off in the middle of the road!'

'It's all right, dear,' reassured her mother, as she surveyed the scene from the front door. 'They're not men. They're runners.'

Road running takes sport to the most unlikely arena: your own doorstep. Any quiet suburban road is liable to become part of a racecourse, as 500 runners line up across Lobelia Avenue at ten o'clock on a Sunday morning for the start of a road race (only to have to part again like the Red Sea a few seconds later to let Mrs Dingleby from number 38 chug through in her Morris Minor, blissfully unaware that she has only just missed crushing one or two well-known feet).

Fortunately, few residents seem to object – vocally, anyway – to the use of their road as a race track. Many come out to watch, a few are oblivious to any sporting event which is not being shown on their TV screens, and just one or two may complain, quite understandably, if they find athletes sitting on their front walls, using their tree branches as coat hooks, or even watering their flowers.

Sadly, some athletes do forget that they are within inches of other people's homes, and treat the surrounding area like a changing room. Tracksuits left on walls or fences without prior permission can be

43

particularly annoying to the residents.

One runner finished a road race to find that his tracksuit trousers had been blown by the wind from a low wall over which he had draped them on to a front lawn, where the owner was mowing the grass. As they were green, explained the gardener to the runner afterwards, only half convincingly, he hadn't seen them and . . .

Then there was the tale of a group of runners who left their tracksuits uninvited on a garden fence during a 10km road race and returned to find that the house owner had collected them up and given them to the vicar for his jumble sale. One of the runners had to queue up outside the church hall the following Saturday and buy them all back for five pence each.

But road running, both training and racing, is the most basic and simple activity within the sport of athletics, and perhaps within any sport. And while you can understand pole vaulters and hammer throwers complaining about the lack of facilities in Britain, a road runner would get little sympathy for complaining that 'those East Germans have got more roads than we have'.

Its sheer simplicity makes it an attraction for a great many club level athletes who seldom if ever set foot on a conventional running track either for training or racing. It is also a particularly satisfying area for those of us with little or no basic speed, for stamina accumulated through regular training can compensate for the inherent lack of swiftness. Most senior club runners can break 6 minutes for the mile, but far fewer can crack the hour for 10 miles. The difference is not speed, but having or gaining the stamina to sustain that limited speed.

The accumulation of stamina results not from any great skill, but simply from regular runs of graduating length and intensity until the body is sufficiently well-trained to achieve the target set for it. After running 10 miles in 1 hour, running 20 miles in 2¼ hours or a marathon in 3¼ hours could be targets at which to aim, or your target could simply be to run those 10 miles faster.

Whatever the goal, achieving it is down to the simplest and fairest give-and-take deal in sport. If you run often, you run faster. All the money in the world, all the friends in high places, all the fast talking and wheeling and dealing that you could imagine, cannot substitute for the only way to prepare to run a long way. Only going out and actually running can do that.

There are, of course, many races shorter than the marathon, and it is in the 10km and half-marathon events that adult newcomers are best advised to obtain their early road running experience before even contemplating a marathon. Details of most of the open road races in the UK (with 'open' meaning open to entry by any amateur runner in the relevant age groups, not a description of the surroundings) are advertised in specialist magazines like *Running* and *Today's Runner*, from which the runner can obtain a great deal of advance information about both road and cross country events.

The organization of road running in the UK comes under the umbrella of the national governing body, which is effectively the Amateur Athletic Association (AAA) during the current restructuring of the sport's administration.

The AAA, established in 1880, took rather a long time to catch up with the present running boom and after abandoning an initial registration scheme designed to enrol the thousands of new runners who preferred to compete outside a formal club, it set up its own Road Race Advisory Committee, which publishes a road race handbook.

This committee nevertheless works in close contact with two other national bodies specializing in road running – the British Association of Road Races (BARR) and the Road Runners Club (RRC).

BARR, to which a specific annual race such as the Thanet Marathon becomes affiliated rather than individuals, was founded in 1983 and is dedicated to improving the overall standard of road race promotion and organization in the UK. In 1989 it began its own grading scheme, whereby races with the best (and worst) organization were accorded a grading.

But the doyen of all the governing organizations is the RRC, which is a national organization of runners from clubs in different locations but with a common interest in road events.

The RRC has really played a significant part in the development of this area of the sport, particularly in the long distance events, since its foundation in 1952. For, although road running had taken place in England since at least 1907, and there were many well-established races long before the early 1950s, interest had not extended very much beyond the classic marathon distance of 26 miles 385 yards.

The father of long distance road running in Britain is acknowledged to have been Arthur Newton, whose exploits in South Africa thirty years earlier were eventually to lead to the foundation of the RRC. Newton, the son of a Norfolk clergyman, was born in 1883 and settled in South Africa in 1901, later buying a farm which produced first-grade cotton and tobacco. He had no background in athletics, and seemed set for a prosperous life as a farmer until a change in government in South Africa put the land he owned and had developed into a 'native territory' belt in 1922, which ended his farming endeavours without compensation.

Searching for a method of getting into the public eye, in an effort to bring attention to his plight, and realizing that successful sportsmen were well-known figures, he decided to enter the Comrades Marathon, a 54 mile event run on rough roads between Durban and Pietermaritzburg. He was thirty-nine and a complete novice at running but, with five months of carefully thought out, graduated, daily training, he managed to win the race and went on to retain the title for the next three years.

Sadly, his success did nothing to help his farming situation, but it did set him off as a prodigious record breaker at long distances, both in South Africa and on return trips to England. He set a world 50 miles best of 5 hours 38 minutes 42 seconds on the London to Brighton road in 1924, and a 100 miles best of 14 hours 6 minutes in 1934.

Newton's ideas, developed through practical experience, and his particularly sharp, reasoning mind, led to the publication of four books and innumerable magazine articles on all aspects of long distance running, although he was not without his critics. Yet even when well into his sixties he would get up at 5.00 a.m. for 12 mile runs, and at his home in north-west London on Sunday afternoons he would hold gatherings of long distance enthusiasts, his disciples.

It was through such meetings that some of his followers had the idea of trying to emulate his feats on the London to Brighton road, which winds for over 50 miles through Croydon, Redhill, Horley, Crawley, Bolney and Pyecombe, taking in three waves of hills.

Ernest Neville, an athletics official with a lifetime of association with that particular road through many walking events held along the route, became involved in organizing a running race from London to Brighton and, with sponsorship from the now defunct *News Chronicle* newspaper, the race was held as part of the Festival of Britain celebrations on 11 August 1951. There were fifty-six entrants, forty-seven starters and thirty-two finishers, with Lew Piper of Blackheath Harriers, a forty-year-old insurance clerk, winning in 6 hours 18 minutes 40 seconds after running the 51¾ miles from Westminster Bridge through wind and rain.

The race was a success, and the only residual problem was to find the means to make it an annual event. Consequently, Neville decided to found a new body, the Road Runners Club, to undertake this task, with the immediate object being to promote the 1952 race. The inaugural meeting of the RRC was held at the Regent Street Polytechnic in London on 30 June 1952, and was addressed by Arthur Newton, who lived to see the race grow from strength to strength before his death at the age of seventy-six in 1959.

Such a long race as the London to Brighton appealed, however, to only a small proportion of those athletes who ran on the road, and so the scope of the newly-formed body was subsequently enlarged to cover

the whole range of distance events from 10 miles upwards. The aim of
the RRC was, and still is, 'To bring together all those interested in long
distance running, to serve their interests, and to act as a forum for all
enthusiasts.'

To this end, the RRC has been a watchdog on such aspects of the
sport as course measurement, and has developed a standards scheme;
it also publishes a high standard club newsletter, operates an insurance
scheme, and organizes film shows as well as a select number of long
distance races, including the annual London to Brighton race each
October, which was, after all, the *raison d'être* of the club.

However, the responsibility for choosing, measuring and marking the
route of a road race remains with the separate race organizers, and
the chief concern of the competitor is simply to run as well as possible.
But advance knowledge of the route and the terrain to be covered are,
at the least, helpful to any competitor, and positively essential to the
ambitious runner. Quite apart from the possible pitfall of leading 2000
other runners into a cul-de-sac, it would be quite conceivable on an
unfamiliar course for a runner to make a hard effort to get away from
the field and then, just as he was intending to ease off slightly to
recover, be suddenly faced with an unexpected hill with no apparent top.

So get to know the course. Most races display some form of course
map at the changing rooms to show competitors the direction and shape
of the route. But such diagrams do not always indicate the uphill and
downhill sections, and a quick trip round the course by car can be
illuminating if it can be arranged. Make mental notes of where the
inclines begin and end, where you can get some form of respite on a
down slope, and what to look for towards the end of the race (or lap,
if several laps are used). There is nothing worse than gathering yourself
up for a final effort towards what you imagine is the finish and then, as
your eyes search in vain for the timekeepers, to be told, 'Only 2 miles
to go!'

It is always possible to jog some of the course as your warm-up, and
in any case the route will be marked in one or more ways. For instance,
a pilot car may drive ahead of the field, and as long as the driver keeps
clear enough of the front runners, so that they do not spend the entire
race breathing in exhaust fumes, this is a good method, as it also warns
oncoming traffic of the approach of a race.

It is not always ideal, however, if the race has to pass through
narrow lanes. I once agreed to pilot a race through a country area and,
while leading the runners down a single track road, met a car coming
the other way. Its driver refused to budge, and I had no alternative but
to reverse up to a passing place some 40 yards back and, while the

offending car went past in the opposite direction, the entire race overtook me, leaving me at the wrong end of a road race field which would be steaming merrily through 20 or 30 miles of little-used Kent countryside if it was not turned left at the next junction. Fortunately, judicious use of another lane just about saved the day.

Police patrol cars and motorcyclists, if the local force can spare the manpower and are asked in plenty of time, are sometimes willing to act as race pilots, while another alternative is the pedal cyclist, as long as there are not too many hills. At a Northern marathon some years back the leading runner was surprised to see the pilot cyclist he had been following for a long way suddenly get off his bike and go into a house. It turned out one of the tyres had punctured and he had gone home to mend it, little realizing that the runners were still following him!

As in cross country, static markers, human or otherwise, are usually positioned at each important junction in a race, and the general rule should be to keep straight on the road you are following until you are directed off. The directions may come from an official, or from arrows, posters or even chalk marks on the road, and again it is essential to familiarize yourself early on with the specific type of markers to be used in that race.

In most events up to 10 miles or so, for the majority of runners it is usually a case of follow-the-leader anyway, but in longer events it is often possible even for big fields to become well stretched out, and then you have to depend solely on how the course is marked. Which brings me back to the original point: knowledge of the course you are about to run can be a great asset in helping to spread your effort most economically over the route and thus improve your time and placing.

So when you are at a race you have never run before, and you hear a lot of changing room talk and nervous jokes about 'Deadman's Hill', or whatever, find out from other runners what they mean. At the Rochester 5 mile road race, for instance, which is one of the country's oldest events, the course starts with a mile-long steady climb and then, just when you think you have reached the top, you are suddenly directed up an even steeper slope called Cookham Hill. It can be a nasty shock if you are not expecting it!

Safety

If we accept that every time we set foot on the road we are entering an arena in which thousands of motorists and pedestrians are killed and injured every year in this country alone, then it is obvious that the appearance of several hundred runners on the scene, if not directly posing danger, is not exactly making the roads safer either.

Road running started before the First World War, when there were few motorized vehicles about, and if the sport has grown considerably since then it is a small expansion compared to the increase in traffic over the same period. Some traditional road races, including the London to Brighton clubs relay, have been discontinued partly because of the traffic problems they created. Others, like the Finchley 20 mile road race, have had to restrict their entry and to switch from a Saturday to a Sunday to conform with local police requirements.

Many other races continue on public roads, usually without incident, but sometimes with a few near misses. And occasionally a runner is badly injured.

The problem may even arise quite unexpectedly. Bolton international Steve Kenyon was leading a Lancashire road race when a well-built spectator inadvertently crossed the road in his path, collided with the slight Kenyon, and sent him somersaulting to land on his head in the road, opening a gash which needed five stitches.

They are the sort of incidents which can never be totally eliminated from the sport, any more than one could have predicted that a rhinoceros would chase Bournemouth's Chris Stewart after 2 miles of a 15 mile road race in Kenya. But there are some common sense rules which can at least help to keep traffic incidents to an absolute minimum.

The most obvious of these is to keep left during races. Yet at many events you can see runners drifting from side to side on the road, often without looking round, to try to take advantage of the bend all the time.

When training for road running, use the pavement as much as possible and, if you have to run on the road where there is no pavement, at least try to face the traffic whenever you can so that you can assess oncoming vehicles. A single runner on a narrow country lane is far more vulnerable to a fast car rounding a bend than when he is running alongside a main road.

At night, wearing a light-coloured (preferably white) tracksuit top or jumper will help motorists to see you, while an alternative is to use fluorescent patches on your tracksuit, or diagonal belts of the type worn by motorcyclists and cyclists.

There are moves afoot to try to transfer, in the interests of safety, as many road races as possible to enclosed circuits in parks or private grounds, and the old motor racing circuit around Crystal Palace National Sports Centre has been successfully used for road races and relays.

But even if it were possible to transfer every road race to traffic-free courses, thousands of runners would still have to train during the week on public roads. As a driver, I have cursed the foolishness of fellow-runners out training when they have suddenly darted across the road, or when I have narrowly missed hitting them because they were running down the middle of the road at night wearing a navy blue tracksuit.

Conversely, as a runner, I have cursed those car drivers whose main ambition in life seems to be to drive as close and as fast as possible to me when out training. In fact, there is probably a proportion of blame on both sides. But the unprotected human body is likely to fare far worse than a mass of fast-moving metal in the event of any collision, and the safest course is for the runner to treat every car driver as a lunatic and to choose the training routes carefully.

Likewise, although training in a group or pack can be particularly enjoyable, you must take care that amid all the backchat and banter which usually accompanies such runs you are not posing a traffic hazard by taking up too much room, straying wide into the road around blind bends, or simply paying insufficient attention to prevailing traffic conditions.

Above all, the runner about to set out on a training run around the local roads can always expect to meet traffic. A driver, on the other hand, will scarcely be setting out on his journey expecting to meet a runner.

5

THE WORLD OF CROSS COUNTRY

Of all forms of running, cross country is the most basic, back-to-nature exercise. The track and road are, after all, simply artificial surfaces developed by man, but the grass and mud of cross country really provide the athlete with a tough, challenging and absolutely natural carpet on which to run.

The elements may make the mud heavier, cover the course in deep snow, or leave it bone hard. The hills provide their own specific challenge. But they will still be there when today's runners have gone; the very grass itself, perhaps churned into mud by hundreds of pairs of feet on a Saturday afternoon, will grow green again when the athletes have packed their kit and left.

While some runners use cross country running and racing merely as a stamina builder for the summer track season, others treat it as a serious form of racing (indeed, often *the* serious form of racing). But, for all of them, the soft surfaces build up leg strength and endurance and help reduce the possibility of injury during a time of year which is usually spent putting in a large amount of background mileage, much of it necessarily on the road after dark.

In the British winter, Saturday and Sunday offer the only chance for many runners to train in the daylight and, if Sunday is traditionally kept for the long, steady road run, then what better mental and physical contrast than to spend Saturday afternoon running cross country and to feel the ground for once yielding beneath your feet?

Organized cross country running has its roots in the mid-nineteenth century when it began as a winter pursuit for members of the Thames

Rowing Club which met at Roehampton in Surrey. They decided to take runs on the nearby Wimbledon Common to keep fit, and in 1868 began to organize paperchases. These events involved several runners setting off as 'hares' and laying trails of pieces of paper cut like confetti, while the other runners had to follow as 'hounds' and there was a prize for the first hound to reach each hare.

From this the club's running section became known, as it still is today, as the Thames Hare and Hounds. The club founder, Walter Rye, was the first president of the English Cross Country Union when it was established in 1883, and he described the club's activities in the 1880s:

> The distance run varies much, and usually consists of a ring of 8–10 miles from the clubhouse, which is generally an old-fashioned suburban inn. The longest run we remember was about 24 miles in a little over 3 hours.
>
> Hares and hounds alike should run in the colours of their club. Canvas shoes with india-rubber soles, worsted socks, flannel knickerbockers, and white or dark blue waterman's sweaters are the best thing to wear for winter, for if a brook has to be forded, or a river swum, the warm wet wool prevents any chill being taken in the coldest weather. And those who have tried it are aware that is *is* cold after sunset, running over 2 miles of heath, fagged out, in wet things.
>
> When the run is over, the tub – lukewarm if it can be had – is in universal request, followed, if possible, by a cold douche by means of a bucketful of water from the hands of a stable helper.
>
> If the run has been extra wet or cold, a steaming glass of port negus may be wisely taken as a precaution. But it is a singular thing that both before and after the meal that terminates the evening, ginger beer and gin is the favourite drink, having probably been found by long experience to best carry off the extra heat of the body caused by a long run. . . .
>
> Tea and a sing-song used to close the evening very pleasantly.

Even earlier, in 1837, a tough cross country race known as The Crick Run had been originated at Rugby School. It was a cross country event too which led to the modern 3000 metre steeplechase. The story is that in 1850 an undergraduate of Exeter College, Oxford, named Halifax Wyatt, was discussing with some colleagues a horse-racing steeple-chase in which his own mount had fallen.

'I'd rather go round the course on foot than ride that animal again,' said Wyatt. This casual remark was taken up by his friends, and later that year a 2 mile foot steeplechase was held on marshy farmland at Binsey, near Oxford. There were twenty-four fences to be jumped and the winner, appropriately, was Wyatt himself. By 1879, a track steeplechase had been established, and that particular type of event was destined to become part of the summer athletics programme. Until recent years the hurdle on the take-off side of the steeplechase water jump even used to incorporate a permanent hedge but now at the majority of tracks it has been replaced by canvas, boards, or just thin air, and so the steeplechase has consequently lost some of its original spirit.

The first English Cross Country Championships as such were staged in Epping Forest in 1876, with all thirty-two competitors going off course and the race being declared void. (Over a century later, the same thing occasionally happens in club races!) The inaugural National Championship is therefore considered to have been the 1877 race, held over 11¼ miles at Roehampton, and won by Percy Stenning from thirty-two other starters on 24 February 1877.

The sport grew, and there were more than 100 starters in the 1881 Championship, 252 in 1908, 544 in 1955, 1046 in 1969, and 2136 finishers in the 1988 Senior Championship event. Over 6600 runners entered the three different men's age group events.

For a short time cross country was also included in the Olympic Games programme, but the occurrences at the 1924 Games in Paris led to its removal. The Olympic race, over a 10,000 metre course which followed the banks of the River Seine for some considerable distance (and was described by one English competitor as 'like a disused brickyard'), was held on a scorching hot July day when the temperature was breaking records itself at 45 degrees centigrade (113 degrees fahrenheit). Many of the competitors suffered heat stroke, dehydration, and several were rumoured to have died, though fortunately these stories proved untrue. But many ran themselves into an advanced and dangerous state of exhaustion in the highly unsuitable conditions, and only fifteen of the original thirty-nine starters finished. Of these, a number were in a very poor state, reeling insensibly around the track at Colombes Stadium, where the race finished, and one competitor actually slumped to the track just 50 yards from the line.

Only the legendary Finn Paavo Nurmi, who won the race by nearly 1¼ minutes and took a total of four gold medals in those Games, appeared unaffected by the weather. Late into the evening officials were searching the course for runners who were still missing, and the scenes at Colombes had so shocked Olympic officials that cross country running was dropped from future Games.

There are now moves afoot, nearly seventy years later, to have it re-admitted to the Olympics and with the considerably greater knowledge of both officials and athletes regarding extremes of temperature it is unlikely that there could ever be a repeat of the Paris race. Cross country running, although essentially a winter sport, is already in the Games in one respect, of course, as part of the modern pentathlon programme.

But exactly what constitutes 'cross country' has been open to many different interpretations over the years. Even the current International Amateur Athletic Federation (IAAF) rules for cross country events are prefaced by the following statement:

> Owing to the extremely varying circumstances in which cross country running is practised throughout the world, especially regarding different seasons, climatic conditions and distances, it is impossible to legislate rigidly for international standardisation of this sport.

Its own definition of a cross country course for championship and international events states:

(a) The race shall be run over a course confined, as far as possible, to open country, fields, heathland, commons and grasslands. A limited amount of ploughed land may be included. The traversing of roads should be kept to a minimum.

(b) The course must be clearly marked, preferably with red flags on the left and white flags on the right, all of which must be visible from a distance of 125 metres. In all other respects, the appropriate rules governing track competitions shall be followed.

(c) When designing the course, very high obstacles should be avoided, so should deep ditches, dangerous ascents or descents, thick undergrowth and, in general, any obstacle which would constitute a difficulty beyond the aim of the competition.

It is preferable that artificial obstacles should not be used, but if the scope of the promotion renders them unavoidable, they should be made to simulate natural obstacles met within open country. In races where there are large numbers of competitors, narrow gaps or other hindrances which would deny to the competitors an unhampered run must be avoided for the first 1500 metres.

(d) The course must be measured and the distance declared at the time invitations are extended, together with a brief description of the course.

(e) The responsibility for providing an acceptable, well-marked course, details of which should appear in the programme, rests with the promoting body, who should appoint clerks of the course, umpires and pointsmen at intricate parts of the course to direct competitors as necessary.

The world Cross Country Championships, which were started in modest form in 1903 but only came under the wing of the IAAF in 1973, have been staged on all types of surfaces, from soft sandy courses with artificial mounds (as in Rabat, Morocco, in 1975), to glutinous muddy puddles (as in Stavanger in 1989).

Often, though, in recent years they have been held on horse-racing tracks, which has resulted in a long, twisting, mainly flat event which is fine for the spectators and TV cameras but less interesting for the runners themselves, and more like a long grass track race.

And this is the dilemma. The more important the race, the greater the number of people who want to see it, either in person or on TV. That means that the course has to be reasonably open and accessible and designed to enable television cameras to cover the whole course as efficiently as possible. That is why televised cross country events tend to be held on short loop courses and why major events like the English National Championship with its 2000 runners is unlikely ever to be covered in the same way. When the World Cross Country Championships were last held in the UK, at Gateshead in 1983, with a typically short lap circuit, it still required a BBC crew of over 100 to televise it.

Some of the best cross country courses in the UK, with their picturesque woodland paths and challenging hills, can only hope to host the smaller, non-televised events. And marking out a cross country course so that no one gets lost can be a long, difficult and thankless activity for the volunteer officials – especially when they have to dismantle it all again afterwards!

Cross country running, therefore, being somewhat off the beaten track, may have far less potential for a commercial 'boom' than road running. But there is no doubt that its attractions remain considerable, especially in a society which displays growing appreciation of the natural environment. If the average runner can accept that the course marking and back-up facilities for some events may be less sophisticated than at most road races, the satisfaction of completing a cross country race is certainly no less than at a road race, and is often greater.

If you feel that you would like a change from training for marathons, half-marathons or 10km road races, cross country is certainly worth considering for a change of scenery.

One crucial difference is that men's and women's races are held separately, rather than simultaneously as in road races.

Although its history is shorter than for men, cross country running for women in Britain goes back further than many people think. It is more than sixty years since the first Women's AAA National Cross Country Championship was held, in terrible weather, at Luton in 1927, when Anne Williams of Littlehampton beat no less than 107 rivals. Even five years before that the ladies of Birchfield Harriers and London

Olympiades AC were including cross country as part of their winter training, while in France a women's national championship had been held since at least 1923. In 1931 an international three-sided match between England, France and Belgium at Douai, France, was staged with Gladys Lunn of Birchfield Harriers leading England to team victory.

Originally, cross country came under the umbrella of the Women's AAA, but a number of enthusiasts felt that it should have its own association. A meeting in Birmingham on 16 September 1950 brought about the formation of the Women's Cross Country and Race Walking Association, with Mrs Dorette Nelson Neal as chairman. The Women's AAA subsequently delegated to the WCC & RWA responsibility for cross country and it has remained there ever since as the winter activity increased dramatically. In 1980 the Association became known simply as the Women's Cross Country Association, but more recently has added Road Running to its responsibilities and title.

So both men's and women's sides of the sport have a strong tradition and substantial organizational network, and over the years the sport has catered for younger and younger athletes. In England, for example, it is theoretically possible for a girl to win a National Minors Cross Country title on her eleventh birthday; in Scotland there is a National Championship for nine- and ten-year-old girls.

But whatever the age, sex, standard or ambition of the runner, and however important or insignificant an event may seem, certain basic approaches to any cross country event apply equally if runners want to get the best out of themselves on the day of a race.

Before the race

Knowledge of the course, its climbs and its descents, surface condition and so forth is of immense value to the cross country runner, and a jog round it can be used as at least part of your warm-up before the race. There is usually a map on display at the changing rooms or near the start (and at larger events, in the programme) setting out the route and distance. Examine this carefully, because sometimes when more than one age group is involved at the same meeting, each age group has its own combination of laps.

There might be a 'small' lap, which leaves out part of the complete circuit, itself known as the 'large' lap. Because different maximum distances are laid out in the rules for each age group, varying lengths of course are needed. For instance, at a women's cross country meeting, the Minors and Girls might run two 'small' laps, the

Intermediates might run one 'small' and one 'large' lap, and the Seniors two 'large' laps. At a men's meeting similarly the Colts, Boys, Youths, Juniors and Seniors might all have different combinations of laps for their respective races.

Consequently, each athlete has to study the map and relate the information given to their own age group. Normally the course will be explained before the start of the race by an official anyway, but it only needs a barking dog or an untimely bout of coughing for you to miss every word of his graphic description. So if you have any doubts just before the start, this is the moment to express them, not halfway round the course, if at all avoidable.

Usually the course is marked by flags of a vivid colour, such as orange or red, strung out in such a way that as the runner reaches each one, the next should be visible. Arrows are sometimes employed too, and it is essential to ensure you know beforehand just what type and colour of markers are being used for your event. Otherwise you might inadvertently start following the signs for a sponsored walk or a guided tour of the New Forest. If the course is indicated along a natural and well-defined path, then you can usually assume that you simply follow the natural line of path until another marker appears. The Scottish CCU has a specific rule which states that competitors have to keep within 10 yards of the markers or risk disqualification, for all over Britain corner-cutting occurs far too often in cross country races. Athletes can be, and sometimes are, disqualified for such an offence if it is deliberate.

Human markers are often posted at strategic or potentially confusing points on a course to ensure that everyone goes the right way, and the best organized races have a profusion of human and static markers around the course. In the unfortunate circumstance that you do go astray, however, it is always better to re-trace your steps once you are sure you are off course, rather than to go on, hoping that you will stumble across the path again. This is partly to minimize the extra distance you will have to run, and partly to avoid leading others off course.

Some events employ the use of one or more runners to act as 'hares', not taking part in the race itself but instead running ahead of the field and leading them round. It is a useful additional method of indicating the route but, if the hare is to be relied upon entirely, there can be hazards. The possibility of the hare losing his way is slight but not unknown, and of course he has to be a reasonable runner himself, especially if senior athletes are involved. It is no good them overtaking him after half a mile and then having to wait for him to come puffing up at every junction before they are able to continue. I remember one race where the hare injured his leg after 1 mile and the entire race had to come to a halt while he was helped back to the start, and a new hare was hastily recruited from the refreshment room.

Far better, then, to study the map, to jog round the course and be absolutely clear in your own mind where you are going. For it is not only the leader who can use the information. Even if you know you are going to be well back in the pack, it is preferable to know exactly how far you have left to run, what hazards if any still remain (are there any more steep hills? any ploughed fields?) rather than come across them as a nasty surprise when you had just imagined that you ought to be finishing. By knowing the course you can spread your effort as efficiently as possible, just as you would in a track race. In that way you can achieve your own best result, which after all is the main aim, whether you are ninth or ninety-ninth.

Competition

Because cross country is a winter sport, the pre-race warm-up needs to be slightly longer than before summer races. The colder weather means muscles take longer to loosen up, and with any sort of race it is essential to be warm and ready at the start, however bitter the day. If it is very cold, additional tracksuits, sweaters and other clothing should be used to keep warm; it is no use standing around shivering and saying 'isn't it cold?' to anyone who will listen. You have to overcome the problem, not discuss it.

There is no limit to how much extra clothing a runner can wear to warm-up or race, and some feel the cold more than others. Lightweight gloves, for instance, are often advisable before a race, and you may even want to race in them. Your hands soon warm up when you are running, however, so the lighter the gloves, the easier it will be to tuck them into the top of your shorts, or to throw them to an official or friend around the course if your hands become uncomfortably warm.

Kit is very much a matter of personal taste, and there is no need to feel that others will think you 'soft' if you wear long-sleeved jumpers, extra T-shirts, mittens, a woollen hat, even tights, if they keep you warm. The body performs much more efficiently when warm, and there is little value in shivering on an icy day in a thin vest and shorts which, in a low temperature, will prevent you from running well. Through experience you will get to know just how much to wear in the different weather extremes so that you will be neither uncomfortably hot nor depressingly cold during the race.

Extremes of temperature and choice of kit are discussed more fully in Chapter 12, but one thing to remember is that, in most club events, and certainly championship races, you have to wear your club colours when competing, and athletes risk disqualification from important races for not doing so. This means that you must decide how many layers of clothing you want to wear in the race, and then put your club vest on top of them, with your number pinned on to it.

Don't worry that you have got a long-sleeved sweater underneath and that the arms of it show! As long as your club colours are on top, with your number clearly visible, you are not breaking any rules.

Put your warm-up gear (i.e. the outer tracksuit in which you will warm up beforehand and discard before the race starts) over the top, and do not take it off until just before the race is due to start. When you do, try to remove it as calmly as possible! You may be in a highly nervous state, particularly if it is an important race, or you are a relative newcomer to the sport, but there is nothing worse than trying to rush and getting in a panic when a zip sticks as you are trying to get your tracksuit trousers off over spiked shoes. You may end up hopping around on one foot, falling in the mud and rolling around like a demented chicken, while 200 other runners shiver on the starting line waiting for the impromptu cabaret to end.

Time must be allowed during the warm-up to stop and change from your warm-up shoes, which will probably be training flats, to your racing shoes. During the warm-up you can assess whether the course surface calls for short or long spikes, or even no spikes at all.

Most modern racing shoes have screw-in spikes, sets of which can be bought in packets in different lengths and are fitted into the sole with a special spanner. It is a relatively easy job to change spikes, but you have to ensure that they are screwed quite tightly in and will not work loose during the race. Conversely, you must be prepared, if trying to unscrew spikes, that one or more may appear to be stuck fast. A pair of pliers can help to shift stubborn spikes, and should become another part of the competitive athlete's permanent kit.

If the course is very wet and muddy, long spikes – say 12 millimetres (½inch), or even 15 millimetres (⅝inch) – should ensure a better grip. But if it is dry or frozen then obviously such long spikes may not go very far into the ground and you would feel instead that you were running around on stilts. In that case, shorter spikes (perhaps 9.5 millimetres/⅜inch), or even studded shoes, known sometimes as 'waffles', would be more suitable.

In the running shoe sense, waffles are not something that you eat, but rather a special type of shoe sole originally developed in the early seventies in the USA by the Oregon coach, Bill Bowerman. It is covered with dozens of small rubber studs which give good traction on most surfaces, and cushioning on hard surfaces by expanding into the space around them. They also have the advantage of providing a uniform grip over the whole of the sole, unlike spikes where the main traction is concentrated to the front of the sole. As distance runners tend to land on their heels first, the advantages of a waffle sole on courses where there are short sections of gravel path or road are clear. Such surfaces are usually discouraged in cross country races, but sometimes inevitable. The latest development is a special cross country shoe which combines the best of both worlds – a studded sole with spikes.

So, when you have made yourself familiar with the course, warmed up thoroughly, and decided what you will wear in the race on your body and your feet, only one other thing remains. The race.

Most cross country races usually begin too fast for the simple reason that the widest part of the course is often the starting area itself. Thus if you are ambitious to do well in a race, it is of little value to get left behind early on, as you will then have to spend the next couple of miles overtaking slower runners. And, if the course gets very narrow in parts, as some do, the overtaking opportunities will be limited, leaving you with frustrations similar to those of a sports car driver who finds himself following a slow-moving load of hay down a country lane. And all the time the leaders are getting further ahead.

In a small inter-club race it may be less of a problem than at the start of the English National Senior Championship where the starting line may be nearly 200 yards long and accommodating more than 2000 athletes. And in that race when the starting maroon explodes (no point in using a pistol) the men who want to get up to the sharp end of the race quickly set off to cover the opening mile in close to 4 minutes 20 seconds, even though there are still 8 more miles to cover afterwards. Thus, although even-paced running is physiologically the most economical method of running any distance race, in practical terms the bigger the race the faster you have to start if you have competitive ambitions, even if it means getting into oxygen debt for a while.

Scoring

The team scoring system in cross country is very simple. If the rules state that, say, three athletes per club will score in the overall result then the judges add together the positions of the first three finishers from each team, and the club with the *lowest* total is the winning side. This result, from a Kent League race, illustrates the three-to-score system:

Seniors

Place		Time
1	D. Goble (*Dartford*)	10.14
2	L. Hall (*Ashford*)	10.20
3	J. Boorman (*Medway*)	10.58
4	K. Hughes (*Medway*)	11.33
5	J. Brown (*Ashford*)	11.44
6	D. Lowings (*East Kent*)	11.59
7	S. Reed (*Wigmore*)	12.13
8	R. Moies (*Wigmore*)	12.35
9	J. Mawgan (*Ashford*)	12.39
10	M. Dye (*Medway*)	13.05
11	J. Ralph (*East Kent*)	13.11
12	L. Dray (*Dartford*)	13.39
13	J. Godden (*Dartford*)	14.05
14	P. Horner (*Wigmore*)	14.27
15	J. Banks (*East Kent*)	15.55

Teams

Place		Score
1	Ashford (2, 5, 9)	16
2	Medway (3, 4, 10)	17
3	Dartford (1, 12, 13)	26
4	Wigmore (7, 8, 14)	29
5	East Kent (6, 11, 15)	32

With relatively small fields, officials can note the finishing position and number of each athlete and work out the team scores afterwards quite quickly. In much larger fields, however, the disc system of scoring is more practical, although it does rely on the co-operation and understanding of every team manager and athlete for it to work efficiently at an event like the English National Championships, where it was first introduced in 1929.

Here, in the Senior 9 mile race, for example, with a six-to-score system, each club is allowed to enter up to fifteen athletes, who will all appear on the programme (Figure X). On the day, however, a maximum of only nine from that fifteen are actually permitted to compete and the club's team manager has to state on a declaration card (Figure Y) handed in to officials before the race starts which nine runners will be taking part for his club. And of those nine, only the first six to finish from each club will be included in the scoring.

As each runner crosses the finishing line he is given a metal disc, about the size of a ten pence piece, on which is stamped his overall position. He hands this to his team manager, who puts all of the discs received by his club's scoring runners into an official envelope (Figure Z), on the outside of which is printed a special form where he must list the competitors' numbers and their finishing positions.

On a separate envelope (Figure Z) he writes down the positions of his 'non-scoring' runners, and when all of the envelopes have been collected in and checked, race officials can sometimes announce the provisional team result before the last runner has even finished the race.

In the event of a tie, with two clubs having the same total points score, the last scoring man home decides which club is placed higher. If, for example, Gateshead Harriers and Folkestone AC both totalled 198 points, but Gateshead's sixth scorer finished sixtieth and Folkestone's sixty-first, then Gateshead would be placed higher.

Knowing that every single place counts gives an added incentive to the later finishing competitors, and even those who know they are not actually in their team's scoring six can assist their clubmates by getting ahead of another club's runners who may be in *their* scoring six and thus push up the total score of their rivals.

FOLKESTONE AC., Light Blue/Black Lettering — 118

922	Allsworth B.	926	French A. K.	929	Temple C. G.
923	Callwell M.	927	Rumsey D.	930	Thompson D. J.
924	Dyer M.	928	Shaxted S.	931	Walsh I.
925	Figgins W. A.				

FRODSHAM H., Black/Orange Badge — 68

932	Jones G. C. H.	937	Wood R.	942	Rowland P.
933	Rose J.	938	Gaynor J.	943	Mather K.
934	Nichelson D.	939	Ratcliffe W.	944	Hayes K.
935	Lloyd P.	940	Butterworth J.	945	Cottrell L.
936	Webster R.	941	Proudfoot C.	946	Stott P.

GATESHEAD H. AC., White Vest, 4" Red Band — 59

947	Foster B.	952	Irvine S.	957	Trainor J.
948	Smith B.	953	Mills J.	958	Coleby M.
949	Coates D.	954	Myatt J.	959	Amos A.
950	Spedding C.	955	Baggaley B.	960	Winter S.
951	Cannon D.	956	Leddicote B.	961	Ainslie H.

Figure X: An excerpt from an English National Cross Country programme. In clubs like Gateshead Harriers there is great competition to make even the 'National' team; clubs like Folkestone AC have to be a little less selective. But both have their place in the race. (The numbers on the right-hand side are those of the starting pens.)

ENGLISH CROSS-COUNTRY SENIOR CHAMPIONSHIP, 197

TEAM CARD

Club *GATESHEAD HARRIERS*

The Competitors running in this team are numbered as under:

947   948   950   952   954
955   956   958   961

Signed

This card must be properly filled in and handed to the Competitor's Steward
Numbers must be given — not names

Figure Y: Before the race the team manager has to hand in this card declaring which runners from those entered will actually be competing.

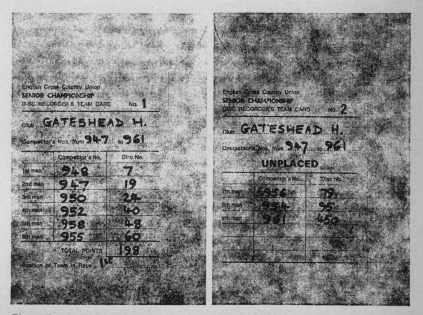

Figure Z: After the race, the team manager puts the finishing discs collected by his athletes into these envelopes, and returns them to the race recorders.

A club does not have to field nine runners to score in the team race: six is the minimum in the English Senior Championships. If, through injury, illness or other circumstances, they cannot even manage six, the surviving athletes can still compete and will receive their discs, but the club will not count in the overall scoring. Likewise, if a club does not have enough runners even to enter a team, it may enter anything from one to five individuals, who will all run and receive discs, which they will hand in to a special steward responsible for collecting the discs of all the individual entries after the race.

Because individual positions play such an important part in cross country scoring, and as in a big race large groups of runners may be finishing very fast and close together, a special system of ensuring their positions are accurately recorded is used. It is the funnel system, and involves the use of roped-off corridors down which the runners are directed as they cross the finishing line.

The narrow part of the funnel is only about 2 feet across, which means it is just wide enough for one athlete at a time, and judges try to ensure that the runners go down the funnel in single file in the same order in which they crossed the finishing line. At the far end of the funnel, which is normally about 30 yards long, officials note down the finishing order of the competitors.

The advantage of the funnel system is that it avoids a bottleneck at the finishing line itself, where it would be impossible to control hundreds of fast-finishing and exhausted runners and still judge them accurately. Indeed, as some of them would not quite reach the finishing line before having to come to a halt, they would not receive an accurate official time. This can still happen if the process is delayed.

As the funnel or chute fills up with runners, so a second parallel funnel can be brought into operation, and then a third and a fourth, with as many as eight funnels or more in operation for the biggest events. By the time the last funnel is filled, the first one should be empty again as the runners have filed through and had their finishing order recorded.

The only disadvantage of the system is that in some international events an unscrupulous runner occasionally tries to move up a couple of places in the funnel itself, which is blatant cheating because the race officially finishes before the funnel entrance is reached. That is where the times are recorded to be matched up later to the finishing order.

But on the short journey to the other end of the funnel, despite its narrowness, an unfair improvement has occasionally been made, with weary runners, many foreign tongues, the general confusion and an unending stream of finishing runners often enabling the action to go unnoticed, or at any rate unpunished.

The IAAF has been investigating ways of tightening up the race finish procedure to eliminate this happening, and fortunately it is a rare occurrence in Britain. But, especially if you are competing abroad, keep your wits about you in the funnel, because the race might not quite be over!

Importance of tetanus injections for cross country runners

The honorary medical officer of the English Cross Country Union, Dr Frank Newton, wrote to *Athletics Weekly* concerning the importance of tetanus injections:

> I write to draw competitors' attention to the fact that it is very much in their best interest that they have full protection against tetanus infection. . . . During last year's National and Inter-Counties Championships I had occasion to stitch quite severe foot injuries sustained from spike wounds. Such wounds frequently become infected since they are often ragged and contain mud, and with the feet cold from snow and frosty ground they are often not noticed by the runner until he has finished his race.
>
> When such wounds do become infected it is on the cards that the athlete may lose several weeks of the most important and competitive part of his season. Almost without exception those who were stitched had not had tetanus injections. Most were about to climb on to team coaches for the long journey back home. They were tired and in some cases, I felt, not in a fit state to receive a tetanus injection, which in some cases can cause some reaction.
>
> The normal routine for protection against tetanus is to have two injections into the arm with a six week interval, followed by a booster six months to a year later, and thereafter one injection every five years. Asthmatic sufferers are not usually given this injection.
>
> I should like to advise all cross country runners to ensure that they commence a course of treatment or update their present protection as soon as possible. One further point: wounds from spikes frequently require stitching. Competitors may not know that stitching should be done quite soon after the injury and that a delay of 12 hours often means stitching will not be carried out. Healing is then significantly delayed, and the resultant scar and discomfort is often significantly larger. Competitors are therefore urged to seek medical attention for such injuries as soon after the race as possible, even if a coach of impatient team-mates is waiting to make the long journey home.

6

ROAD RUNNING AND CROSS COUNTRY:

Preparing for Competition

There is a saying, which should not be taken too seriously, that a sprinter is an athlete who has speed but no strength, a marathon runner is an athlete who has strength but no speed, and a middle-distance runner is an athlete who has neither strength nor speed. It does, though, highlight the problem facing most athletes training for cross country and road running. Both forms of competition require stamina, but the shorter distances especially require some element of speed too.

Stamina can be accumulated by regular long runs at a steady pace, and the more frequently you run, the stronger you become. But, if you want to include some speed work too, then a place has to be found during the week for that. And what about hills? Inevitably you will face hills of varying gradients during the competitive season, and training on hills at least once a week will help you to cope with them. Then of course there is the need for rest, and easing down before competition. . . .

How on earth do you fit it all in? If you are keen to build up your mileage to gain stamina, then you will not be too anxious to spend a great deal of time on speed work which does not add up to many miles. But if the race is short, what point is there in being strong and slow? So the dilemma continues, with the athlete or coach facing a constant struggle to fit a quart's worth of training into a pint's worth of time, and still come up fresh and smiling on Saturday for a race.

In this section, we examine some of the possibilities facing the athlete, and for convenience it is separated into three broad sections:

66

the senior male athlete, the senior female athlete, and the young athlete.

Men

The first important decision to be made is the level at which you hope to be competing in the forthcoming season. If your ambition is to challenge for a place in the UK team for the World Cross Country Championships in March, then your approach will be quite different from the club runner who is quite happy maintaining a reasonable level of fitness which will help him get through a weekly succession of low-key road and cross country races without too much discomfort.

But let's start with the ambitious runner, whose planning will have begun before the previous track season had ended. Through his club officials, he will know the dates of all the major cross country championships of the winter, most of which come after Christmas, with the UK selection race normally held in February.

From that, he can work backwards and decide how many weeks he is going to allow himself to build up for such races. For the Trial, for example, the period from the beginning of September to the middle of February would give him twenty-four weeks, with another week of easing down before the race itself. In the initial period he will want to gradually build up his training mileage towards, and perhaps above, its previous highest ceiling, and then once he has put a lot of miles 'in the bank', he will introduce more sessions involving faster running and his overall mileage total may fall slightly.

That twenty-four-week period could be subdivided, perhaps just into two periods of twelve weeks each, with speed work being introduced in the second period. Or it could be further divided into four periods of six weeks each, with one week's training repeated six times and then amended. Or, to get a wider variety of training, a fourteen-day cycle could be repeated three times over a six-week period, and then amended. The latter could look something like the table on page 68.

The schedule is only a guide, of course, and some runners have achieved a great deal on less; others have had to do a lot more. Adjustments also have to be made for mid-season races in which the athlete wants to do well, and will therefore have to ease down, for you cannot train at your greatest volume and compete at your highest level simultaneously. When you are building up your training mileage, you will be tired for most of the time. You will be tired before you train, you will be tired afterwards and, if you line up for a race on Saturday afternoon, you will probably still be tired.

Day		Period One *Early Sept. to Oct.*	Period Two *Nov. to mid-Dec.*	Period Three *Mid-Dec. to Jan.*	Period Four *Feb. to mid-March*
1	Sun	Long run: 15 miles	Long run: 16 miles	Long run: 18 miles	Long run: 20 miles
2	Mon	(a.m.) 5 miles (p.m.) 8 miles	(a.m.) 5 miles (p.m.) 10 miles	(a.m.) 8 miles (p.m.) 10 miles	(a.m.) 5 miles (p.m.) 8 miles including hills
3	Tue	(a.m.) 5 miles (p.m.) 12 miles	(a.m.) 5 miles (p.m.) 12 miles	(a.m.) 5 miles (p.m.) 12 miles	(a.m.) 5 miles (p.m.) 12 miles
4	Wed	2 × 5 miles	3 × 5 miles	(a.m.) 8 miles (p.m.) 10 miles	(a.m.) 5 miles (p.m.) 5 miles including 3 × 1200 metres fast
5	Thur	(a.m.) 5 miles (p.m.) 10 miles	(a.m.) 5 miles (p.m.) 10 miles	2 × 5 miles, including 4 × 600 metres strides	(a.m.) 5 miles (p.m.) 10 miles
6	Fri	7 miles	(a.m.) 5 miles (p.m.) 7 miles	1 hour fartlek	(a.m.) 5 miles
7	Sat	Race, or 10-12 miles cross- country	Race, or 12 miles cross-country	Race, or 12 miles cross-country	(a.m.) 5 miles (p.m.) Race or 10 miles (or 12 × 400 metres) on country
8	Sun	Long run: 17 miles	Long run: 18-20 miles	Long run: 20 miles, hilly course	Long run: 15 miles hilly course
9	Mon	(a.m.) 5 miles (p.m.) 8-10 miles	(a.m.) 5 miles (p.m.) 10 miles	(a.m.) 5 miles (p.m.) 10 miles	(a.m.) 5 miles (p.m.) 1 hour fartlek
10	Tue	(a.m.) 5 miles (p.m.) 1 hour fartlek	(a.m.) 5 miles (p.m.) 90 mins. fartlek	(a.m.) 6 miles (p.m.) 12 miles	(a.m.) 5 miles (p.m.) 12 miles steady
11	Wed	(a.m.) 5 miles (p.m.) 12 miles	(a.m.) 5 miles (p.m.) 10 miles	(a.m.) 5 miles (p.m.) 8 miles	(a.m.) 5 miles (p.m.) 8 miles fast
12	Thur	2 × 5 miles	3 × 5 miles	(a.m.) 5 miles (p.m.) 10 miles	(a.m.) 5 miles, including hills (p.m.) 10 miles
13	Fri	Rest	Rest	Rest	Rest
14	Sat	Race	Race	(a.m.) 5 miles low-key (p.m.) Race	(a.m.) 5 miles (p.m.) Race or 10 miles cross-country

Day	Period One Early Sept. to Oct.	Period Two Nov. to mid-Dec.	Period Three Mid-Dec. to Jan.	Period Four Feb. to mid-March
	Average: 85 miles a week	Average: 96 miles a week	Average: 97 miles a week	Average: 91½ miles a week
	Repeat cycle three times	Repeat cycle three times	Repeat cycle three times	Repeat cycle three times

A sample twenty-four week winter training plan for a male athlete aiming to race well in the UK Trial and National Cross Country Championships (see page 67).

Thus the races which are included in the training programme shown are not those of great importance, but rather the low-key inter-club events which will provide a mental break from training. If the athlete feels particularly strongly about going into a race in which he knows he will probably not do particularly well because of residual fatigue, then he can easily substitute a training run for the race.

In fact, it is now a frequent and rather ironic sight to see the number of athletes busy training round a cross country course on a Saturday afternoon, cheering on their clubmates, but not joining in the race themselves because they are 'too busy training'! As long as the athlete is honest with himself, and the reason genuinely is one of fatigue, then it can be justifiable for him to become a mobile spectator in this way. Pushing your body to the limit in training two or three times a day, particularly in winter, can be a very trying exercise, guaranteed to test the resolution and fortitude of any athlete, regardless of the eventual results it produces. But perspective must always be maintained.

It can be harder still for the summer-minded athlete, of course, as he tries to improve his track ability by increasing his winter training volume. But take heart from the fact that even Brendan Foster admits he had his blackest moments during his winter preparation for the 10,000 metres at the 1976 Montreal Olympic Games, where he eventually was Britain's only athletics medallist, and also broke the Olympic record in the 5000 metres.

'Very tired tonight' and 'very fatigued over the last few miles' were the sort of comments he was putting in his training diary as he logged over 130 miles week after week. But when he eased down again, it all paid off, as he knew it would from his years of experience as a club runner and an international.

Foster had built up over fourteen years to reach that level of 130 miles a week, and the worst thing the club runner could do would be to copy faithfully that amount simply 'because Brendan Foster does it'. A gradual increase in your average mileage over the winter is always the safest and most sensible way of improving and trying to stay clear of the injury you will almost certainly sustain by suddenly jumping from, say, 50 miles to 100 miles a week.

Just consider: if you increased your average winter mileage from 50 to 70, a reasonably large jump in one season, then over a six month period you would still have run well over 500 miles more than the last winter. But the chances are that if you tried to go from 50 to 100 miles a week you might manage it for three weeks, get injured, and end up with an actual average nearer 25! Gradual improvement over a long period has been the story of anyone who has made a lasting impression in distance running at any level. And remember, the world is not generally expected to end tomorrow.

Obviously, though, the higher the total mileage you undertake, the more your life has to revolve around running instead of the other way round. Each athlete develops a training pattern which suits him individually, even if it may not suit anybody else. Many of our leading runners adopt programmes which are similar in volume but different in detailed breakdown.

A great many club runners, of course, train in high volume with no illusions about their ability but just a desire to lower their best road times, improve their best cross country places, and perhaps one day to have a go at the marathon. They prefer LSD running for the most part, and do very little, if any, speedwork because, although they realize that it can help them become faster runners if applied properly, they simply do not enjoy it or want to risk injury to legs which are quite comfortably churning out 7 minute miles in training, and 6 minute miles in races.

A regular level of around 70 miles a week of steady running, even without speedwork, should still be enough to place most runners quite respectably in club races.

But if you are looking for a weekly mileage of 70, how should you break it down? Theoretically, it averages 10 miles a day, but actually doing a 10 mile run every single day would not only be monotonous but would probably have less conditioning effect than this possible schedule:

Sunday	15 to 18 miles
Monday	8 miles
Tuesday	12 miles
Wednesday	two runs of 5 miles each
Thursday	12 miles

| *Friday* | 3 to 4 miles easy |
| *Saturday* | race, or 10 miles |

That would give you a chance to run for the best part of 2 hours on Sunday, still leaving the rest of the day free, although you could always tack on a few extra miles in the evening if you wished.

Doing two runs on a Wednesday might mean getting up early, or squeezing one into the lunch hour, but it would still keep most of the evening free and allow you to run a little faster because of the shorter length of runs. Friday would give you a chance to relax with just a jog to get any stiffness out of your legs (or could even be a complete rest) before Saturday, where a low-key race could become the speed session of the week. By adopting this sort of approach, you would give yourself a varied programme, leave yourself some time for social activities, and still get in your 70 miles a week.

But 70 miles a week takes a fair bit of time, and it is by no means the minimum amount of training. Some runners regularly cover 20 miles or less a week, and enjoy a club race at the weekend, where they may even fare better than a rival who covers 30–50 miles a week for a few weeks, then stops altogether for a couple of weeks.

Obviously results and improvement are subject to an imaginary sliding scale and, if you run only 20 miles a week, you cannot expect to finish near the front in 10km races or half marathons. But it would still be possible to improve your own best time for a particular course from year to year on such a distance if it was carried out consistently. A typical 20 mile week might break down like this:

Sunday	5 to 6 miles steady
Monday	rest
Tuesday	4 miles steady, including several hills if possible
Wednesday	2 to 3 miles a little faster, or 12 × 200 metres fast strides, with 200 metres jog in between
Thursday	3 miles steady
Friday	rest
Saturday	5 mile club race on road or in country

In planning your own individual target you simply have to decide how much time and effort you are willing to put into your running, be realistic about the sort of results you can expect for that input, and then stick to it.

In the next chapter I give sample 12 week training schedules for both the 10km and half marathon at three different levels: beginner, experienced, and elite.

Women

The first tip one could give any ambitious female distance runner is to re-read the section on men's training, and then to work out in her mind how *she* would fit two or three sessions a day into her routine. For, at the highest levels, women must accept that they need to train more and more like their male counterparts and, if they cannot hope to match the actual pace, then at least they can attempt to put in the same volume and intensity of work.

In cross country events, the distances may be shorter than the men's races, but the competition is equally fierce and well-prepared. There is less time to correct errors in tactics or pace and the battle is on from the starting gun. In international races there are very few second chances.

In the UK some people have perhaps become conditioned to the rather irrational thought that there will always be someone else with a better training set-up, probably state-aided, and ready to run the legs off our women athletes. In certain female track and field events it may even be true that we are not competing on an equal footing, and perhaps never will. But in distance running the limitations are inside the head of the athlete, not imposed by the finance department of a state-controlled sports federation.

Sadly, the drop-out rate among young athletes in general, and young women in particular, is already too high for the sport's own good. The particular problems of young athletes are considered more fully in the next section, but basically the tremendous enthusiasm of junior girls sometimes wanes a fair bit in the Intermediate age group (over 15 and under 17) for reasons which are not all that difficult to understand. Leaving school, starting work, meeting with a wider social circle, subsequent pressure from friends outside the sport to give up running and do something else on a Saturday, and even a mistaken belief that running is 'only for kids', all contribute in their varying ways to the drop-out rate. No one can blame them, because there *are* other things in life, and it must be admitted that training hard to become a top-class athlete can be a time-consuming, tiring, restricting pursuit, albeit a rewarding one in its own way.

Also, because running needs a regular training regime of some description to be a comfortably enjoyable pastime, even if only two or three times a week, while other activities like recreational swimming or badminton can be picked up and put down at will, some drift towards the latter.

Making the switch from school life to working life is discussed more fully in the section on young athletes, but girls seem to find it even harder than boys to make the transition. Because, unlike boys, for most teenage girls sport is still fairly low on the list of priorities. In a *Sunday Times* survey more than half of 185 female students questioned admitted that they rarely or never took any exercise. Thus a female runner, when she leaves school, may find herself not just the only athlete at her place of work, but also the only female participant in any type of competitive sport. And that situation can occur whatever the age of the runner. Thus, she is likely to keep her sporting interest well separated from her work, and in her spare time, of which she will now have less anyway.

In fairness, some bigger firms do organize sports and social clubs, and a few even have specialist athletics sections, but very many do not, and even the opportunity to run to and from work as part of training presents itself less to a girl than a boy, with its accompanying problems of showers and changing. A male runner can cope with a quick change and a wash-down in the gents' toilet if necessary, but although the same should theoretically be possible for the girls (in the ladies', not the gents'!), few seem to do so because 'it's just not done'.

Some are in the apparently ideal job of a physical education teacher, with access to showers and changing rooms. But against that must be set the tiring effect of spending most of the day on your feet, organizing physical activity, so that by the evening it takes some extra determination to go out training.

If you look for them, there are 101 different reasons why training for distance running is difficult for a girl once she has left school. But few of them can be more of a problem than having to run at 6.00 a.m. on snow and ice in dark, sub-zero Norwegian winters, as both Ingrid Kristiansen and Grete Waitz had to in order to become the best female distance runners in the world.

And, even if you have not got that particular degree of dedication and determination, there is probably no absolute reason why you could not still train regularly at some stage of the week, and put up very reasonable performances in open races. If you can train at least two, or preferably three, nights during the week, and use the weekend as well, then it should be possible to maintain a degree of fitness which will see you comfortably through cross country and the shorter road races.

Suppose you are an athlete whose training has become erratic and without specific direction at the moment. You may have been training only when the mood takes you, and consequently your fitness has suffered, which in turn makes you feel even less like training. Can you pull together the threads and get yourself back into racing shape? Of course you can, but the first essential is to make a training plan and stick to it. Too many runners still expect results to follow a haphazard training pattern in which they only train when they feel like it, and only do what they feel like. If that is the way in which you are satisfied to approach your running, then that is fine, as long as you do not believe that consistent improvement will automatically result from it. Haphazard training produces haphazard results, and some runners are quite content to accept that fact.

But the point is that, just because you do not commit your life to becoming a world class runner, you do not have to accept the 'haphazard' approach to training as the only possible alternative. It just needs a methodical way of training, a framework on which to build the rest of your weekly activities, to be able to enjoy both your running and your life outside running.

Say you start the week on a Sunday. Most people can find some spare time to run on that day, so let us establish it as your regular 'long run' day, as it is for thousands of others already. 'Long' is only relative to what you have done before, of course, so if 2 miles is the furthest you have ever run then a 3 mile run will seem long. Whatever the distance, it should be covered just at a steady pace, not a flat-out effort, and you should finish feeling you could have gone just a little bit further. Then the next week you could try to go that little bit further, but again keeping the pace down so that you do not finish exhausted.

If you do feel that the first run you undertake is about your current limit, then just repeat it the following week instead of increasing it, and perhaps take it a little easier this time. Gradually it should become more comfortable anyway.

If you intend to run on Saturdays too, then we can call Monday a rest day, and spread your other training days over the midweek: Tuesdays and Thursdays, if you intend to train twice during the week, or Tuesday, Wednesday and Thursday if three times is possible.

The Tuesday sessions could be a shorter, faster run than Sunday, perhaps even broken up into two sections with a short recovery phase in between – medium-paced runs of about ¾ mile each, with ¼ mile jog in between, for instance. When you can handle that comfortably, you could increase the number of runs to three, or the length of the runs to a mile, or amend the session to any combination which allows a gradual progression in distance, speed or volume.

Thursdays could be earmarked as the interval session day, with perhaps 10 runs of about 100 metres at a fast stride, with a walk/jog back between each run as recovery. Again, as the weeks pass and you can handle the session comfortably, you can gradually increase the number of runs, or the individual distances, or cut down the recovery slightly – though not all at the same time. When you reach a combination which you feel is pretty close to the limit, then do not make it harder until you can manage it comfortably.

Assuming that you are normally going to train quite hard on Tuesdays and Thursdays, then the Wednesday session should be a light one, with perhaps just a couple of miles at a very steady pace being sufficient.

With Friday as another rest day, Saturday will either be a race or another longish run, perhaps with a complete change of scenery. A form of gentle fartlek (see page 16) might make a good alternative to just running at a steady pace again, and the length of time can be gradually increased over the weeks.

By establishing some sort of routine like this, you are far more likely to appreciate that there is an overall meaning and progression to the training and perhaps will be more inclined to get out and run than if your normal decisions about if and what come only when you poke your nose out of the front door to see whether it has stopped raining yet. The sort of routine outlined here will not make too much of a dent in your social life and, if it will not guarantee that you win the National Cross Country title either, it should at least ensure that you run reasonably well.

But, in turn, encouraging results in races will help you out of that front door more quickly, and your thoughts may turn to ways of eventually increasing your training still further, rather than which excuse to use to avoid going out tonight.

Graduation over a period of weeks or months is very much a personal thing, and your body will tell you whether you are ready to increase the load or not. But the sort of progression shown on the table overleaf over a ten week period might not be unreasonable.

The problem of monthly periods affects some female runners more than others. In one questionnaire given to women athletes, 20 per cent felt that their performance was worse during a period, while 10 per cent actually thought it was better and 70 per cent noticed little difference. Another survey revealed that Olympic gold medals have been won by athletes at all stages of the menstrual cycle.

In recent years some female competitors, particularly those who suffered badly from severe period pains which forced them to stop training for a day or so, have used the contraceptive pill to regulate their periods and ensure that one did not coincide with a major championship race.

Other physical disadvantages appear to be a slight increase in weight and a bloated feeling, due to the greater water retention which occurs during a period, and the risk of anaemia caused by blood loss. In the latter case, a simple iron supplement will help to offset the loss.

It has also become apparent, as a result of the increasing opportunities for women in long distance events, that a considerable proportion of female runners have no periods at all while training hard for an extended time. This condition, known as amenorrhoea, is reversed once the training load is reduced, with no apparent negative effect on fertility.

Some years ago, the very idea of a pregnant woman running would have been rejected out of hand, and brought forth a flurry of old wives' tales about such exertions being liable to induce a miscarriage or at least jar the foetus. Now, though, greater medical research has indicated that not only is easy running during pregnancy not harmful, but it can actually contribute to the health of mother and baby.

The limitations are not the pregnancy itself, but rather the discomfort of running with an increasingly large bulge in front of you! The foetus is well protected in the early days by the muscles and bones of the mother's pelvis, and in later stages of pregnancy by the sea of amniotic fluid which cushions it from shock.

With the agreement of the doctor (whose main problem with expectant mothers may well be persuading them to take any exercise, not stopping them), it should be possible to run for five or six months into the pregnancy, or even longer if there are no complications, and if it is not too uncomfortable. In the USA at least one woman athlete continued running right up until the day before the birth of her fine, healthy son, although by that stage alternate 100 yard walks and jogs were about her limit.

My own wife, Clare, a county-level runner with no burning ambition but a love of running, kept jogging into the fourth month of her first pregnancy and even took part in a 1½ miles fun run at Gateshead. She only stopped running when it became too uncomfortable to do so, but kept up an exercise programme and surprised the doctors with the speed and ease of the delivery of our first son. Within six weeks of the birth she was running again. We now have four children, and she is in training for the London Marathon!

Some doctors are convinced that a mother can actually become a better runner than she was before giving birth, but the practical demands of motherhood often result in female athletes ending their competitive careers when they first become pregnant.

Joyce Smith is an example of what can be achieved by a mother who manages to look after a family, run a home and still train. In 1959 she first won the National Women's Cross Country title; in 1968 she gave

Day	Type of Training	Week 1	Week 2	Week 3	Week 4	Week 5
Sun.	Steady run	3 miles	3½ miles	4 miles	4 miles	4½ miles
Mon.	Rest	Rest	Rest	Rest	Rest	Rest
Tues.	Medium-paced runs with 2 min jog	2 × 4 mins	2 × 4 mins	3 × 4 mins	3 × 4 mins	2 × 6 mins
Wed.	Easy, relaxed run	1½ miles	1½ miles	2 miles	2 miles	2½ miles
Thurs.	Interval fast strides	10 × 100 metres	10 × 100 metres	12 × 100 metres	10 × 120 metres	8 × 150 metres
Fri.	Rest	Rest	Rest	Rest	Rest	Rest
Sat.	Race, or fartlek for time	15 mins fartlek	20 mins fartlek	25 mins fartlek	Race	30 mins fartlek

Day	Type of Training	Week 6	Week 7	Week 8	Week 9	Week 10
Sun.	Steady run	4½ miles	5 miles	5 miles	5½ miles	6 miles
Mon.	Rest	Rest	Rest	Rest	Rest	Rest
Tues.	Medium-paced runs with 2 min jog	3 × 4 mins	2 × 6 mins	4 × 4 mins	3 × 6 mins	4 × 4 mins
Wed.	Easy, relaxed run	2½ miles	2½ miles	2½ miles	3 miles	3 miles
Thurs.	Interval fast strides	12 × 120 metres	15 × 100 metres	10 × 150 metres	12 × 120 metres	10 × 150 metres
Fri.	Rest	Rest	Rest	Rest	Rest	Rest
Sat.	Race, or fartlek for time	Race	35 mins fartlek	Race	40 mins fartlek	Race

A typical ten week progressive training plan for a female club-level runner.

birth to Lisa; and in 1972 won the World Women's Cross Country title, set a UK 1500 metres record on the track and captained Britain's Olympic team.

The following year she finished second in the World Cross Country Championship behind the Italian Paola Cacchi, who herself had interrupted her athletics career to become a mother, and in 1974 Joyce became the first British woman to break 9 minutes for 3000 metres on the track. In 1976 her second daughter, Lia, was born, and within three months Joyce was competing again in the National road relays. During 1979 she set British best performances on the road at 10 miles, 20 miles and the marathon, and in 1984 she finished 11th in the first Olympic women's marathon in Los Angeles at the age of 46. In her case, her age is just a measure of years rather than fitness.

Young athletes

The huge expansion of events for youngsters in recent years has reflected the growth of interest in cross country and road running among school-age children, and fields of several hundred boys or girls are now commonplace all over the country on a winter Saturday.

Few seniors throw as much undiluted energy into their events as these young runners, whose main tactic often seems to be to run as fast as possible for as long as possible, then slow down and hope they can make it to the finish! It is refreshing to watch such unbridled enthusiasm as they charge across the fields, a waist-high swarm of colour, all running like there was no tomorrow.

It would be satisfying to think that they are all just running for fun, gradually learning about the sport, and not worrying about winning or losing. Many older runners, asked for advice, often tell such youngsters, boys and girls alike, just to play around with running and not get caught up with a preoccupation over success or failure. Between the ages of eleven and sixteen, sport should be basically nothing more than recreation. But the reality can be slightly different.

For few areas of athletics generate the amount of emotion which sometimes surrounds young athletes' races. At women's cross country meetings, a vast number of parents, coaches and club officials often swarm round the Minors and Girls fields as they line up for the start, collecting tracksuits, issuing last-minute instructions, encouragement and threats, before galloping off to vantage points around the course. By the time the Intermediate and Senior athletes are lining up, the spectators have thinned out dramatically and some of them are already in their cars heading home and holding a post-mortem with little Sally on today's race.

The similarly large fields which turn out for Boys and Colts cross country and road events again attract this big following of adults who sometimes become as involved in the race, if not more so, than the athletes they have come to support.

Undoubtedly, such a healthy sport as running is ideal in itself for youngsters who are overflowing with energy and who are so often being accused of being part of a generation of overweight telly addicts. But unfortunately it sometimes seems difficult, by the nature of the activity, to promote any sort of low-key running event for them. Competitions involving young athletes rarely have the same relaxed atmosphere of some senior inter-club meetings, and I frequently feel that this is not due to the over-enthusiasm of the athletes themselves, but that it owes more to the constant worrying and fussing of the parents and coaches of the youngsters. They are the people who spend a lot of time and money in the preparation and transportation of the athletes, and in some cases they are the same people who have created the very competitions for which they are now urging little Jimmy to run himself into the ground.

There are extremes, of course, and it is the extremes which concern me, rather than the many reasonable parents and coaches. But there are parents so obsessed with their son/daughter obtaining success as a runner that it spoils the whole week for them if little Jimmy/Sally performs below the high standard sometimes unreasonably expected of them. But then are they any worse than the parents who take absolutely no interest at all in their son or daughter's sport, and rarely even ask them how they got on when they get back from a race on Saturday evening?

It is a very complex situation, but the ones who eventually suffer most are the youngsters themselves, who are being made to believe by the tune of the surrounding adults (who are usually right about everything else, after all) that it really matters whether they win or lose, when it patently does not matter. The youngsters will simply not possess the mature reasoning powers to work out that in many cases it matters only to the parent or coach because of their own frustrations or lack of success in sport or elsewhere, and that in broad terms it does not actually matter to the future of civilization whether they finish first or fiftieth.

If I feel that any of my own young athletes are beginning to come under some pressure over a particular race, I just point out to them that 54 million people in the UK will not even know that the race took place, never mind where he or she finished. I try to throw it back to the athlete: never mind what anybody else wants or thinks, what do *you* want to do? How well do *you* want to run? By letting them set their own targets, even if sometimes they are too high or too low, I believe the athlete can develop a much better judgement value than by simply relying on someone else to tell them whether or not they have done well. In dealing with young athletes especially, I feel sure that their whole long-term commitment to the sport could be favourably affected if parents and coaches associated with these impressionable youngsters used variations on just three short phrases: *Good luck. Well done. Never mind.*

It could be worse, of course. In the USA, where there are four-year-olds running marathons and eight-year-olds covering 100 miles a week in training, surveys have shown that very few of the prodigious runners ever made the transition to success even in their teenage years. And adults must take the blame for that because no four-year-old sets out to run a marathon, or eight-year-old to run 100 miles a week, on their own and without a good deal of adult prompting and supervision.

Fortunately in Britain a four-year-old, or even a seventeen-year-old, cannot race a marathon, and in general the rules governing age and distance limits for young athletes are based on common sense and protect the athletes from themselves, or at least ambitious adults.

But if I now start to talk on the next page about the sort of training young athletes could do to improve their performances, am I not setting myself up as just another 'pushy adult coach'? I hope not, but I acknowledge the possibility and answer it as follows.

Thousands of boys and girls all over the UK enjoy taking part in cross country and road running races. That is healthy. Like everyone else, they would like to improve and to run faster and to do better next time. That too is natural and healthy and to be encouraged.

My reservations come when, instead of simply letting nature take its course, adults expect constant success, often without considering what is involved in obtaining it. In a field of fourteen-year-old boys, are they really all equal? Will that skinny little lad have a chance against that well-built boy showing the first signs of a moustache? In a field of fourteen-year-old girls, how will the runner with the slim boyish figure fare against her close rival of last season, who has put on over half a stone in a few months?

In the school years, running should be just a sport to be mixed in as part of life, together with exams, TV, discos and other recreations, and not an end in itself. Some adult runners may decide to abandon everything for athletics, to work only part-time, refuse promotion or even remain unemployed in order that they may train longer and harder. They may deliberately go to live at altitude, or follow the sun to the other side of the world in winter, just to help them eventually run faster in competition. They may devote a period of some years just to running, and if they do then they have the right to decide whether the result of a particular race at the end of it was a success or a total disaster, in view of their sacrifices.

But no one is likely to win an Olympic gold medal for distance running under the age of sixteen, whatever happens in swimming or women's gymnastics. They are different sports, with separate specific physical demands, in which a youthful body may be a distinct advantage, and in which consequently serious training has to start very much younger than athletics. Few swimmers or girl gymnasts compete internationally in their late twenties – a time when runners are usually reaching their physical peak.

Training for distance running involves a gradually increasing workload over a long period. To do too much too soon means it is unlikely that the full potential will ever be reached – like a car with just sufficient petrol for a particular journey which is then driven too quickly early on, burns up too much fuel and stops before its destination.

There are many different reasons why runners eventually drop out of the sport. Business reasons, family reasons, injury, lack of time, and so on. But the saddest of all is the athlete who showed promise early on but was simply ground down by constant demands for more records, more victories and more titles, while receiving scant praise for winning and only loud criticism for losing. It is sad, because with a little thought and consideration it could have been avoided and that same athlete might have carried on to achieve performances which would be remembered much longer and further afield than his or her youthful activities which will probably be forgotten as soon as the next wonder child comes along.

Statistics show that an athlete who displays tremendous ability as a runner in early teens will be less likely to make an eventual impact as a senior than the less talented runner who works away regularly at a gradual improvement on performance over a period of some years. Runners like Brendan Foster and Bernie Ford, both of whom were destined to become English National Cross Country Champions as Seniors, never even qualified for their county team at the English Schools Cross Country Championships when they were teenagers.

But how does the young athlete start in the first place? What do you do if you are a boy or girl around twelve years of age, and you think you want to become a distance runner?

The first step, if it has not already been taken, is to get in touch with the local athletics club. Often, if there is a running track or sports centre nearby, the club will be based there for at least part of the year. If the youngster is new to the sport, it is the best way to find out about competitions in the area, to receive on-the-spot coaching advice, and to meet others of their own age group who also enjoy running and with whom they will be able to train.

Training sessions are often held three times a week, with Sunday mornings and Tuesday and Thursday evening the popular, but not arbitrary, choice of many clubs. With races usually held on Saturdays (although there are now an increasing number of Sunday events too), that spreads the activity out over the whole week, and gives the runner a chance to recover on Mondays, Wednesdays and Fridays. As he or she gets older and fitter, runs from home on Mondays and/or Wednesdays may become part of the training pattern too.

Many clubs organize coach travel to meetings outside their own locality, as well as fund-raising activities like discos and jumble sales, so there is often an active social side to club athletics too.

Attendance at every training session is not compulsory, but at least twice a week should be a minimum if possible. Athletes are usually organized in groups according to their age and ability, and the coach in charge of the group should be kept informed about the athlete's availability to compete, forthcoming holidays, colds, injuries or anything else relating to the long- and short-term planning. Each coach may have twenty to thirty separate athletes to keep tabs on, but each athlete only has the one coach, and it should be the athlete's responsibility to keep the coach informed.

The amount of actual training at each session will depend very much on the coach in charge, but no one will expect a newcomer to break any world records – in their first week, anyway! During the summer, most of the races available to the young distance runner will be on the track at 800 metres and 1500 metres, with the occasional 3000 metres for boys.

Don't ignore these events just because you want to be a cross country runner. Such track races are good background for the winter season, and a good start to competition.

For an athlete of eleven or twelve years of age, the two or three training sessions at the club, together with a race on Saturdays, should be quite sufficient to get him or her basically fit for running and able to cope with competition. There is no point trying to do more in the first year or so, and progress can be made by attempting to do the same training faster rather than increasing the volume.

The advantage of training with a club group is that the coach can introduce some activities into training like the caterpillar or shuttle

nning has never been so
pular, with 30,000 participants
ing part in both the Great
rth Run (below) and the
ndon Marathon (right) each
ar, and many thousands more
ned away.

You are never too young to derive enjoyment and satisfaction from running, even if it sometimes needs a strong element of determination.

Opposite: But at the highest levels of youthful competition great care is needed to protect runners from too much pressure from coaches and parents ... even if they can't get enough mud and water (below)!

Cross country frequently provides a thorough testing, whether it is the mud, snow or gradients.

relays, which get the athletes running hard and having fun at the same time. In the caterpillar, for instance, a single file of any number of runners jogs around the track or the outside of a field, and when the coach gives the word the runner at the back of the line sprints to the front, joins on, and resumes jogging. Then the next runner does the same, and so on. It is a gentle introduction to interval training, and could possibly be described as 10 × 60 metres sprint, with 200 metres jog between. But to the participants it is virtually a running game and not a hard training exercise.

The same applies to the shuttle relay, in which teams of roughly equal ability are divided into two halves, facing each other about 50 metres apart, and then race, one runner at a time, in a continuous relay backwards and forwards across the 50 metres. It could be reduced clinically to something like '12 × 50 metres, with 90 seconds' rest in between', but it will be remembered by the young runners as another enjoyable running game. At the same time, though, it is developing their ability to cope with harder sessions later in their athletics career.

As time passes, a gradual increase in the training load must be made because the body adapts to the stresses placed on it by training and needs a new level of work to continue the adaptation process. The extra runs on Mondays or Wednesdays can be introduced in the second or third year of training, and the amount of work at the club should be slowly increased. But there is no need to reduce the fun element too much. By this time the athlete will probably appreciate the benefits which training produces, and if they are keen to progress they will work hard anyway, but an exercise like the shuttle relay can be as fast as you want to make it and still provide a refreshing break.

Sometimes the need to increase the training load is overlooked, and a young athlete may find their form has tended to stagnate. In one case I came across, a girl who had been an outstanding Minor in her county when she was eleven and twelve seemed to be making very heavy weather as she moved in to the Intermediate age group. Some of the girls she had beaten easily as a Minor were now finishing ahead of her.

Examination of her training diary revealed that she was doing virtually the same training as four years previously, and had reached a level of fitness at which that amount of work no longer stretched her. Thus her progress had stopped.

She had beaten the other girls in the early days by having more natural talent, and in the Minor Girls and Colts age groups success frequently comes down to natural talent because few of the runners have been training long enough to have significantly improved otherwise. Her natural talent plus a light training load was eventually not enough to hold off the girls who had less talent but trained harder over a long period. Yet by gradually increasing her own training she was eventually able to get back close to where she had been in the county as a Minor.

The schedules shown overleaf are provided purely as an example of how the training of an eleven-year-old boy or girl can be graduated over a period of seven years, from three days a week training to six, with relevant increases in the amount of work. I am not a great advocate of vast amounts of mileage in this age range, not because I do not think that youngsters can cope with it – I am sure even the youngest could, physically, if asked – but because of the races in which they are competing, which are all relatively short and sharp. Consequently, the training, while allowing for overall strength increase, must give them a chance to run at or above their racing pace several times during the week.

There are a large number of cases where an athlete has just not been able to adapt to a higher training load after achieving a fair amount of success on natural ability plus light training. It is not that the athlete is physically incapable of hard training, but mentally it is something which is alien to them, not through arrogance but simply because it was not a necessity for success.

A few athletes in that situation are able to change course in midstream, and reorganize their training to a higher volume, but the majority, experience seems to tell us, are not. They tend either to carry on at the same rate, or drop out of the sport altogether. For that reason it is probably fair to say that the majority of those most physically capable of becoming top-class runners as seniors in the UK do not reach their potential.

And, while that is frustrating for the sport in many respects, it also offers great encouragement to those who do not excel in their first season or two as runners. They are the athletes who realize very early on that the only way they will achieve great improvement is by consistent training. The realization itself may even put a few off, but it steels the rest to their task and their long-term prospects are in consequence relatively high.

Which comes back to the problem of striking the right balance between too much pressure to succeed in the early days, and the need to graduate training over a long term. Let me put a hypothetical question. Suppose you had three young athletes of the same age, but in different situations:

Athlete A is a natural runner, who wins everything at school sports days, trains only lightly but seems unbeatable.

Athlete B is less talented but is under great pressure from home to train flat out every day with the express intention of beating athlete A next winter.

Athlete C also has limited talent, but enjoys training and has gradually increased it season by season. The performances of Athletes A and B are, he knows, irrelevant as long as he keeps improving.

Of those three, which would you think was the most likely to be still around and running well in five years' time?

A hurdle which has to be tackled at some time by both boys and girls in the Intermediate and Senior age groups and boys in the Youths or Junior age groups, concerns leaving school. Quite a few coaches and athletes barely even consider this giant step when planning future races and training, but the fact is that the major upheaval which can result may be enough to throw some athletes off course for some time.

Again it all depends on the individual and the circumstances, but the potential hazards must at least be acknowledged. Even if the school-leaver gets a job which is enjoyable and not physically taxing, the new experience of working longer hours with fewer holidays, and having greater responsibility, will be somewhat tiring at first. It may mean getting up earlier and it will almost certainly mean getting home later. It could involve a journey of some length and, instead of being home by 4.30 p.m. and finished training by 6.00 p.m. with the whole evening free, he or she may not arrive home until 6.00 p.m. or even later, perhaps very tired.

Possibilities of training during school hours, such as in PE or games periods, will no longer exist, holidays will be much shorter, and training will have to be fitted into reduced leisure time.

The problems are not insurmountable if the spirit is willing, and the body and mind will adjust to the different situation (and the new financial opportunities . . . new running shoes . . . a new tracksuit . . .). But some form of allowance for fatigue has to be made in the first few weeks of work. Training should be reduced and competition results not taken too seriously until the adjustment is made. A reassessment of sleep and diet may be necessary after a couple of weeks. Does the new way of life need more hours of sustained sleep? Is there any skimping of meals now that school lunches are no longer being eaten?

Many thousands of runners do work full-time, often commuting some distance every day, then train in the evenings and still compete at weekends. It just needs some time to make the adjustment from school life to working life, and it only has to happen once.

Of course, some jobs are more suitable than others for distance runners. Anything involving a lot of hard physical activity, like labouring

Day	11-12 years	13 years	14 years	15 years
Sun.	Club session or 2 to 3 miles steady	3 to 4 miles steady	4 to 5 miles steady	5 to 6 miles steady
Mon.	Rest	Rest	Rest, or 2½ miles easy	2 miles warm-up, then 10 × 120 metres on hills. Warm-down
Tues.	1½ miles fast on road circuit	2 miles fast on road circuit	Warm up, then 'up the clock' session: 100, 200, 300, 200, 100 metres	3 miles road circuit fast
Wed.	Rest	2½ miles steady on road	3 miles steady on road	30 minutes fartlek (in woods if possible)
Thur.	10 × 150 metres fast, on grass, jog between runs	10 × 200 metres on grass, jog between runs	4 × 600 metres approx, on grass. 4 minutes rest between runs	'Up the clock' session: 100 up to 500 metres, back to 100 metres
Fri.	Rest	Rest	Rest	Rest
Sat.	Race or rest	Race or 2½ miles fast on country	Race or 3 miles fast on country	Race, or 4 miles fast on road or grass

or bricklaying, is not going to allow the athlete to feel very fresh or inclined to run a long distance in the evening, although it has been done. Likewise, anything which involves standing for long periods, such as working in a shop, will leave the athlete thinking only about an arm chair when he or she gets home. Naturally, it is not impossible for someone in one of these jobs to become a successful distance runner, but it would need a lot of dedication because their daily occupation will hinder rather than help.

A sedentary job, perhaps at a desk, could be more suitable and a large number of runners choose to work in insurance, banking or the civil service, all of which have very active athletics sections, including annual cross country championships, and are sometimes more helpful with time off for competition than other employers.

In some areas of the country there is little choice, or indeed very little employment unfortunately, and to talk of desk jobs may seem ridiculous. But the determined athlete generally gets what he or she is after eventually, even if it takes a little while and other work has to be accepted temporarily in between.

Day	16 years	17 years	18 years
Sun.	6 to 7 miles steady	7 to 8 miles steady	(a.m.) 7 to 10 miles steady (p.m.) 3 to 4 miles steady
Mon.	3 to 4 miles easy	40 minutes fartlek, including hills	60 minutes fartlek, including hills
Tues.	5 miles on road or country, with 4 × 300 metres efforts	3 × 1 mile hard effort, 10 minutes walk/jog between	3 miles steady then 6 × 600 metres on grass, jog 400 metres between
Wed.	2 × 1½ miles road circuit hard. 8 minutes recovery	4 miles road circuit hard	6 miles road run, including hills
Thur.	12 × 200 metres, jog 60 seconds between	8 × 300 metres approx. on grass, 90 seconds recovery	15 × 200 metres on grass or track, jog 200 metres in between
Fri.	Rest	Rest	Rest
Sat.	Race, or 4 miles fast on road or grass	Race, or 5 miles fast on road or grass	Race, or 6 miles fast on road or grass

A sample training plan for a young athlete, aiming to build up volume and ability over a period of years.

One problem which affects girls in particular when they take on sedentary jobs is an increase in weight. At school they may have been active all the time but, once seated at an office desk, particularly if the job is not very interesting and breaks for coffee and buns come round every couple of hours, they may put on half a stone or a stone, much of it around their hips and bottom. This will do nothing for their running except slow it down, and attempts to crash diet it away may result in a loss of energy, or even anaemia. Often the weight increase may be primarily related to the hormonal changes associated with puberty. The best cure is really prevention by recognizing the dangers of this adjustment in daily life, and taking it easy with the calories in the first place.

A period of transition in which running has to take a back seat for a while must also be allowed for the new student athlete who is attending college or university for the first time. It particularly applies if he or she is living away from home for the first time, which can be a very difficult transitional period because not only is the educational establishment a new world to which they have to become accustomed, but normal everyday chores like shopping, washing and cooking are new energy-consuming challenges to the student on their own for the first time.

Again, some individuals will cope better than others, and some will find their running actually improves while others will note, temporarily anyway, a slight decline. In itself, that doesn't matter.

What does matter is that every one of us who at some time puts any degree of pressure on a young athlete, either as a parent, coach or club official, must remember that in producing good results there are a lot more factors to take into account than simply the right training schedule.

Dos and Don'ts for Young Athletes

Do remember to warm up well before your race, with at least 1 mile of steady jogging and a few fast strides covering 80–100 metres as the very minimum. Keep on the move and keep warm right up to the time you are called for your race.

Don't stand around talking before the start, getting cold and losing the value of the warm-up.

Do make sure your spikes are tied firmly with a double knot so they don't come undone in the race, or get pulled off in the mud.

Don't warm up or warm down in your spikes; warm up in flat shoes at a cross country race, and then change into your spikes before doing your strides.

Do make sure you are wearing your number securely pinned at both sides (not top and bottom, because it folds over and officials can't read it). Make sure that it is the right way up and that you really are number 66 on the programme, not number 99.

Don't eat crisps, Mars bars, sandwiches, chips, or indeed anything for at least two to three hours before the start of your race. You won't have time to digest it; it will just feel heavy in your stomach and could even make you sick.

Do hand your disc quickly in to your team manager at the end of a big race if the disc system is in operation. Don't take it home to show Mum.

Don't collapse in a heap on the ground at the end of a race. You really aren't as exhausted as that (it is amazing how quickly 'dead bodies' recover and are soon chasing around watching the other races). More importantly, it will cause a bottleneck at the finishing funnel which may wreck the whole results system, stop other runners from getting an accurate time, and anyway give officials another problem they could do without.

Do take a complete change of clothing to races with you, including underwear, plus a towel, even if you travel to the event in your running kit and tracksuit. There might be torrential rain and ankle-deep mud when you get there, and it won't be much fun travelling home in that kit then.

7

ROAD RUNNING
Training for the 10km and Half-marathon

The two distances which have taken over in mass popularity from the marathon in recent years are the 10km (6.2 miles) and the half-marathon (21km/13.1 miles). These have become by universal acclaim today's equivalents of the 5 and 10 mile road races which used to dominate the British road running fixture list until the early eighties.

The aesthetic challenge of breaking the hour for 10 miles was always somewhat akin to breaking three hours for the marathon for the club runner and, indeed, being able to run ten consecutive 6-minute miles has the same symmetrical appeal of running a four-lap mile race in under 4 minutes. These mathematical teasers should help to keep both events alive in the future.

But the great surge of participation in the 10km and half-marathon events has come from several directions simultaneously. For a start, many of the new breed of runner originally attracted by the London Marathon, and whose sole running ambition initially centred on completing 26 miles 385 yards, began to look for a new challenge once they had conquered their personal Everest. And while for most runners completing a marathon always gives enormous satisfaction, it also tends to create a post-marathon vacuum.

Time is needed to recover fully from the physical effort of the marathon, and to overcome the running equivalent of post-natal, post-Christmas blues which frequently attends the aftermath of a marathon. But running in half-marathons and especially 10km is physically far less taxing and allows a much quicker recovery.

These events are also where running is now gradually returning to its upright stance after some years of being upside down. For in the past the marathon had always been the event to which you only graduated after years of experience and competition at shorter road distances. The marathon boom changed that, with beginners sometimes breezing straight into marathon training after 20 years of physical inactivity. But while it was the marathon and its particular mystique which first attracted them, once into the sport they soon became just as obsessed with the act of running as any previous generation had. Breaking 90 minutes (or two hours) for the half-marathon became a new target. So did cracking 40 minutes (or the hour) for 10km.

But the growing popularity of these distances also brought forward a quite separate brigade of runners, people who had neither the time nor inclination to train for a full marathon, but to whom the idea of tackling a local 10 km road race had just enough possibility about it to make it worth undertaking.

And once these runners began clicking up the 10km races, or the occasional 10-miler, their thoughts soon switched to the half-marathon as the next step. From there an eventual attempt at the marathon becomes virtually inevitable!

With such emphasis on participation and improvement at the two new 'classic' distances, I have devised a three-tier training schedule for each one. These schedules are based on a 12-week preparatory period which culminates in the target race itself.

For Beginners at both distances the schedules consist simply of a prescribed daily dose of steady-paced running, which is structured to allow an overall gradual progression in volume while encompassing as much recovery as possible. The main aim of this schedule is simply to get through the race comfortably.

For the Experienced runners, their 12-week programmes introduce some faster sessions, such as interval training and fartlek, which have their essential place in the schedule of any ambitious runner. Races at other distances can also be sprinkled judiciously into the programme with beneficial effect.

But the hardest schedules, naturally, are those for the Elite runners – men aiming for sub-35 minutes for 10km and sub-80 minutes for the half-marathon and women with targets of sub-40 minutes and sub-95 minutes respectively.

All three schedules are, of course, open to amendment by the individual runner according to their current fitness level. But I hope, even if you are not able to follow the schedules to the letter, that they will indicate the way to progress once constant steady–paced training no longer appears sufficient to make further progress at these distances.

10 KILOMETRES: 12 week schedules

BEGINNER – *aiming to complete 10 km comfortably*
All running should be at a steady, even pace

WEEK 1
Sun:	5 min
Mon:	5 min
Tues:	8 min
Wed:	5 min
Thurs:	10 min
Fri:	Rest
Sat:	8 min

WEEK 2
Sun:	15 min
Mon:	8 min
Tues:	Rest
Wed:	12 min
Thurs:	10 min
Fri:	Rest
Sat:	15 min

WEEK 3
Sun:	20 min
Mon:	10 min
Tues:	Rest
Wed:	15 min
Thurs:	10 min
Fri:	Rest
Sat:	15 min

WEEK 4
Sun:	25 min
Mon:	10 min
Tues:	Rest
Wed:	20 min
Thurs:	15 min
Fri:	Rest
Sat:	15 min

WEEK 5
Sun:	25 min
Mon:	10 min
Tues:	15 min
Wed:	20 min
Thurs:	10 min
Fri:	Rest
Sat:	15 min

WEEK 6
Sun:	30 min
Mon:	20 min
Tues:	Rest
Wed:	25 min
Thurs:	10 min
Fri:	Rest
Sat:	20 min

WEEK 7
Sun:	30 min
Mon:	20 min
Tues:	15 min
Wed:	25 min
Thurs:	20 min
Fri:	Rest
Sat:	20 min

WEEK 8
Sun:	35 min
Mon:	10 min
Tues:	Rest
Wed:	25 min
Thurs:	20 min
Fri:	Rest
Sat:	20 min

WEEK 9

Sun:	35 min
Mon:	15 min
Tues:	20 min
Wed:	30 min
Thurs:	25 min
Fri:	Rest
Sat:	20 min

WEEK 10

Sun:	40 min
Mon:	25 min
Tues:	Rest
Wed:	15 min
Thurs:	30 min
Fri:	Rest
Sat:	20 min

WEEK 11

Sun:	45 min
Mon:	20 min
Tues:	30 min
Wed:	Rest
Thurs:	25 min
Fri:	10 min
Sat:	20 min

WEEK 12

Sun:	30 min
Mon:	15 min
Tues:	Rest
Wed:	25 min
Thurs:	10 min
Fri:	Rest
Sat:	Rest
Sun:	**The Race**

EXPERIENCED – *40 min men / 45 min women*

WEEK 1

Sun:	7M steady
Mon:	4M fast
Tues:	4×800m, 800m jog recovery
Wed:	30 min fartlek
Thurs:	6M steady
Fri:	Rest
Sat:	3M fast

WEEK 2

Sun:	7M steady
Mon:	4M fast
Tues:	3×1000m, 600m slow jog
Wed:	6M steady
Thurs:	35 min fartlek
Fri:	Rest
Sat:	3M fast

WEEK 3

Sun:	8M steady
Mon:	5M fast
Tues:	5×800m, 800m slow jog
Wed:	6M steady
Thurs:	40 min fartlek
Fri:	Rest
Sat:	3M fast

WEEK 4

Sun:	8M steady
Mon:	5M fast
Tues:	4×1000m, 600m slow jog
Wed:	6M steady
Thurs:	40 min fartlek
Fri:	Rest
Sat:	3M fast

WEEK 5
Sun: 9M steady
Mon: 5M fast
Tues: 6×600m, 400m jog recoveries
Wed: 6M steady
Thurs: 40 min fartlek
Fri: Rest
Sat: 40 min steady, including 4×400m (approx) bursts

WEEK 6
Sun: 9M steady
Mon: 5M fast
Tues: 6×800m, with 400m slow jog
Wed: 7M steady
Thurs: 40 min fartlek
Fri: Rest
Sat: 40 min steady, including 4×600m (approx) bursts

WEEK 7
Sun: 9M steady
Mon: 6M fast
Tues: 6×600m, with 400m slow jog
Wed: 7M steady
Thurs: 40 min fartlek
Fri: Rest
Sat: 40 min steady, including 4×800m (approx) bursts

WEEK 8
Sun: 10M steady
Mon: 6M fast
Tues: 6×800m, with 400m jog recoveries
Wed: 7M steady
Thurs: 40 min fartlek
Fri: Rest
Sat: 45 min steady, including 3×1,000m (approx) bursts

WEEK 9
Sun: 10M steady
Mon: 5M fast
Tues: 3×1000m, with 600m slow jog
Wed: 6M steady
Thurs: 30 min fartlek, a little faster overall than previously
Fri: Rest
Sat: 5M fast, or race

WEEK 10
Sun: 10M steady
Mon: 5M fast
Tues: 4×800m, with 400m slow jog
Wed: 6M steady
Thurs: 30 min fartlek
Fri: Rest
Sat: 5M fast, or race (up to 5M)

WEEK 11
Sun: 10M steady
Mon: 4M fast
Tues: 5×600m, with 400m slow jog
Wed: 6M steady
Thurs: 30 min fartlek
Fri: Rest
Sat: 3M fast

WEEK 12
Sun: 8M steady
Mon: 4M fast
Tues: Rest
Wed: 2×2M fast, with 10 min recovery
Thurs: 6×200m strides, with 200m jog
Fri: 20 min jog
Sat: Rest

Sun: **The Race**

ELITE – sub-35 min men / 40 min women

WEEK 1
Sun: 12-15M steady
Mon: 7M fast
Tues: 3×1000m, with 6min recovery
Wed: 35-40 min steady
Thurs: 6×300m, 200m jog recovery. Then 4×200m, 200m jogs
Fri: Rest or 5M steady
Sat: (a.m.) 7M steady
        (p.m.) 10×100m hills, plus 4M fast

WEEK 2
Sun: 12-15M steady
Mon: 7M fast
Tues: 6×600m, with 4 min recovery
Wed: 8M steady
Thurs: 8×300m, 300m jog recovery
Fri: Rest
Sat: (a.m.) 7M steady
        (p.m.) 12×100m hills, plus 4M fast

WEEK 3
Sun: 12-15M steady
Mon: 7M fast
Tues: 2×600m, with 4 min recovery. Then 2×1000m with 6 min recovery
Wed: 40 min fartlek
Thurs: 12×200m, 200m jog, plus 4M fast
Fri: Rest
Sat: (a.m.) 8-9M steady
        (p.m.) 12×100m hills, plus 3M fast

WEEK 4
Sun: 12-15M steady
Mon: 7M fast
Tues: 3×1000m, 6 min recovery
Wed: 8M steady
Thurs: 12×60 sec hard on grass, with 90 sec jog recoveries
Fri: Rest
Sat: Short road race (up to 10M), or hard 8M

WEEK 5
Sun: 12-15M steady
Mon: 6M fast
Tues: 4×1000m, with 6 min recovery
Wed: 40 min fartlek
Thurs: 10×400m, jog 200m recovery
Fri: Rest
Sat: (a.m.) 7M steady
        (p.m.) 12×100m hills, plus 3M fast

WEEK 6
Sun: 12-15M steady
Mon: 6M fast
Tues: 5×800m, jog 400m recoveries
Wed: 45 min fartlek
Thurs: 10×300m, 200m jog
Fri: Rest
Sat: Road race (5-6 miles) or 8M hard

WEEK 7

Sun:	12-15M steady
Mon:	6M fast
Tues:	4×1000m, 6 min recovery
Wed:	45 min fartlek
Thurs:	12×400m, 200m jog recoveries
Fri:	Rest
Sat:	(a.m.) 7M steady (p.m.) 15×100m hills, plus 3M fast

WEEK 8

Sun:	12-15M steady
Mon:	6M fast
Tues:	6×800m, 400m jog recoveries
Wed:	45 min fartlek
Thurs:	12×300m, 200m jog
Fri:	Rest
Sat:	Road race (5-6M) or 8M hard

WEEK 9

Sun:	12-15M steady
Mon:	5M fast
Tues:	4×1000m, with 6 min recovery
Wed:	10M steady
Thurs:	8×300m, 200m jog
Fri:	Rest
Sat:	Track race at 3000 or 5000m or 4M fast

WEEK 10

Sun:	12-15M steady
Mon:	5M fast
Tues:	30 min fartlek
Wed:	3×1000m, with 6 min recovery *or* find an open track meeting 3000m race
Thurs:	10×400m, 200m jog
Fri:	Rest
Sat:	(a.m.) 6M steady (p.m.) 15×100m hills, *or* 3000m track race (if not on Day 4)

WEEK 11

Sun:	12-15M steady
Mon:	5M fast
Tues:	30 min fartlek
Wed:	3×1000m, with 6 min recovery
Thurs:	15×100m hills
Fri:	Rest
Sat:	(a.m.) 5M steady (p.m.) 3M fast

WEEK 12

Sun:	10M steady
Mon:	5M fast
Tues:	1×800m (6 min recovery) 1×600m (4 min recovery) 2×400m (3 min recovery)
Wed:	1500m track race or 4M fast
Thurs:	8×200m strides jog recoveries
Fri:	30 min jog
Sat:	Rest
Sun:	**The Race**

HALF-MARATHON: 12 week schedules

BEGINNER – aiming to complete comfortably
All running should be at a steady, even pace.

WEEK 1
Sun:	25 min
Mon:	15 min
Tues:	30 min
Wed:	20 min
Thurs:	25 min
Fri:	Rest
Sat:	(a.m.) 20 min
	(p.m.) 15 min

WEEK 2
Sun:	35 min
Mon:	20 min
Tues:	30 min
Wed:	25 min
Thurs:	30 min
Fri:	Rest
Sat:	35 min

WEEK 3
Sun:	40 min
Mon:	20 min
Tues:	30 min
Wed:	15 min
Thurs:	35 min
Fri:	Rest
Sat:	(a.m.) 25 min
	(p.m.) 15 min

WEEK 4
Sun:	45 min
Mon:	20 min
Tues:	35 min
Wed:	20 min
Thurs:	35 min
Fri:	Rest
Sat:	30 min

WEEK 5
Sun:	45 min
Mon:	25 min
Tues:	35 min
Wed:	15 min
Thurs:	40 min
Fri:	Rest
Sat:	(a.m.) 25 min
	(p.m.) 20 min

WEEK 6
Sun:	50 min
Mon:	15 min
Tues:	35 min
Wed:	20 min
Thurs:	40 min
Fri:	Rest
Sat:	35 min

WEEK 7
Sun:	45 min
Mon:	20 min
Tues:	35 min
Wed:	20 min
Thurs:	45 min
Fri:	Rest
Sat:	35 min

WEEK 8
Sun:	60 min
Mon:	15 min
Tues:	30 min
Wed:	20 min
Thurs:	40 min
Fri:	Rest
Sat:	(a.m.) 30 min
	(p.m.) 15 min

WEEK 9
Sun:	50 min
Mon:	20 min
Tues:	35 min
Wed:	10 min
Thurs:	45 min
Fri:	Rest
Sat:	40 min

WEEK 10
Sun:	70 min
Mon:	20 min
Tues:	40 min
Wed:	20 min
Thurs:	50 min
Fri:	Rest
Sat:	(a.m.) 35 min
	(p.m.) 20 min

WEEK 11
Sun:	60 min
Mon:	25 min
Tues:	40 min
Wed:	25 min
Thurs:	60 min
Fri:	Rest
Sat:	45 min

WEEK 12
Sun:	45 min
Mon:	Rest
Tues:	30 min
Wed:	25 min
Thurs:	20 min
Fri:	Rest
Sat:	Rest
Sun:	**The Race**

EXPERIENCED – *men, 85 min +; women 95 min +*

WEEK 1
Sun:	6M steady
Mon:	4M fast
Tues:	6×2 min hard effort, 2 min jog recovery
Wed:	5M steady
Thurs:	25 min fartlek
Fri:	Rest
Sat:	4M steady

WEEK 2
Sun:	7M steady
Mon:	4M steady
Tues:	4×3 min hard effort, 3 min jog recovery
Wed:	5M steady
Thurs:	30 min fartlek
Fri:	Rest
Sat:	4M fast

WEEK 3
Sun:	8M steady
Mon:	5M fast
Tues:	8×90 secs hard effort, 2 min jog recovery
Wed:	5M steady
Thurs:	30 min fartlek
Fri:	Rest
Sat:	5M fast

WEEK 4
Sun:	9M steady, or 10km race
Mon:	5M steady
Tues:	8×2 min hard effort, 2 min jog recovery
Wed:	6M steady
Thurs:	4M time trial
Fri:	Rest
Sat:	5M steady

WEEK 5
Sun: 8M steady
Mon: 6M steady
Tues: 5×3 min hard effort,
       3 min jog recovery
Wed: 6M steady
Thurs: 35 min fartlek
Fri: Rest
Sat: 5M fast

WEEK 6
Sun: 10M steady
Mon: 6M fast
Tues: 8×90 secs hard effort,
       90 secs jog recovery
Wed: 6M steady
Thurs: 4M time trial
Fri: Rest
Sat: 7M steady

WEEK 7
Sun: 9M steady
Mon: 5M fast
Tues: 8×2 min hard effort,
       90 secs jog recovery
Wed: 6M steady
Thurs: 40 min fartlek
Fri: Rest
Sat: 6M fast (or 4M steady if
       racing next day)

WEEK 8
Sun: 11M steady, or 10M race
Mon: 6M fast
Tues: 4×3 min hard effort,
       2 min jog recovery
Wed: 7M steady
Thurs: 4M time trial
Fri: Rest
Sat: 5M steady

WEEK 9
Sun: 10M steady
Mon: 5M fast
Tues: 6×90 secs hard effort,
       60 secs jog recovery
Wed: 7M steady
Thurs: 40 min fartlek
Fri: Rest
Sat: 4M fast

WEEK 10
Sun: 12M steady
Mon: 6M fast
Tues: 2 sets of 6×1 min hard
       effort, with 1 min jog
       between runs, and 5 min
       jog between the two sets
Wed: 8M steady
Thurs: 4M time trial
Fri: Rest
Sat: 6M steady

WEEK 11
Sun: 10M steady
Mon: 5M fast
Tues: 4×3 min hard effort,
       90 secs jog recovery
Wed: 6M steady
Thurs: 40 min fartlek
Fri: Rest
Sat: 6M fast

WEEK 12
Sun: 8M steady
Mon: 4M fast
Tues: 4×2 min hard effort,
       2 min jog recovery
Wed: 5M steady
Thurs: 20 min fartlek
Fri: 2M jog
Sat: Rest

Sun: **The Race**

HALF-MARATHON: 12 week schedule

ELITE – sub 85 min men; sub 95 min women

WEEK 1
Sun: 8M steady
Mon: 5M fast
Tues: Intervals: 6×600m at 75 per cent effort, with 2 min walk/jog recovery
Wed: 8M steady
Thurs: 10×150m hills
Fri: Rest
Sat: 45 min fartlek

WEEK 2
Sun: 10M steady
Mon: 5M fast
Tues: Intervals: 4×1000m at 75 per cent effort, with 4 min walk/jog recovery
Wed: 8M steady
Thurs: Intervals: 12×300m, jog 200m recovery
Fri: Rest
Sat: 45 min fartlek

WEEK 3
Sun: 10M steady
Mon: 5M fast
Tues: Intervals: 6×600m, 75 per cent effort, with 2 min walk/jog recovery
Wed: 8M steady
Thurs: 12×150m hills
Fri: Rest
Sat: RACE 5M/10km if possible; otherwise 45 min fartlek

WEEK 4
Sun: 12M steady
Mon: 5M fast
Tues: Intervals: 5×800m, 75 per cent effort, 3 min recovery
Wed: 8M steady
Thurs: Intervals: 10×400m, 75 per cent effort, 200m walk/jog recovery
Fri: Rest
Sat: RACE 5M/10km if possible; or 45 min fartlek if raced last week

WEEK 5
Sun: 12M steady
Mon: 5M steady
Tues: Intervals: 5×1000m, 4 min walk/jog recovery
Wed: 8M fast
Thurs: Intervals: 12×300m, 300m walk/jog recovery
Fri: Rest
Sat: 45 min fartlek

WEEK 6
Sun: 14M steady
Mon: 5M steady
Tues: Intervals: 6×600m, 75 per cent effort, 2 min walk/jog recovery
Wed: 18×150m hills
Thurs: 7M fast
Fri: Rest
Sat: RACE 5M/10km or 45 min fartlek

WEEK 7
Sun: 12M steady
Mon: 5M fast
Tues: Intervals: 6×800m, 75 per cent effort, 400m walk/jog recovery
Wed: 10M steady
Thurs: Intervals: 10×400m, 75 per cent effort, 200m jog recovery
Fri: Rest
Sat: RACE 5M/10km if possible; otherwise 45 min fartlek

WEEK 8
Sun: 15M steady
Mon: 5M fast
Tues: Intervals: 4×1000m, 75 per cent effort, with 3 min walk/jog recovery
Wed: 8M steady
Thurs: 20×150m hills
Fri: Rest
Sat: RACE 5M/10km if possible; or 45 min fartlek

WEEK 9
Sun: 12M steady
Mon: 5M steady
Tues: Intervals: 8×600m, 75 per cent effort, 2 min walk/jog recovery
Wed: 8M fast
Thurs: Intervals: 10×300m, jog very slow 100m recovery
Fri: Rest
Sat: 40 min fartlek (or rest if race tomorrow)

WEEK 10
Sun: 15M steady, or RACE 10M if possible
Mon: 5M steady
Tues: Intervals: 5×1000m, 75 per cent effort, with 3 min walk/jog recovery
Wed: 8M steady
Thurs: Intervals: 20×150m hills
Fri: Rest
Sat: 45 min fartlek

WEEK 11
Sun: 12M steady
Mon: 5M fast
Tues: Intervals: 6×800m, 75 per cent effort, 3 min recovery
Wed: 10M steady
Thurs: Intervals: 10×300m, 75 per cent effort, slow 100m recovery
Fri: Rest
Sat: RACE 5M/10km, or 35 min hard fartlek

WEEK 12
Sun: 8M fast
Mon: Rest
Tues: Intervals: 6×400m slightly faster than before, jog 200m recovery
Wed: 7M steady
Thurs: 4M fast
Fri: 2M jog
Sat: Rest

Sun: **The Race**

8

THE WORLD OF
THE MARATHON – 1

In the small hours of a summer Monday morning, a crowd of around 4000 is gathered outside an hotel in Stockholm, cheering and serenading the two slim young men who stand on the balcony. It is 1912, and the pair of them have just been carried shoulder high from a banquet at the Swedish capital's Olympic Stadium.

Their names are Kenneth McArthur and Chris Gitsham, and a few hours earlier they finished first and second for South Africa, overcoming the oppressive heat, in the Olympic marathon.

The warm night sky is illuminated with fireworks, honouring the winners, and the vivid reds and yellows briefly light up a room at the nearby Serafino Hospital, where the singing and applause for McArthur and Gitsham are clearly audible.

Unhearing, on a bed in the room lies a feverish twenty-one-year-old Portuguese runner named Francisco Lazaro, who lined up with his sixty-seven marathon rivals opposite the Royal Box in the Olympic Stadium at 1.45 p.m. the previous day. Like them, he passed a medical inspection, and even declared that the course looked much easier than those he was used to in Portugal, where he had three times been national champion.

But after 19 miles of the race, he crumpled in the unremitting heat and was rushed to the hospital. Now, news of his grave condition is kept quiet in view of the festivities taking place after the race.

Later that day, as a result of sunstroke and heart failure, young Lazaro dies. 'In his delirium,' an eye-witness says, 'he seemed still to be struggling in the marathon.'

Before we move on to the question of how best to prepare for the marathon, it is worth looking briefly back to see who was responsible for the invention of the wretched race in the first place. And, despite its aura and mystique, to reduce it clinically to what it is: simply a long road race, whose exact distance lies not in Greek history but within this century, and whose origins as a sporting event barely stretch into the last. Only the occasion it symbolizes goes much further back.

The race commemorates a run supposed to have been made by a Greek messenger named Pheidippides in 490 BC, from the village of Marathon, some 23½ miles north-east of Athens. The Athenians had defeated the Persians in a great battle there, and Pheidippides is said to have run all the way to Athens with the news; around the latter stages of a modern marathon, most competitors probably wish he had just sent a telegram instead.

However, on arrival in Athens, Pheidippides gasped out the news of the victory to the city elders, and then collapsed dead (at which point I always envisage the elders looking at each other and asking '*What did he say?*').

Something which tends to keep Pheidippides firmly in the area of legend rather than fact is that his run was not mentioned by historians until nearly 600 years after the battle, although a courier named Pheidippides is said to have run from Athens to Sparta, covering 120 miles in two days, to request military help *before* the battle.

One theory is that the Roman historian and storyteller Plutarch created Pheidippides' run from Marathon to Athens simply as a means of transferring his tale from the battlefield to the city, instead of resorting to whatever was the Roman equivalent of 'Meanwhile, back in Athens . . .' Another theory is that Pheidippides' run is not mentioned by contemporary Greek historians because he was a deserter.

Whatever the truth, and we shall never know, what is certain is that the distance from Marathon to Athens is not the classic 26 miles 385 yards (42.195 km) which the race has become. As a sporting event, its roots are relatively recent, springing from the preparations which were being made by the Frenchman, Baron Pierre de Coubertin, for the staging of the first modern Olympic Games at Athens in 1896.

A friend of de Coubertin, named Michel Breal, who was an historian, linguist and professor at the Sorbonne, suggested to the organizing committee the inclusion of two athletics events in the Games which would particularly reflect the glories of Ancient Greece. One was the discus throw, and the other was an endurance run along the original route supposedly taken by Pheidippides from Marathon. Both ideas were accepted and the endurance race, the marathon, eventually provided the highlight of those inaugural Games when the Greek shepherd Spiridon Louis gave the host nation its first and only victory of the Olympics in 2 hours 58 minutes 50 seconds. Greek runners also took second and third places on a course which was just under 25 miles.

The marathon quickly became an integral part of the Olympic Games on courses around that distance. But not without incident. At the 1904 Olympics in St Louis, the first runner into the stadium was an American named Fred Lorz, who was subsequently disqualified when he admitted that he had dropped out of the race with leg cramp at 10 miles and accepted a lift in a car, which had churned up clouds of dust from the unmade roads all over his rivals before ultimately breaking down at 22 miles. So Lorz apparently ran the last three miles to the stadium and pretended to be the winner, until the other runners arrived. He explained later that it had been meant as a joke, but his national federation took a dim view, and suspended him from competition.

A little-known sequel to the story is that the incident weighed so heavily on Lorz's conscience afterwards that he literally ran himself into the ground in winning the 1905 Boston Marathon as a form of redemption. His feet were blistered and bleeding, and he collided with his own bicycle attendant in his exhausted state at the finish, falling heavily.

The Boston Marathon, the world's oldest annual marathon, was established in 1897. Almost all of the US competitors at the 1896 Olympics had been members of the Boston Athletic Association, and upon returning home had urged the Association to stage a marathon in the city, as they had been so enthralled by it. The first Boston Marathon was less than 25 miles, and it was only when the Olympic Games came to London in 1908 that the first ever race over the now-standard distance of 26 miles 385 yards was held.

The London event was due to begin in Windsor and finish at the White City Stadium, Shepherd's Bush, in west London. The actual start was staged on the private lawns of Windsor Castle because the children of the Royal Family wanted to see the runners, and it was also decided that the race should end opposite the Royal Box in the Stadium, so that Queen Alexandra could see the finish clearly.

That 1908 Olympic event also became widely known as 'Dorando's Marathon'. A diminutive Italian pastrycook from Capri, named Dorando Pietri, was the first runner into the White City Stadium, as a contemporary newspaper account relates:

> With 75,000 people in the seats and nearly 25,000 more packed into every inch of standing room all round the enormous amphitheatre of the Olympic Stadium, with the Queen of England in the Royal Box, surrounded by

many members of her own and other Royal families, a miserable little figure tottered in at the North-Eastern entrance of the stadium. For a moment, as the news of his approach drew nearer, there had been a muffled roar of anticipation that rolled from tier to tier of iron and concrete, and re-echoed across the vast expanse of turf in sullen waves of sound.

But there was a sudden hush, almost a strangled sob of overwrought suspense, in all those hundred thousand throats when that small, withered man fell forward on to the first visible yard of cinder track, dizzy with excitement, devastated by the utmost atrocites of fatigue, but indomitable still. It was the Italian, Dorando Pietri. What followed was the most poignant scene that has ever been witnessed. It might have been beneath the skies of the South that we were all watching the struggles of some wounded toreador.

The wretched man fell down, incapable of going on for the two hundred yards that alone separated him from the winning post opposite the Royal Box. He was lifted up, and fell again. He struggled pitifully along to within fifty yards of the finish and collapsed. At that moment another competitor was seen struggling through the entrance, and after a terrible effort the Italian rose up and hurled himself with the last fragment of expiring will-power past the post.

He was carried away on a stretcher. After some twenty minutes the doctor was able to announce that he was going on well. But his stupendous efforts had been thrown away. Even at the price of a gold medal and the victory of the marathon race such agonies were too dearly bought. But Dorando was not even to get that. The doctor's testimony that the Italian, after he had fallen the last time on the track, would have been utterly unable to move without assistance was sufficient to prove – when proof was asked for – that the rule had been broken which clearly sets forth: 'No attendant will be allowed on the track in the Stadium'.

So the race was awarded to the second man home, Johnny Hayes of the USA, but Dorando had been taken to the hearts of the British people. When, three days later, Queen Alexandra presented the Olympic medals to the winners (as was the custom then), there was a special award for him: a gold cup, accompanied by a card headed Buckingham Palace, and in the Queen's own handwriting:

> For P. Dorando
> in remembrance of the Marathon race,
> from Windsor to the Stadium
> from Queen Alexandra.

The entire awards ceremony was brought to a halt by the acclamation given to the tiny Italian as he walked forward, clutching his cloth cap, and with a sprig of the King's oakleaves in his lapel, to receive the cup. The official with the megaphone simply couldn't make himself heard.

Now Dorando remains, more than 80 years later, one of the most famous Olympians of all. The following year he and Hayes, the eventual gold medallist, both turned professional as a marathon craze swept the USA, and in 1909 they were racing marathons involving 260 laps on an indoor track at Madison Square Garden!

The scenes of Dorando's collapse remain among the most famous in athletics history, and the opening ceremony of the 1974 European Athletics Championships, which were staged in Rome's Olympic Stadium, included a 're-creation' by Italian athletes and officials of that dramatic finish 66 years earlier.

The exact distance between the private lawns at Windsor and the Royal Box at White City was measured as 26 miles 385 yards, and although the 1912 and 1920 Olympic marathons were held over courses of slightly different length, from 1924 onwards the curious distance set in 1908 was adopted as the standard marathon length.

The ultimate irony came many years later, when the 1969 European Athletics Championships were held for the first time in Athens, and the marathon, along the classic route, had to include a detour of several miles in order to bring it up to the required standard length! Appropriately, in the circumstances, it was an Englishman, Ron Hill, who won that race.

While times for the marathon are always difficult to compare because of the varying terrain of different courses (not to mention the differing lengths of those earliest races), one of the most significant performances between the wars came from a man considered to be the first of the great Finnish distance runners, Hannes Kolehmainen. In the 1912 Olympics he had won gold medals in the 5000 metres, 10,000 metres and (now discontinued) cross country events.

A vegetarian in his earlier years, Kolehmainen had actually run his first marathon at the age of seventeen, before concentrating on track racing. But in 1920 he won the Olympic marathon, held that year over its longest-ever distance of 26 miles 990 yards, in 2 hours 32 minutes 36 seconds, which would be equvialent to around 2½ hours for the now-standard length.

Times improved along with training methods, as in every event, but in the marathon there was still the chance for the winner to come from practically anywhere, and from any background. The Argentinian Juan Carlos Zabala, for instance, could scarcely have had a worse start in life after being abandoned by his parents as a baby. But he took up competitive running at the age of sixteen in 1927, and in 1932 at Los Angeles the foundling became the youngest-ever winner of the Olympic marathon title.

Always the marathon provided high drama. For few other moments in sport can ever match the emotional charge of the entry into the

Olympic stadium by the marathon leader. All eyes are fixed on a narrow tunnel entrance, the track has been cleared in readiness, and the announcement is made that the leader is now approaching the stadium. Who will the first runner be? And will he come shambling on to the track with weak, rubber legs, like Dorando Pietri? Or will he stride strongly into the arena, with a confident wave, and be able to enjoy the luxury of those final yards knowing that he is going to win?

As a boy I lived in Wembley, and often on summer evenings or winter mornings I found myself drawn to run the two miles to Wembley Stadium, turning down the long, deserted Olympic Way which leads to the slope up to the gates of the giant stadium which was the venue of the 1948 Olympic Games. It has been the scene of many other great sporting events, like the epic 1966 World Cup soccer final between England and West Germany. But always I was aware that I was exactly retracing the steps of the Olympic marathon runners, and I tried to imagine what it must have been like that day – not for Delfo Cabrera, the Argentinian whose name is immortalized nearby on a special plaque as marathon winner, along with the other 1948 champions – but for the Belgian runner Etienne Gailly.

Gailly, who had escaped from occupied Belgium during the war and served in Britain as a lieutenant in the Belgian Parachute Regiment, had led that Olympic race for so much of the way, around Mill Hill, Radlett, Elstree, Stanmore and Kingsbury, and up that slope to the stadium. He entered the arena in the lead, but barely moving at a shuffle, and Cabrera took the lead from him some 300 yards from the line. A few seconds later, Britain's Tom Richards came past to take the silver medal. Gailly (who was killed in a road accident in Brussels in 1971) held on for the bronze medal, and was carried out of the stadium on a stretcher, barely conscious. Cabrera's name is on the plaque outside, but Gailly is the man remembered.

By contrast, the 1952 Olympic title in Helsinki was won with great ease by the remarkable Czech Emil Zatopek, who had already won the 5000 and 10,000 metres titles before lining up for his first-ever marathon.

Zatopek recalls now that his entire plan in what was, for him, unknown territory was based on following Britain's pre-race favourite Jim Peters ('I didn't want to follow a nobody'), and that he had checked Peters' number – 187 – beforehand. Then, just to be sure, he had gone up to the athlete wearing 187 at the start, extended his hand and said, 'Hello – I'm Zatopek.'

'Hello, I'm Jim Peters' replied 187. And then Zatopek knew that he had the right man in his sights.

Peters, who had set a world best of 2 hours 20 minutes 43 seconds the previous month, led the early stages of the race, but by the halfway mark Zatopek had joined him. The Czech looked across at Peters and asked, 'The pace? Is it fast enough?'

Already feeling the effects of his earlier exertions, but not wanting to show it, Peters answered, 'The pace is too slow.' A few minutes later Zatopek put in a burst which took him clear of the Englishman, who eventually dropped out at 20 miles. Zatopek went on to win by 2½ minutes in an Olympic record of 2 hours 23 minutes 4 seconds, while the defending champion, Cabrera of Argentina, ran 8 minutes faster than at Wembley and yet was placed only sixth.

The name of Jim Peters is so well known in connection with another race that he did not finish – the 1954 Empire Games marathon in Vancouver – that his enormous contribution to the progress of world marathon-running is sometimes overlooked. But the Essex runner had set new levels of training mileage in the early fifties, and his 1952 run of 2 hours 20 minutes 4 seconds had clipped no less than 5½ minutes off the previous world best. He improved it three more times, down to 2 hours 17 minutes 39 seconds in 1954, prior to his last race on that sweltering day.

Peters had always believed in pushing himself to the absolute limit, and although even he realized that the 80°-plus heat in Vancouver meant that record-breaking would be impossible that day, he still ran so hard in the conditions that by the time he reached the stadium, his legs were no longer capable of supporting him.

He fell on the cinder track, rose, staggered, and then fell again, and again. The crowd, who had earlier that afternoon thrilled to the 'Mile of the Century' between history's only two sub-4 minute milers at that time, Roger Bannister and John Landy, were now stunned, some almost hysterical, at the new drama before them. They were torn between admiration for this stubborn rag-doll figure, desperately trying to finish the race (oh, those 385 yards!), and a wish to save him from further suffering.

Peters later recalled falling only about three times. In fact, it was nearer a dozen, and alongside him a troupe of officials and athletes matched his every agonized step, willing him on, but none daring to touch him, mindful of the Dorando Pietri incident (the name Pietri, incidentally, is the Italian version of Peters).

Finally, Peters reached the apparent haven of the finishing line, and the English team's masseur Mick Mays grabbed him as he was about to fall again, and helped carry him off. He was rushed to the Shaughnessy War Veterans Hospital, where he was put into an oxygen tent and injected with considerable quantities of saline solution to counteract the effects of dehydration.

'Did I win?' he asked a nurse when he came round.

'You did very well,' she replied.

For he had not won. Instead, the finishing line for the marathon had been another 200 yards further round the track, rather than at the point where all the track races finished. He had not been disqualified for receiving assistance to finish, like Dorando. Tragically, he simply had not finished.

The race itself was eventually won by Scotland's Joe McGhee in 2 hours 39 minutes 36 seconds, as only six of the sixteen starters completed the course in the oven-like conditions. The irony was that McGhee was still some three miles behind Peters when the Englishman staggered into the stadium. Peters would theoretically have had time, had he only known, to have rested in a shaded part of the track, and walked the rest of the way.

As a result of his harrowing experience, Peters retired from competitive running, although he made a full and complete recovery from his collapse. And his run, like Dorando's nearly half a century before, did not go totally unrewarded. On Christmas Eve 1954, a parcel arrived at his home, bearing a Buckingham Palace postmark. Inside was an Empire Games gold medal, mounted on a base, which was inscribed:

> This gold medal was given to HRH the Duke of
> Edinburgh at Vancouver, and presented by him to
> J. Peters
> as a token of admiration for a most gallant
> marathon runner

A decade later, two other British runners helped to take the world's best marathon time for the distance towards the 2 hours 10 minutes mark. Coventry draughtsman Brian Kilby ran a world best of 2 hours 14 minutes 43 seconds in 1963, a year after winning both the Commonwealth and European titles (within six weeks), but this record was taken by his own Coventry Godiva Harriers team-mate Basil Heatley in 1964, with a run of 2 hours 13 minutes 55 seconds from Windsor to Chiswick.

Heatley also finished second that year in the Tokyo Olympic Games marathon (Britain's fourth silver medallist in the event) but his world best was in turn broken by the winner, the brilliant Ethiopian Abebe Bikila. His performance of 2 hours 12 minutes 11 seconds put him more than 4 minutes ahead of Heatley, and never was there a more relaxed winner. He even went through a session of vigorous exercises on the infield after the race, before Heatley arrived, to show how fresh he was feeling. Even more remarkably, his performance came just six weeks after he had undergone an appendicectomy. Yet Bikila had recovered quickly enough to become the first man ever to retain the Olympic marathon title, having won (barefooted!) in Rome four years earlier.

His attempt to complete the hat-trick had seemed quite feasible, as the 1968 Games would be staged at 7000-feet-high Mexico City, and Bikila was himself a high-altitude dweller. But the attempt ended when severe leg pains forced him to drop out of the race after 10 miles. The following year he was badly injured in a car crash, receiving spinal damage which paralysed him from the waist down, and he died in 1973 at the tragically early age of forty-one.

The first man to average under five minutes per mile for the full distance (a pace which equates to 2 hours 11 minutes 6 seconds) was Derek Clayton of Australia, who clocked 2 hours 9 minutes 36 seconds in 1967. Clayton, a native of Lancashire who emigrated to Australia in 1963, has completely the opposite build to the normally accepted world class marathon runner's light frame. He stands 6 feet 2 inches and weighs 11½ stone, and his heavy physique, together with his aggressive way of training – always hard, high quality and high quantity running – probably contributed to his frequent injury problems. These involved nine surgical operations altogether, and partly led to his competitive retirement in 1974, although he still runs regularly and maintains his racing weight.

Despite these injuries he apparently improved his world best to 2 hours 8 minutes 34 seconds at Antwerp in 1969, a performance which has been surrounded by controversy ever since. In England the meticulous Road Runners Club has never recognized the mark on the basis of lack of evidence of accurate course measurement, and in the USA the 'bible' of the sport, *Track and Field News*, dropped the performance after nearly twelve years from its world record lists in 1981 in the light of a new investigation by the Road Runners Club of America. No relevant documents from the Antwerp race now exist, but the conclusion was that the course may have been short by one kilometre, and that it was measured by a car, which is not acceptably accurate.

In his defence, Clayton points out that the second and third runners in the race did not set personal bests, that he had warned the organizers that he would be trying for a world best, and had been told that the course had been measured with a calibrated wheel. 'I'm as certain as I can be that my record is accurate,' he says. 'I never thought the record would last this long. Otherwise, I might have measured the course myself. I only wish it could be proved that it is accurate.' It will almost certainly remain an unresolved area of controversy, because no more evidence is likely to be produced one way or the other. Certainly, Clayton's ability to run a time of 2 hours 8 minutes 34 seconds is not really in question.

But if the Antwerp course *was* short, then two of Britain's greatest marathon runners of the seventies, Ron Hill and Ian Thompson, have been denied the chance of being acclaimed 'world's fastest marathoner'. Hill, the Lancashire textile chemist and more recently a highly successful running goods businessman, was the instigator of many marathon innovations during the peak of his competitive career. He ran 2 hours 9 minutes 28 seconds in winning the Commonwealth Games title at Edinburgh in 1970, to add to his European title of the year before, and only Clayton's controversial run in Antwerp was faster at that time.

Then, in January 1974, Luton's Ian Thompson leapfrogged over Hill on the ranking list to take the Commonwealth title at Christchurch, New Zealand, in 2 hours 9 minutes 12 seconds. Again, only Clayton's 'record' was faster.

The rise from obscurity of Ian Thompson, real comic book stuff, inspired club-level runners all over the world for years afterwards. Never really excelling on the track or cross country, and describing himself only as a 'scrubber', Thompson, then twenty-four, ran his first-ever marathon at Harlow in October 1973, simply to help out his Luton United AC clubmates in the team race.

The race was also the selection event for England's Commonwealth Games team but, totally unexpectedly in the star-studded field, Thompson won the race in 2 hours 12 minutes 40 seconds, then the fastest marathon debut of all time. Even he couldn't believe it. He had never raced further than 10 miles, and was merely aiming for 2 hours 20 minutes.

But the story gets better. Four months later, he won that Commonwealth Games race in the second fastest time ever, and another eight months on, in the sticky heat of Rome, he ran right away from Europe's best to win the gold medal in the European Championships by 1½ minutes in 2 hours 13 minutes 19 seconds.

All it then needed was for him to win Britain's first-ever Olympic marathon gold medal at Montreal in 1976 to complete the fantasy. 'All' it needed. But on a nightmare day at Rotherham in May 1976, suffering from leg cramp, he failed even to qualify for Britain's Olympic team, finishing seventh in the AAA Marathon, his first defeat at the distance in five races.

Yet runners like Thompson, who has since been a consistent

international performer if never reaching those early heights again, help to keep alive the magic of the marathon. What he did in 1973 and 1974 was in many respects illogical. Yet as long as someone can still achieve the illogical, the unexpected and the unpredictable in the event from time to time, the fascination of the marathon will not fade, and there is hope for everybody.

In contrast to Thompson's sudden rise to fame, the emergence of Charlie Spedding and Steve Jones as world class marathon runners in 1984 was, in both cases, the result of long careers spent learning their trades in the less glamorous world of road and cross country races.

Spedding, who had long filled a supporting role at Gateshead Harriers as one of their most consistent performers, always ready to contribute a solid leg to a road relay or a high position in the National Cross Country Championship, never found himself in the limelight as much as some of his clubmates. But his victory in the 1984 London Marathon in 2hr 9min 27 secs finally brought him, at the age of thirty-one, out of the shadows and into public recognition.

Later that year in Los Angeles, Spedding confirmed his talent for the event by taking the Olympic bronze medal, Britain's first Olympic marathon medal for 20 years, and was only beaten for the silver by Ireland's John Treacy in the last half mile. The Olympic champion that year was an even more mature runner; Portugal's Carlos Lopes who had made, at thirty-seven, a remarkable comeback.

Lopes had been the Olympic silver medallist at 10,000m and World Cross Country champion in 1976 but his career had then been curtailed by injury and it was generally considered that he had retired. But he reappeared as a world force at 10,000m in 1982 and in 1984 regained the World Cross Country title after eight years. In the Los Angeles Olympics he always had the measure of the field, breaking away over the final five miles to win in 2hr 9min 21 secs.

But the biggest surprise of 1984 was still to come. Steve Jones, a twenty-nine-year-old RAF corporal from Ebbw Vale in South Wales, was another runner in the Spedding mould, with years of running well at track and cross country events but only rare success in major events. He had been at the Los Angeles Olympics as a 10,000m runner and finished eighth, a solid enough performance for him. But two months later he not only unexpectedly won the prestigious Chicago Marathon, but did so in a world best of 2hr 8min 5secs. Like Spedding before him, Jones had found his true event at last.

His reign as world record holder lasted just six months. For, instead of retiring with his Olympic victory, the evergreen Carlos Lopes went into 1985 better than ever. In March he retained his World Cross

Country title and in April took the world marathon best into new areas by recording 2hr 7min 12secs on an ideal flat course in Rotterdam, where he was paced by two Belgian 'hares'.

The very next day Jones was due to run the London Marathon, and although he was unable to respond to this latest performance by Lopes, he still set a UK all–comers record of 2hr 8min 16secs. He had eventually prevailed after a classic stride–for–stride battle with Olympic bronze medallist Charlie Spedding, who was a close second in 2hr 8min 33secs, an English record.

By October Jones was ready to have a proper crack at the new Lopes mark on his return to Chicago and produced another major improvement of his own time. He went through halfway in an unprecedented 61min 43secs (sub 2hr 4min pace!), yet held on sufficiently in the second half to fail by just one tantalizing second to match the world best, clocking 2hr 7min 13secs – just a stride or so short of a world best after 26 miles!

Jones had also discovered that success in the world of international marathoning was highly financially rewarding; one estimate of his road racing prize money between 1984 and 1988 was put at $194,000. But money was always secondary to achievement to the modest Jones, a quiet family man with two young sons, who chose to continue his job as an aircraft technician at RAF St Athan long after his arrival on the lucrative world marathon stage.

Rather than keep piling up dollars, Jones really wanted to win a major championship gold medal and his best chance appeared to be in the 1986 European Championship marathon in Stuttgart. The clear favourite, he set off at world record pace. At halfway he was already two minutes ahead of the field and looked unstoppable. But the unexpected so often happens in the marathon. It had nothing to do with his running. Instead, he found it impossible to stomach the fizzy mineral drinks provided at refreshment stations, and from 20 miles began to suffer from dehydration. He slowed dramatically, and was caught by the field. A lesser man would have quit as they poured past but Jones was determined not to drop out and staggered into the stadium in 20th position in 2hr 22min 12secs.

Finishing in that state was as brave a piece of running as any of his world class performances and such is his character that when he finally crossed the line in the stadium after his nightmare experience he insisted on standing to attention as the British national anthem was being played for an earlier track success before being helped into the medical room.

Sadly, the Stuttgart experience rocked his confidence and began a down period in his career. He was selected for the 1987 World Championships, but had to withdraw beforehand because of an injury and then failed to earn selection for the 1988 Olympic marathon. But Jones is not a man who gives up easily.

The runner who benefited most from the collapse of Jones in the 1986 European marathon was the Italian Gelindo Bordin, who won that race in 2hr 10min 54sec, three seconds ahead of compatriot Orlando Pizzolato. Bordin was to become the new star of the marathon and although the twenty-seven-year-old surveyor from Verona was only able to finish third in the 1987 World Championship marathon in Rome behind the unknown Japanese-based Kenyan Douglas Wakiihuri, Bordin was destined to be the 1988 Olympic champion, winning a dramatic race in Seoul from Wakiihuri after taking the lead only in the last mile.

In doing so, Bordin became the first Italian to win the Olympic marathon title, exactly 80 years after the exhausted Dorando Pietri had victory taken from him in London in 1908 by those well-meaning officials.

There was one note of uncertainty about Bordin's status. For although the Seoul Olympics were largely unaffected by boycotts, one missing nation was Ethiopia, and in April 1988 a little-known Ethiopian, Belayneh Dinsamo, had broken the world marathon record on the fast Rotterdam course with 2hr 6min 50secs, also pulling Djibouti's Ahmed Salah (2hr 7min 7secs) under the old record set in 1985 by Lopes. Salah was to be bronze medallist in Seoul, less than half a minute behind Bordin, while the new world record holder Dinsamo had to remain in Ethiopia with his boycotting teammates.

Would Dinsamo have beaten Bordin in Seoul? We will never know. But then that, surely, is the fascination of the event, where the unexpected is always expected.

For the unexpected has been the life blood of the marathon's history. Like the time Scotland's Jim Alder led up to the stadium at the 1966 Commonwealth Games at Kingston, Jamaica, but could not find any markers to show him the entrance. He ended up running along a corridor and down a flight of steps before finally emerging on the track in the daylight to discover he was now only the second man on the track, as England's Bill Adcocks had taken a different route. But Alder, in his desperation, managed to close a 50-yard gap on Adcocks in the 300 yards before the finish, and win the race.

The unexpected. Like the time American Frank Shorter approached the Munich Olympic Stadium nearly two minutes ahead of the rest of the 1972 Olympic field. The eyes of 80,000 spectators inside turned in eager anticipation towards the tunnel, out of which emerged to great acclaim . . . a heavily-built West German student named Norbert Sudhaus, clad in the blue and orange colours of his club, who ran almost a full lap of the stadium before running off the track and revealing his 'joke' to embarrassed officials and security guards. It left Shorter (who was actually born in Munich) totally bewildered as he then entered the stadium to a baffling torrent of booing and whistling directed, he was later relieved to learn, not at him, but at the student who had stolen his thunder and fooled so many of the crowd.

The unexpected. Like the occasion, four years later, when a little-known East German named Waldemar Cierpinski won the same Olympic title in Montreal. But as he crossed the line after completing the requisite one circuit of the track, he noticed that the lap marker still showed '1'. So he kept on running, just to make sure, by which time defending champion Frank Shorter had come in for second place, completed the correct distance and stopped. It must have been the first time that an Olympic marathon gold medallist had found the silver medallist waiting for him on the finishing line!

But Cierpinski made no mistake four years later in Moscow, where he became the second man (after Bikila) successfully to defend the Olympic title.

The unexpected. Like the time that a totally unknown twenty-six-year-old Cuban-born New Yorker named Rosie Ruiz crossed the line as first woman to finish the 1980 Boston Marathon, recording 2 hours 31 minutes 56 seconds, which six months earlier would have been a world best. But there was something a little suspicious about Rosie . . . she certainly didn't look like a world-class runner, either in build or style. On a hot day, she was barely damp from her efforts. And no one actually remembered seeing her at any point of the course before 24 miles or so. Some spectators even claimed they saw her join in then. She protested her innocence, and that she had indeed run the full distance.

But a few days later, amid much speculation, she was officially disqualified as the winner, and the race awarded instead to Canada's Jacqueline Gareau. (Ms Ruiz still maintains she ran the whole way, but I watched that race at various points around the course, and I'm afraid I don't believe her either.)

The unexpected. Like the time at an earlier Boston Marathon, in 1967, which was then still for male runners only, when race official Jock Semple jumped off a following bus and tried to push one of the athletes off the road. He had just realized that, horror of horrors, the figure in a baggy, shapeless tracksuit was a *woman* who had gatecrashed the race. She had even obtained a race number by entering as 'K. Switzer'.

The K stood for Kathrine.

However, Kathrine's boyfriend, a 15-stone hammer thrower, was jogging alongside her at the time, and he removed Mr Semple bodily from the road instead. So Kathrine finished the race, and she and the hammer-thrower later married. Later she became the best of buddies with Boston official Jock Semple, who died in 1988 and women are now, of course, officially welcome to run in the Boston Marathon, and in the Olympic Games Marathon. Such is life.

Those early days of women in the marathon consisted entirely of female runners gatecrashing men's races, at the risk of incurring the wrath of their own officials, never mind the men's. But it was then the only way they had of demonstrating that they could run the distance too.

The first such incident is as old as the race itself: a Greek girl called Melpomene (named after the Greek muse, Tragedy) joined in the first Olympic marathon at Athens in 1896, finishing the course in 4½ hours.

A French girl, Marie-Louise Ledru, finished 38th in a men's marathon in 1918, and there is a record of a Violet Piercey, in 1926, covering the Windsor-to-Chiswick course in 3 hours 40 minutes 22 seconds. Women began gatecrashing men's marathons in the USA in 1963, while a Scottish girl, Dale Greig, set an unofficial world best of 3 hours 27 minutes 45 seconds on the Isle of Wight in 1964. An ambulance followed her all the way!

A Canadian, Roberta Bingay, joined in the 1966 Boston Marathon unofficially, and it was the following year that Kathrine Switzer managed to line up with a number and survive that little roadside scuffle.

Meanwhile mounting physiological evidence pointed to the fact that a woman could run a marathon as efficiently, if not quite as quickly, as a man. In 1972, as the women's best fell below three hours, American women were allowed to run marathons officially. In 1973 West Germany became the first country to hold an official national women's marathon championship. And in 1975, the Women's AAA introduced experimental rules to allow British girls over the age of twenty-one to run the distance.

The 'experiments' proved a success, no one collapsed and in 1978 the Women's AAA introduced an official national championship at the distance. Back in the USA, at the New York City Marathon, twenty-six-year-old Grete Waitz, an Oslo schoolteacher and a classical Scandinavian blonde, who had already established herself in European track and cross country running, smashed the women's world best in her first marathon by running 2 hours 32 minutes 30 seconds. 'Who are you?' asked the American journalists. Over 1100 American women had entered that New York race, alongside 13,000 men, as the US running boom of the seventies continued unabated, and was about to cross the Atlantic.

In 1980 Professor Ludwig Prokop, an Austrian member of the International Olympic Committee's Medical Commission, reported to the IAAF on the subject of women's marathon running:

Contrary to the traditional opinion that the physical performing capacity of woman is limited and that she cannot be exposed to greater strain mainly with respect to her endurance, sports physiological research and experience show completely different results. Apart from the fact that her muscular strength is less, physical performing capacity of women with respect to endurance is absolutely, as well as relatively, equal to that of men. Under extreme conditions of constant performance, women must even be rated higher than men. This is explained by the fact that the female heart may be excellently trained just like that of a man.

According to examinations carried out in the USA, Czechoslovakia, Federal Republic of Germany and German Democratic Republic even in child age endurance performances only slightly differ between boys and girls aged between seven and thirteen years. Therefore, after equally long periods of training, women develop an oxygen absorption per kilogram of bodyweight nearly similar to that of men. Another decisive characteristic, which is probably sex-linked, is oxygen utilisation being more favourable in women than in men. This is also confirmed by the fact that women are at least as resistant or even more resistant to high altitudes than men; mountain sickness (hypobaropathy) is less common in women than in men.

Practical experience with women as long distance runners confirms performance physiological results. Although the marathon race for women has been carried out as a regular competition only for a few years and only by a few women, there are already about 30 women running the marathon under 2 hours 40 minutes, and a best performance of well under 2 hours 30 minutes has been achieved. So far no accidents have been observed during marathon races for women, so this is no argument against competition for women over longer distances. Experiences with long distance swimming for women are similar. In swimming as well as in running, women approach the performances of men as the distances increase, and going over extremely long distances they often achieve better results than men.

Professor Prokop concluded, 'There are no relevant sports medical grounds against marathon running for women.'

At their meeting in Los Angeles in February 1981, the International Olympic Committee decided that the case for women had been proved. At the 1984 Olympic Games in that city, 88 years after Melpomene had gatecrashed that original marathon race in Athens, women would be allowed to compete for the first time in the Olympic Games over 26 miles 385 yards.

Before that, in 1982, the first ever fully-fledged women's marathon championship was held during the European Championships in, appropriately, Athens. In the city where the marathon had its roots two thousand years earlier, the first gold medal was awarded at the finish in the 1896 Olympic Stadium to an unknown Portuguese girl from Oporto called Rosa Mota, who could not conceal her delight at winning.

A year later, the IAAF took a lead by including the women's marathon in the first World Track and Field Championships, held in Helsinki. It was the tough Norwegian Grete Waitz, who had missed the 1982 European race through injury, who took the gold medal. She had dominated women's long distance running for years and at last she had a gold medal which she could never hope to have earned at the previous longest championship distance for women, which was just 3000 metres on the track.

Grete and her compatriot Ingrid Kristiansen were among the favourites for the inaugural women's Olympic crown at Los Angeles in 1984. But instead, and to the delight of the partisan US crowd, the diminutive American Joan Benoit established an early lead which she held to the end, receiving an enormous ovation as she trotted into the Los Angeles Coliseum, nearly 1½ minutes ahead of silver medallist Grete Waitz.

In the following years, however, it was the waif-like Mota who dominated the championship scene, even though she failed to share the passion of Waitz, Benoit and Kristiansen for attempting to break the world record. Following her bronze medal in Los Angeles, Mota retained her European title easily in 1986, succeeded Waitz as World Champion in 1987, and crowned her collection by winning the 1988 Olympic title in Seoul.

Meanwhile, the women's world best had been steadily improved, with Ingrid Kristiansen, disappointed at failing to gain a medal in the 1984 Olympics, reducing the mark to 2hr 21min 06secs in winning the London Marathon in April 1985. The first sub-2:20 marathon by a woman seemed not likely to be far away, but it was to prove somewhat elusive. Kristiansen's record withstood a whole series of attacks, primarily by the Norwegian herself, but by the beginning of the nineties it still stood.

Kristiansen, who also simultaneously held the world track records at 3000m, 5000m and 10,000m, was a splendid role model for female distance runners, always unafraid to attempt to set records in uncharted waters but ever-mindful of her motherly duties.

The 1984 Olympic champion Joan Benoit, by now Mrs Samuelson, returned to competition after becoming a mother herself in 1987, and the message was clear. Any remaining medical concern that hard training and severe physical effort might permanently affect a sports-woman's ability to become a mother appeared groundless. Kristiansen and Benoit typified women fulfilled both as competitors and mothers, and nearly a century after the first sporting marathon, the right of the female long distance runner to take her place alongside the male had been firmly established.

9

THE WORLD OF
THE MARATHON – 2

'Whatever you do, don't drop out,' an athlete destined to be a winner tells me before the start. He can see I am definitely a loser. 'If you do, you'll regret it for months afterwards. And you'll still have to go through it all again another day.'

There are more than 250 of us, a record entry, lining up for the start in the private grounds of Windsor Castle. This year the traditional Goldenlay Polytechnic Harriers Marathon also includes the inaugural women's race: I look round the faces for one in particular, but she hasn't entered.

Several hundred yards after the start we pour through the George IV gates, which are fortunately open, and pass a large group of spectators who stand beside the ironically named Long Walk wearing that kind of pitying expression adopted when someone says: 'Well, I suppose you know what you're doing'.

At 300 yards I spot my wife, who is obviously confident that I will at least get that far. She is poised with the camera, ready to take a last photograph, but looking the wrong way. When she spots me, she panics and takes a colour picture of her left foot instead. 'Okay,' a runner beside me calls out. 'We'll all have to go back and start again.'

At 7 miles, the first refreshment station. It looks easy in the Olympic films: take a quick drink from the plastic cup on the run, then toss it down. What you actually do is to snatch a cup from the table; then the orange squash sloshes over the sides and sticks your fingers together, and if you try to drink while running, you end up spilling it up your nose and down your chest.

So for weeks I have been practising on training runs: my wife standing beside the road, holding a squirty plastic bottle, and myself attempting to grab it and propel a jet of liquid in the vague direction of my mouth, which I would simultaneously try to remember to open. Coordination was never my strong point, but eventually it works. So for four of the refreshment stations we label squirting bottles with my race number, 187, and hand them in before the start.

As you approach each station, a strategically placed advance official shouts out to other officials manning the drinks table: 'One hundred and eighty-seven!'. This gives the others time to sort through the labelled bottles and then, as you arrive panting in front of them, to shout back to the first official: 'Pardon?'

So this is the marathon, 26 miles and 385 yards. 16 miles gone, legs not too bad, breathing okay. But there is a long way to go. The mind wanders as we pass through leafy lanes, the nose twitches at the smell of cut grass. Wearing two big number cards, front and back, I feel like one of those playing cards in *Alice in Wonderland*. The numbers are big partly because they carry the names of both the race sponsor and the organizers. Goldenlay Poly? It sounds like a particularly randy parrot. I come up behind a runner whose own number is hanging down from his back by one pin, flapping up and down like a single wing.

'These numbers are a problem, aren't they?' I say in a spirit of that camaraderie which grows richer as the race progresses. If I had been sitting opposite him on a train, I wouldn't have dreamt of speaking. I tear it off for him like a Good Samaritan, and continue on my way, wondering if I ought to report him for not wearing a race number on his back. If I can help somebody . . .

Between 6 and 19 miles, I have actually been overtaking a few of the runners who started too fast. I have no thoughts of the dreaded 'Wall', which is supposed to hit you in the closing stages. But suddenly I realize that the runner in front, a greying man in a purple vest, who is apparently only shambling along, is not getting any nearer to me. I am going at the same pace. I do eventually catch him, talk to him, pass him, am passed by him, and make a bid to get away from him in the last mile. Only to be overtaken again in the final half-mile, as he finishes ahead of me. So at around 19 miles, we must both have hit that 'Wall'.

Looking back, I don't quite know what I expected to happen at that point, when the glycogen reserves run out. Was it a symbolic sheet of tissue paper stretched across the road, a flash of lightning, or a road-sign showing a pile of bricks? I noticed none of these things. I just became slower in return for more effort.

Our tour of the Berkshire lanes is over. We return to suburban Windsor. And at 24 miles I walk briefly for the first time, to ensure taking in some liquid at the last refreshment station. The last mile seems to take an age, and is not helped when, three-quarters of a mile from the end, a well-meaning spectator says, 'Come on, only a mile to go.'

We come into the finish area at the Windsor, Slough and Eton Athletic Club track. Seven hundred yards to run. There are spectators, applause and the drone of a loudspeaker. It is a scene with which I am familiar, having seen dozens of marathons. The clubmen are finishing; down the field, but finishing. These men on the track with me are the ones I have watched before, more often than the stars who can break 2 hours 20 minutes at the drop of a hat. Why do they do it? They're never going to win anything, are they?

But as I cross the line, feeling a sense of relief, emotion, and for a few seconds, the most intense kind of insularity, perhaps I know why they do it. I walk on, then slowly lie down on the grass. My time is 2 hours 52 minutes 27 seconds – over half-an-hour behind the winner, but who cares? A friend comes over, picks up my hand, shakes it and lays it down on the ground again. At that moment, I am not sure if I am still attached to it. The tiredness in my legs, though, is a wonderful feeling. I have run a marathon. Okay, so it's been done before. But not by me.

(Reprinted from The Sunday Times, June 1978)

Whatever other possibly unattractive aspects I may hereinafter mention about the tantalizing, glorious, strength-sapping challenge called the marathon, I must make clear from the outset my belief that in sport, perhaps even in life itself, it is actually the fairest event of all in terms of pure give and take.

Respect the marathon, be fair to it, and it will be fair to you. It will allow you to experience from running its demanding course a sense of physical achievement you will never forget, nor want to. Treat it too lightly, however, and underestimate the surreptitiously fatiguing effects of those 26 miles, and that long, silent ribbon of tarmacadam will suck you towards it, like the Devil's vacuum, long before the end.

Don't be put off. Completing the distance doesn't need magic potions or anything other than a progressive build-up of steady running over a sustained period, starting and finishing at your own doorstep. I know. Even I've done it, and I'm probably the slowest, least skilful, most unco-ordinated physical specimen you're likely to come across outside a cemetery; two left hands, two right feet. So for me the appeal of long distance running events like the marathon is simply everything about it.

Not everyone who starts running later in life will achieve the success of men like Jack Foster, who emigrated from Liverpool to New Zealand at the age of twenty-four. By thirty-two this former cyclist was the overweight father of four children. As he tells in his book *Tale of the Ancient Marathoner*:

'One day I had the bright idea that I'd have a run for a while. It was summer time and the good weather inspired me. We were out for a picnic and a swim. I set off before lunch, thinking I'd have a run, then a swim. What I thought to be many miles later, I arrived back at the car.

'"What's wrong, have you forgotten something?" my wife asked.

'I didn't understand.

'"You've only been gone seven minutes," she said.

'Impossible. I was sure I'd run at least six or seven miles. I was soaked in perspiration and felt tired. I'd thought I wasn't in too bad shape physically. Not really overweight, though heavier than when I was riding the bike regularly. Now I was worried. If I was like this at thirty-two, how would I be when I was forty, or worse still fifty? So I began running – or jogging as I realize it was now.'

Nine years later, at the age of forty-one, he was the silver medallist in the 1974 Commonwealth Games marathon at Christchurch with a time of 2 hours 11 minutes 19 seconds, which put him among the ten fastest marathon runners of all time. Fifteen years later it remained as the World Veterans record. And in 1978, at forty-six, he finished sixth of the 11,000 starters in the New York Marathon in 2 hours 17 minutes 29 seconds, in 80 degrees of heat. A runner literally half his age finished just 35 seconds in front of him. 'Perhaps what I've achieved as a runner may have inspired some other thirty-five-plus men to get up and have a go. I'd like to think so,' he says.

Men like Foster underlined the need to re-evaluate the accessibility of the marathon. We used to think that it was only suitable for hard training runners, sometimes nearing the end of their careers, who would inevitably, we imagined, be reduced to a staggering jelly by the demands of the race.

More recently, as beaming mothers-of-six have come jogging cheerily across the finish line, we have come to acknowledge that it was the intensity at which the marathon was habitually run which wrought the most draining physical effects, not the distance.

Once the mass marathons took off, and allowed – indeed encouraged – thousands more runners to participate at their own more gentle pace, the event took on a whole new perspective. Those established marathons which failed to adapt to their new potential entry by opening their doors withered; and a new type of mass participation event, far more attractive to commercial interests and television, grew up.

This change did not meet with unanimous approval. The major international marathons, like the New York and London races, were accused of being little more than circus events. Whether or not that is fair, the fact is that people like circuses; they come to watch, and perhaps some of those spectating will become sufficiently inspired to want next year to become part of that circus.

A circus needs its strong man, its glamour, its clowns and its spectacle. For the crowd along the route of such 'mass' marathons, there is the same excitement of the sawdust ring in waiting for the leading international runners, the quickest woman, the characters like the waiter and his tray, the personalities, like the Jimmy Saviles, and the oldest runners, and the backwards runners, and the slowest runners.

Watching a marathon confined to just several hundred reasonable standard male runners, which had been the traditional pattern of the pursuit in Britain until then, can still be fascinating enough for those of us deeply involved in the sport. But to the casual observer, it must be about as riveting as watching paint dry. There is room for both types of races, of course. But everyone vividly remembers the day the circus came to town.

On the wall above my desk is a large colour poster of the start of the New York Marathon. It has two purposes. It covers a damp patch quite nicely, but more importantly it provides constant inspiration. For both carriageways of the shimmering, silver-grey Verrazano-Narrows Bridge, which connects the start on Staten Island with Brooklyn, are obliterated by two broad streams of humanity climbing the rise and disappearing into the horizon on the start of a journey which will leave them exhausted, blistered, and, for those who reach the finish in Central Park, fulfilled.

All over the world, similar scenes take place annually. In Paris, Stockholm, Oslo, Rome, Melbourne, Los Angeles, thousands and thousands of runners, joggers and even non-runners are lining up to tackle an event which has commanded the deepest respect of some of the world's greatest athletes for almost a century. Bus drivers, insurance clerks, students, bricklayers, housewives, and people from every other walk of life with no previous experience of running are being taken over by a personal compulsive urge to train for the marathon. (You wondered why you had to wait so long for a number 36 bus? Now you know.)

As you look at the poster of that New York start, you can pick out the individual anonymous heads. Every one of that multitude must have been deeply motivated to be on that starting line in the first place, but no-one will ever know the full total of physical, mental, social and environmental difficulties which these runners collectively had to overcome along the way to be in a position even to face the 26 miles 385 yards with that mixture of fear and anticipation which pervades every marathon starting line. But perhaps all that is certain is that for every single one of those 18,000 runners in the race, there was at least one other somewhere in the world desperately disappointed because his or her entry for the same event had been rejected.

It would be the same deep sense of disappointment and rejection felt by those whose entries for the London Marathon are returned. A frustration that they will not be permitted to share in what is always a real occasion as much as a pure running event. But then the marathon has become a victim of its own success.

The curiosity as to why such a hard test of physical endurance and mental tenacity became so attractive to the British in the eighties is a topic for future generations of sociologists. It could provide material for a book in itself, and still not reach a specific conclusion. But there were 25,000 starters in the 1989 London Marathon, and 25,000 unique sets of circumstances which caused them to line up at Blackheath in the first place. Very, very few of them were there to try to *win* the race. And that surely is the key. But one inescapable fact constantly faces you when preparing for the marathon. You cannot realistically hope to run the distance at all, let alone well, unless you are willing to put in a considerable amount of training mileage beforehand. The event, after all, tests endurance to a high degree and, without running regularly in training, and including some long runs in that training, your level of aerobic fitness will not be sufficiently high for a confident approach to the race. Even allowing for the probability that most first-time marathon runners will be satisfied simply to finish, the point is that, unless some reasonable degree of preparation has been undertaken, the chances are that you will either not finish, or else do so in such a fatigued state that you may not wish ever to attempt it again.

The marathon is not an event to tackle on the spur of the moment. A graduated approach to it is essential and, even if you have been running shorter road races for years, some sort of stepping stones to the full 26 miles are advisable: several races at 10 miles or so, and at least one each of around 15 and 20 miles before the big day, just to assure yourself that you will be able to get within a reasonable reach of the full distance. If you cannot run 20 miles, or even 15, then you certainly will not be able to run 26.

But, having established that, the marathon offers more chance of success to those runners who are usually well down the field in shorter road races. It requires less speed, less skill and less technical ability than any other event. But what it does need is a great deal of preparation through sufficient steady-paced running, a graduated race programme, and long-term overall planning if you are to get full satisfaction and success out of it.

So how much training is sufficient? The real answer is that there is no real answer. Some top international runners may train as much as 140–160 miles a week, others may achieve reasonable results on 70–80 miles a week, and there will always be a few who will tell you that they got by in a marathon on 30 miles a week. Perhaps, but such people usually have a much longer history of running over a period of years which helped them through, and in any case such a modest preparation is not to be recommended.

In general, I am against the application of rigid formulae and equations in working out potential, because such things cannot take into account so many minor yet relevant factors (sleep, diet, injury, illness etc.). But one rule of thumb which often seems to work is an American theory that a distance runner's 'collapse point' is three times his average daily mileage for the past two months. In these terms, collapse point does not refer literally to collapsing, nor is it exactly the same as 'hitting the Wall' in a marathon, which is discussed later in this chapter.

Instead, it refers to the point at which the life and bounce leave a runner's legs in a steady-paced race. For example, if your average daily training for two months has been 4 miles, then by this theory you should be able to run 12 miles in a race reasonably comfortably before reaching the collapse point, after which running becomes a much harder physical effort for less result. From this it can be seen that someone who had only averaged 4 miles a day for two months would have a hard time in the marathon, because the life will have left their legs before even the halfway mark.

Yet joggers and runners who do average less than 4 miles a day – sometimes considerably less – are entering marathons everywhere, and they are the ones who are taking 16 minutes per mile to complete the course.

Using the same theory, therefore, a potential marathoner should average at least 9 miles a day (or 63 miles a week) for the two months before the marathon to be reasonably confident of being able to run the distance ($3 \times 9 = 27$ miles).

9 miles a day may not sound too much, just an hour or so of steady running each day. But remember it is an *average*, based on seven days a week for eight consecutive weeks. In practice, few runners will run literally 9 miles a day like that (nor would they necessarily be advised to) but, in order to allow for the occasional rest day, the odd ache and pain, or the unavoidable social occasion, the daily total must often be higher than that. And to make up for any below-par weeks, the total mileage on other weeks may have to be bumped up a little to ensure an average of 63 miles plus and, since the runner will want to ease down on training before the actual race, some extra miles will have to be allowed for in the early weeks to maintain the average all the way through. Remember, too, that the 63 miles a week is the *minimum* recommended amount to be reasonably confident of being able to run the whole distance at a steady pace. Theoretically, it allows very little margin for error, such as misjudging the starting pace of the race and going off too fast.

Obviously, there will be people who have run marathons on less and lived to tell the tale. But if you intend to tackle the marathon, you should always be asking how you can fit in more training, not how little you can get away with.

To ask an under-conditioned body to run a marathon is like placing a huge load on a table with weak legs: it might just hold, but it won't be happy about doing so.

Whatever the level of training, the runner must aim to build up stamina, which is the single most important factor in marathon running. Long steady runs at a comfortable pace will help to build the foundations, and will strengthen the muscles for the constant repetition and increase the efficiency of the cardiovascular system in transporting oxygen economically to the muscles, while all the time adding the type of mental confidence to cope with the challenge which can only be accumulated by many hours of such running.

Ninety-nine per cent of the marathoner's efforts are aerobic. In other words, the demand for oxygen should not exceed the supply at virtually any stage of the race, and if a marathon runner does get into oxygen debt he will have to reduce his pace until the debt is paid, and then concentrate on staying on that side. A pace which may seem ridiculously slow in the early miles of a marathon can become very difficult to maintain in the closing stages but, through training and performances in shorter races during the build-up for the marathon, the runner should have a rough idea of a target time at intermediate points in the race.

The charts on page 206 show what average pace in miles and kilometres is needed, and the cumulative splits, on an even pace schedule for the final time in the right-hand column.

In terms of breaking down the training mileage into manageable units, one significant question would be: when does 20 miles not equal 20 miles? The answer is when it is made up of two tens or four fives. In other words, whatever your total training mileage for the week, it should include at least one long run, rather than consist entirely of a great many shorter runs.

Bill Adcocks, another of Britain's best ever marathon men, once said that in some respects it was easier to run a 2 hours 10 minutes marathon than a 3 hours 10 minutes one 'because you're on your legs for an hour longer'.

A world class marathon man will be running hard for nearly 2¼ hours, and a top woman marathoner will take between 2½ and 2¾ hours. Those are the minimum lengths of time; for most of us, it takes a lot longer, so the body needs to get used to running continuously for a long time. The Sunday morning 20-miler has long been part of the British distance runner's routine, especially for marathoners, and, apart from the benefits to the cardiovascular system, just being on your legs for several hours of easy paced running helps to build a special endurance which could not be equalled by four separate runs of 5 miles, nor two of 10.

Not that 20 miles is by any means the upper limit, and runners like Ian Thompson had covered 30 miles at a stretch in training several times before his dramatic breakthrough in the 1973 Harlow Marathon, which was in turn a springboard to his gold medals in the 1974 Commonwealth and European Marathons. There is no reason why such 'overdistance' training should not work as effectively for the marathon as it does when applied to the track events, but one would need to be very careful to avoid injury and to allow for the extra fatigue such runs would produce.

But to run regularly 30, or even 20, miles also needs a special type of mental toughness and dedication to the task which is frequently found in marathoners. Natural physical ability counts for less than the determination and willingness to churn out a high mileage day after day, when on some days things go well and some days not so well. We all have days when we don't feel like training, but the marathoner has to accept that his or her feelings may change maybe three or four times during the course of a single long run, as they might in a race. Successful marathon runners are not the ones who sometimes have to be goaded into training; they are the ones who sometimes have to be held back from over-training.

Remember the formula: hard work plus rest equals success. It applies to the marathon runner as much as anyone, yet because of the nature of the event, the training and the number of occasions on which you can race a marathon flat-out during one year, the preparation has to be viewed over a much longer time scale than shorter events. You have to think in terms of seasons and years rather than weeks and months if you are considering dramatic improvement.

Even international marathon runners had to run a first marathon at some point, and for many club runners that might in itself represent the ultimate challenge: simply to run the distance, to feel that, even if you could not cover it anywhere near as fast as the top men, you could still condition your body sufficiently well for it to be able to conquer the distance.

But, unless you are already doing a fairly high mileage, at least six months would be a reasonable minimum amount of time to allow yourself to prepare for a first marathon. Select the race in which you want to make your debut six months hence, and then spread out on a table some sheets of ruled paper, a calendar, your diary, your club's fixture list, the current year's road race fixture list, and some recent copies of athletics publications like *Running* or *Today's Runner*, which will contain advertisements for forthcoming races.

Suppose you are a keen club runner, whose longest ever run has been 11 miles and whose average training mileage is around 40 per week. You may decide that you want to run in the Maidstone Marathon, which is normally held in June. So working back from the actual date, you should try to find a 20 mile road race some 4–6 weeks beforehand, a 15 mile road race about 2–3 weeks before that, and then several half-marathons spread over several months before that. These will then become your stepping stones to the marathon, wellspaced to allow recovery, a return to hard training and an easing off in between. Some possibilities might be:

24 February:	Woking 10 miles
17 March:	Fleet Half-marathon
31 March:	Folkestone 10 miles
13 April:	Bracknell Half-marathon
5 May:	Chichester to Portsmouth 25 km (16¼ miles)
20 May:	Pembroke 20 miles
16 June:	Maidstone Marathon

Next, mark in some other reasonably accessible road races between now and your planned marathon. These will be alternative events to help you across any voids, or to take the place of any race you have to miss unavoidably, even though you may not end up doing any of the alternatives unless you want to.

17 February:	Hillingdon 5 miles
24 February:	*Woking 10 miles*
17 March:	*Fleet Half-marathon*
24 March:	Guernsey Half-marathon
31 March:	*Folkestone 10 miles*
7 April:	Reading Half-marathon
13 April:	*Bracknell Half-marathon*
14 April:	Newport 10 miles
15 April:	Cambridge 10 miles
21 April:	Solihull 10 miles
28 April:	Havant Half-marathon
5 May:	*Chichester–Portsmouth 25 km*
7 May:	Trowbridge 10 miles
12 May:	Croxdale 10 miles
19 May:	Beccles 10 miles

20 May:	*Pembroke 20 miles*
26 May:	Newport 15 miles
28 May:	St Neots Half-marathon
3 June:	Michelin 10 miles (Staffs)
9 June:	Canterbury 10 miles
16 June:	*Maidstone Marathon*

(NB. Dates are examples only)

The task is then to work out a training plan which will enable you to increase your mileage gradually over six months but will also allow you to ease off before the 'stepping stone' races so that you can judge the benefits of the training without feeling too tired, while still graduating by stages to your longest racing distance.

If your main ambition is to run a reasonable marathon in six months' time, then it is best to accept from the start that you may not necessarily be able to turn out your most sparkling performances at shorter distances week after week if you are also trying to build up to your highest ever training mileage. You cannot always produce your best when your body is still recovering from being pushed to its maximum load.

Thus it is a personal choice whether you will want to run in any or all of the other races you have listed. Almost certainly it will not hurt you, and it may well provide a mental break from the training efforts; some people thrive on racing and would wither without at least one race a fortnight. Others might prefer to race very sparingly and not risk any possible depression if they did run a slower time than the previous year despite their extra training. In many cases, it may even be considerably faster, but the overall plan cannot be judged on such intermediate races. A very practical alternative, of course, is that the athlete might prefer to use the Saturday for a long run, or several shorter sessions, thus totting up more miles than they might get in a race.

A further choice is to train on the morning of a race, or after a race, if travelling does not make it too difficult. It is a matter of personal preference, and there is no specific 'right way'; the right way is the one which suits you.

A simple but effective way of working out the overall training plan is to number the weeks between the present moment and the marathon, in this case from 1 to 24, and list the numbers down the side of a piece of ruled paper, together with the relevant dates, the stepping stone races, and the alternative races. Then with this framework, a pencil (and a rubber!) you can produce a training plan which might look something like the chart on pages 132–133.

It cannot be stressed too much that the figures are just a guide, and that some runners will want to do fewer miles and some will want to do more. But if, as in the imaginary example I have used, the runner was only averaging 40 miles a week before the build-up, with a longest run of 11 miles, then I feel the figures quoted may well be the maximum load he or she could attempt without very greatly increasing the chance of injury. The key is to build up gradually over a long period, going close to the border of breakdown without actually stepping over it.

The training chart could apply equally to women marathoners too, if not all of the races (although some are open to female runners). The length of the marathon is exactly the same for women as it is for men, and so they need to train in the same volume, though their pace may be slower than that of a male counterpart. Some of the top American women marathon runners are covering 120 miles a week themselves now.

Another aspect of the chart should be particularly noted. After a few weeks of gradually increasing the load, the total occasionally drops back down for a week, either to accommodate an easing down period for a race, or simply to allow some slight recovery from the highest mileage weeks, mental as much as physical.

Some years ago a young distance runner showed me his planned weekly mileages for the forthcoming winter. He had never run more than 85 miles in a week before, and he intended to start, quite reasonably, with several weeks of 40–50, building up through 70 and 80 miles a week, but increasing the totals every single week until he planned to be doing 110, 120, 120, 130 and 130 in successive weeks. As I pointed out to him, he was planning to run at least five consecutive weeks at a load over 50 per cent in excess of the most he had ever run in a week before, straight after a string of consecutive weeks also well above his previous maximum. Could he imagine, I asked, going to bed exhausted on the final night of his second 120 mile week, then waking up next morning and having to start the first day of another two weeks at a still greater, and even more fatiguing, target?

By not considering such practical factors, he was setting himself a far too ambitious load, which was likely to end in physical breakdown or high mental fatigue. If he was going to attempt to increase his mileage drastically, it would be far better to allow for breathing spaces in between, dropping the mileage down to a lower level every third week or so to allow the body a chance to recover, repair damaged tissues, and generally prepare to face another push forward, rather than force an already tired body to perform continually and reluctantly at a level currently beyond it.

These are principles which have to be considered. There is no foolproof guide to the point at which your body is being asked to do too much. Perhaps, if it was ever discovered to be, say, 89⅞ miles a week, then a lot of the fascination would go out of the sport.

But 'too much' is only relative to what you would have done in the past and your current capabilities. Every runner is a separate case, with a different background, but by understanding the problems in general terms it is possible to work out a training programme which will most likely be of the greatest benefit to you *at the moment*.

The young runner, incidentally, was named Mike Gratton. A few years later, in 1983, he won the London Marathon in 2hr 09min 43 sec.

There *are* marathon runners who can pile up 150 miles a week, week after week, but they have built up to it over a period of some years, not a few months. If you respect your body, its current capacity, and do not ask it to become a world class marathoner's body overnight, progress will be steady but relentless. Like the race itself, you will get there eventually, but not by sprinting the first 100 metres. The marathon runner who started his preparation last year may be ahead of you, but if you start now, you'll be ahead of the runner who is going to start next year.

Week No.	Dates	Stepping Stone Races	Planned Total Weekly Mileage	Long Sunday Run	Alternative Races
1	31 Dec–6 Jan		40	10	
2	7–13 Jan		45	11	13 Jan: Cross country relay for club
3	14–20 Jan		50	12	
4	21–27 Jan		55	12	27 Jan: Cross country league for club
5	28 Jan–3 Feb		50	12	
6	4–10 Feb		60	14	Feb 10: Southern Cross Country Championship
7	11–17 Feb		65	14	17 Feb: Hillingdon 5 miles
8	18–24 Feb	24 Feb: Woking 10 miles	55 incl. race	15	Feb 24: National Cross Country Championship
9	25 Feb–3 Mar		65	15	

Week No.	Dates	Stepping Stone Races	Planned Total Weekly Mileage	Long Sunday Run	Alternative Races
10	4-10 Mar		70	16	
11	11-17 Mar	17 Mar: Fleet Half-marathon	65 incl. race	16	
12	18-24 Mar		75	17	24 Mar: Guernsey Half-marathon
13	25-31 Mar	31 Mar: Folkestone 10 miles	65 incl. race	17	
14	1-7 Apr		80	18	7 Apr: Reading Half-marathon
15	8-14 Apr	13 Apr: Bracknell Half-marathon	70 incl. race	18	14 Apr: Newport 10 miles
16	15-21 Apr		85	20	15 Apr: Cambridge 10 miles 21 Apr: Solihull 10 miles
17	22-28 Apr		80	20	28 Apr: Havant Half-marathon
18	29 Apr-5 May	5 May: Chichester-Portsmouth 25km	75 incl. race	18	
19	6-12 May		90	22 (Sat 12 May)	7 May: Trowbridge 10 miles 12 May: Croxdale 10 miles
20	13-19 May		60	18	19 May: Beccles 10 miles
21	20-26 May	20 May: Pembroke 20 miles	70 incl. race	20	26 May: Newport 15 miles
22	27 May-2 Jun		80	22-24	28 May: St. Neots Half-marathon
23	3-9 Jun		50-60	15	3 Jun: Michelin 10 miles 9 Jun: Canterbury 10 miles
24	10-16 Jun	16 Jun: Maidstone Marathon	60 incl. race	–	

A sample twenty-four week build-up to a first marathon (see page 130).

The 'Wall' and the Carbohydrate Loading Diet

The simple question of 'How can I run faster?' when posed by some of the world's leading international marathon runners is not that simple any more. But in the past decade or so it has led to the widespread adoption of (and in some cases disenchantment with) various 'carbohydrate loading' techniques, which have helped some runners achieve quicker times, others to perform well below their best, and generally caused a great deal of controversy in the marathon world.

The relatively recent introduction of such techniques, whose principle is to manipulate the diet into providing additional energy fuel, has meant that even physiologists, let alone the runners themselves, are still somewhat divided on the relative merits and drawbacks of the system. No one knows, either, whether there are any long-term effects of what is actually a method of deliberately tampering with the body's chemistry.

The background is this. Marathon runners have long recognized that there comes a point in the later stages of the race, usually between 18 and 23 miles, when running suddenly becomes very much harder. From running quite comfortably they are suddenly, without warning, dragged down to a much slower pace, despite increased effort. The change is accompanied by weak legs, acute muscle discomfort and fatigue, together with doubts about even finishing.

That sensation in the race is commonly known as 'hitting the Wall', because that is very much what it feels like. Every race in athletics has its equivalent crucial moment. A 400 metres runner hits it around 300 metres, and it has been said, graphically and accurately, that the winner of a 400 metres race is not the athlete running the fastest, but the one who slows down the least. That description could apply equally well to the marathon.

For what has happened is that after approximately 20 miles of hard running, the muscles have used up all their chief energy-providing source, glycogen (which is stored carbohydrate, in the form of sugar), and a chain reaction sets in as new stocks of fuel are urgently sought by the muscles.

The body switches to a readily available, but less efficient, alternative: fat. The fitter and more experienced in long runs you are, then the quicker and more easily this transition takes place. No one, claim physiologists, can avoid hitting the Wall at some stage, using up all of their glycogen, if they have run hard for the full 26 miles. But some hit it harder than others.

The leading runners sometimes tend not to notice. Some even claim they have never hit the Wall. What they mean is that they have not *noticed* the effects of doing so, probably because they were concentrating so hard on the race itself. But they will still have had to work that much harder in the closing miles just to maintain an even pace, while those who hit the Wall hardest may slow by anything up to 3 minutes a mile or more.

So that was the problem which faced the world's fastest runners at the end of the sixties, when they were already doing a tremendous volume of training mileage, which could scarcely be increased significantly without openly inviting leg muscle or bone injury from overuse.

The whole field of 'carbohydrate loading' diets was first opened up by Swedish physiologists who were experimenting at that time with ways of increasing the muscle glycogen content in long-distance cyclists. They developed a method of deliberately depleting the glycogen some time before competition, and then boosting the replacement stores by dietary adjustment.

The first link with marathon running came through Ron Hill, who was told of the experiments by an international team-mate.

Appreciating its value in possibly delaying the moment in a marathon race at which the runner hits the Wall, Hill tried out the technique for the first time in the 1969 AAA Championship race in Manchester, and beat Australia's Derek Clayton by 2 minutes, moving into the lead at 15 miles, and winning in 2:13.42 (then the second fastest-ever time by a British runner).

Two months later he tried it again in the European Championships race in Athens. Although by the 19 miles mark he was in third place, feeling tired, and had already settled for the bronze medal, in the last 7 miles he found himself sweeping through with apparent ease into first place. He turned a deficit of 1½ minutes on the leader into a winning margin of 45 seconds by the finishing line, to record the first of a series of major international marathon victories.

The Techniques:

The fullest and most severe version of the carbohydrate loading diet technique is divided into three distinct sections, as follows:

1. Seven days before your race (say the Sunday before a Saturday marathon) you take a very long run, perhaps 20 miles or more, to deliberately deplete the glycogen currently in your muscles. You 'run to the Wall', in fact. (Some physiologists suggest a shorter distance, but followed by a series of hard interval runs over, say, 400 metres, will also result in sufficient depletion.)

2. After that session, and for the next three days, you take very few carbohydrates in your diet, but live on a mainly high protein and fat diet, while continuing to train very lightly.
3. From Wednesday lunchtime you switch to a high percentage carbohydrate diet (bread, cereals, cake, doughnuts, chocolate etc.), while still taking in fats, proteins, vitamins and minerals, and still training lightly.

The theory behind this is based on the Swedish experiment which showed that by intentionally using up all the glycogen first (a process known as the 'bleed-out'), followed by a near abstinence from carbohydrates for three days, you can stimulate the body into producing extra glycogen-storing enzymes, and these will eventually allow the muscles to store an even greater amount of glycogen than they could before.

Then, when the diet is switched back to its high carbohydrate level from lunchtime on Wednesday, the amount of stored glycogen can reach almost double the normal level.

But, like everything in this world, it is not quite as simple as that. Otherwise it would undoubtedly be in wider use than it is. But for a start the athlete using the most severe form of the system has to endure three days of possible depression, while feeling jaded, tired, irritable, possibly sleeping badly, and being particularly prone to catching any flu or cold germs which may be in the vicinity, as the body is so low in its resistance at that time. From Wednesday, the intake of cakes and Mars bars can be very enjoyable, but because training all week is kept to a very light level, partly to preserve the maximum of glycogen for Saturday, but partly too because the runner may not be feeling very energetic for much of the time, there is often a weight increase. A higher liquid intake is necessary too, because stored glycogen needs a considerable amount of water (3–4 lbs of it may be stored per lb of glycogen) and if that water is not provided by the diet, the body will take it from elsewhere, leading to possible dehydration.

So you go to the starting line, not having run particularly well, or far, for nearly a week, feeling somewhat lethargic and bloated, and knowing that you are several pounds heavier than usual. It needs a great deal of confidence in those circumstances to feel that you are still going to run well.

Some athletes have survived the diet regularly with honour; others now feel that an illness suffered just before a major international race was due entirely to the 'early week blues'; and still others point out that their best time in a marathon using the diet, and their best time without it, are just a few seconds apart.

In fact, no two athletes probably react in exactly the same way. And there is medical opinion that the diet should not be used more than two or three times a year, because any possible long-term effects which this repeated 'fooling' of your body may cause are unknown, and because of the fact that in any case the body soon realizes its chemistry is being manipulated, and adapts accordingly. Then the method is not so effective. In any case, it should never be tried by anyone suffering from a condition like diabetes.

Ron Hill, with 20 years of international marathoning behind him, has now modified his own views on the diet through his varied experiments, trying different combinations of depletion and high and low carbohydrate diets. For a start, he says, he has never been an advocate of the initial 20 miles 'bleed-out' run, because 'to me it seems crazy to run 20 miles at any pace only a week before a marathon'. He feels that the glycogen can be depleted on less, and he brings about depletion by running twice each day (his normal routine) with hard runs on the second session of the first and second days of the week; then he runs easily on the third.

During these first three days, on the low carbohydrate phase, he still eats eggs, cheese, bacon, ham, cooked meats (boiled ham or tongue), butter, fish, other meats (chicken, steak, chops) together with green salads, tomatoes and other vegetables, such as carrots, turnips, cabbage, cauliflower, peas and beans (but no potatoes). He avoids the obvious sweet and starchy foods, but permits himself four Ryvita biscuits (instead of bread), an apple, an orange and a yoghurt each day.

He emphasizes that carbohydrates should not be totally eliminated from the diet during the first phase, because some are needed just to support the vital life processes. In his early days with the diet, though, he went beyond this.

'After the initial successes, the more I refined the diet, up to the 1972 Munich Olympics, the worse it became. I simply didn't understand what was happening, or the fact that if you cut out carbohydrates completely during the early part of the week before the race, still train hard and deplete your glycogen level, but go past that point, then you're actually harming yourself.'

When he switches back to carbohydrates on the Wednesday now, he satisfies the immediate craving for sweet foods, but takes care not to overstuff himself on the next two days because he has experienced indigestion problems, and in any case feels that his normal diet is sufficiently high in carbohydrates to 'load' the muscles when combined with his lighter pre-race training programme. His own experiences have indicated that, while it is not for everybody, the diet has certainly worked for him in the past, and he notices a quicker recovery rate after the race than when he doesn't use it.

A warning on the effects of overloading came from Dr Gabe Mirkin, an American running nutrition expert, who pointed out that once the enzymes in the muscle tissue are 'overprimed' to receive extra glycogen stores, they will store all that is offered to them: 'And once glycogen is stored, it cannot get out. You have to burn it off, otherwise it will keep accumulating until the muscle tissue bursts. Runners who have loaded for more than three days, or whose muscles fill to capacity in only two days, have done themselves considerable damage on the diet.'

Because of its possibly negative psychological effects in the early part of the week, more and more runners are turning instead to an abbreviated version of the diet, where a depletion run of around 12 miles is done four days before the race. No carbohydrates are eaten for the rest of that day, but the athlete switches *next* day to the high carbohydrate intake, and can still achieve a relatively high proportion of the loading effect.

Other runners are simply content to eat more carbohydrates in their normal diet in the last three days before a marathon (pizza and pasta are popular eve-of-marathon dishes) without depleting at all. The night before the race is the last to eat heavily; on the morning of the race, light foods like cereal, toast or scrambled eggs should suffice, so that the stomach is not still trying to digest heavy food when the race starts.

The term 'placebo' has even been used of the full carbohydrate loading system by the more cynical. But if you can survive the traumatic period between the bleed-out stage and getting to the 20-mile point in the race itself, then it may suddenly become a big mental, as much as physical, boost.

Another simpler, and more recently proposed, recipe for delaying the arrival of the Wall is the good old cup of coffee. The noted US physiologist David Costill has recommended two cups of black coffee, drunk about an hour before the start, as possibly helping the athlete to run faster. The caffeine in it apparently allows the burning of a greater amount of the free-floating fats in the blood system for energy earlier in the race, thus helping to postpone the eventual exhaustion of available glycogen.

'I play down the caffeine now, because it's a drug,' says Costill, 'and I don't want anyone to feel they have to do the equivalent of taking a pill in order to turn in a good performance. But it does seem to facilitate fat metabolism, and that in turn delays glycogen depletion.'

What must never be forgotten, though, is that the whole idea of the carbohydrate loading diet was originally taken up by international runners *who had reached the virtual limit of their possible training load.*

What it can never, ever do is to replace the hundreds and hundreds of training miles which you have to put into your marathon preparation first. It is no good spending time, effort and discomfort arranging in advance for your triumphant blast through the infamous Wall at 22 miles if you have to drop out exhausted after only 8 miles through lack of fitness. And in any case such diets are definitely not recommended for first-time marathoners.

Sometimes we may even put too much emphasis on diet, shoes, and so on. Of course they have to be right too, and you won't get far if you don't normally eat a reasonable, balanced diet, or if your shoes are too tight. But above all, even if you have the right diet and the right shoes, you will still not get anywhere if you haven't made your main priority training sufficiently hard in the first place.

The Last Week

There is no doubt that the more seriously you take the marathon, the more it dominates your life. But because it is not an event which you can throw off at frequent intervals, or with the minimum of physical effort, you owe it to yourself (and your family!) at the end of a long training regime to use every single opportunity to increase your chance of achieving a performance as near to your optimum as possible, no matter how fast or slow.

So it is worth spending a little time considering some of the external factors which could affect your run on the day, and how advance planning and attention to detail can help.

The Week Before the Race

As the day of a marathon draws nearer, so you must physically and mentally prepare to meet it. Still feeling the effects of tiredness from fatiguingly long training runs immediately before the race will not help, so in the final week training mileage should drop away to around half the normal load, with the majority of it coming early in the week. The longest run could come on the Sunday before a Saturday marathon, with another medium-length run on Wednesday, but on other days, particularly Thursday and Friday, you should do little more than jog. Remember the equation: hard work *plus rest* equals success. The last few days before a marathon are too late to do runs of sufficient length to have any positive effect on your stamina and still recover before the race.

If you decide to undertake the carbohydrate loading diet, then Sunday will be the occasion for your long 'glycogen bleed-out' run, and Wednesday lunchtime will be a high point of your week as you switch to stuffing yourself with carbohydrates. But for a first-time marathoner, that type of diet is best left alone.

The final few days are simply a time to conserve energy, to be a little lazy, and catch up on some of that reading you have been meaning to do, all those letters you should have written, and finally to see the films everyone else is talking about. And as you ease off training, so you should feel a little more lively than usual, and going out for a walk to burn up a little excess nervous energy won't hurt.

Everyone has their own way of relaxing. Some might prefer early nights in the final week, which is fine as long as you can sleep and not spend the extra time restlessly. Others may find that going to bed a little later than usual may help them to get off to sleep more quickly.

This is the period when you should check on details for the race. Are you absolutely sure you have got the date and the starting time right? Check your official instructions, which will have been sent in acknowledgement of your entry. What do you mean, you haven't had an acknowledgement of your entry? Check with the organizers straight away to ensure they received it; don't leave it until the day of the race, when it may cost you valuable energy.

Are you sure you know exactly where the changing rooms and the start are? You won't want to waste energy on the day walking miles looking for them.

If you are travelling to the race by public transport, inquire in advance about train or bus times, and make sure they give you sufficient breathing space before the race to go through all the pre-race preparations without rushing them. It is better to arrive half an hour early than ten minutes late. Have you checked for the possibility of weekend railway engineering works on the route you are using, which will not be shown in timetables, but could delay you? If you're going by car, does the driver (if it's not you, or even if it is) know the best route, and how long it will take?

All these things may seem trivial, obvious items. But when your mind is on the race itself, they can be overlooked, and the one thing you want on the day of the event is the absolute minimum of unnecessary hassle. You want to get to the venue as quickly and smoothly as possible, to concentrate on the race, and not to have to worry overmuch on the day about fringe details, like travel.

Sometimes, if a long journey is involved, you may need to stay overnight beforehand. If so, try to stay away from town centres, which can be noisy places, especially on Friday and Saturday nights when the pubs empty. Choose the best accommodation you can afford, because after the months and months of training, for whatever level of result you are aiming, you will not want to undermine your chances at the eleventh hour by sacrificing the peace and comfort of your own home for somewhere which may be noisy and depressing.

Early in the week, start making a check-list of all the items of kit you want to take with you. Take a bit too much, rather than too little, and keep adding to the list as you think of things while on a training run, washing up, or travelling home from work. Then, before you leave, go religiously through the list as you pack your bags. It won't be much fun to arrive at the race and realize that your shoes are still under the kitchen table.

In addition to the usual items of kit, you should include Vaseline, an emergency plastic bag for storing your tracksuit if necessary, spare shoelaces (they always break at the wrong moment), a tin of assorted plasters (for use before or after the race), plus any other medical items you may feel necessary, wads of toilet paper (it frequently runs out in the changing rooms, and some tucked into your shorts during the race may prove a blessing too), and your favourite refreshments for after the race.

If you are running abroad, remember that in Europe, for example, it is often impossible to get cereal for breakfast. So take your own, together with any other accustomed items of pre-race food you feel you need. Don't rely on being able to get them at the race venue. I remember Joyce Smith sitting in the hotel on the morning of the 1979 Avon International Women's Marathon in West Germany, making up sandwiches of brown bread and honey which she had brought specially from England, while other runners watched, goggle-eyed. But it was ideal for her, psychologically and nutritionally, and she won the race in a Commonwealth record of 2 hours 36 minutes 27 seconds.

If you are going to tape your toes as a precaution against blistering, the night before is often a good opportunity. Wind short overlapping lengths of half-inch sticking plaster around each toe individually, firmly, but not cutting off the circulation! Overnight it will set and mould to your toes like an extra layer of skin.

This is a particularly therapeutic occupation. For not only are you concentrating your mind on the race, and doing something of practical value in preparation for it, but you are also substituting a kind of related physical activity. It is often difficult to concentrate fully on anything other than those 26 miles getting nearer and nearer.

The Day of the Race

On race day, aim to arrive at the changing rooms some 90 minutes before the start. Collect your number from the officials' table, and if you have personal drinks remember to mark your race number (which you may not know until you arrive at the venue) on your bottles before handing them in.

You may find yourself visiting the toilets several times as nerves increase, but take every opportunity to clear bowel and bladder 'ready for action'. Re-read the instructions sent to runners, which may explain all you need to know about the race. Surprisingly, not everyone does.

Decide what you are going to wear in the race itself, based on how hot/cold/wet/windy it appears to be, and pin the numbers to whatever will be your top layer in the race. If it is hot, stay in a cool place for as long as possible, not in the sun, and sit or lie down for part of the time, trying to relax as much as you can.

Study a course map, because even if you are not going to be in the lead, it will be a great help to know roughly where you are in relation to the finish at any point. The better-organized races will have regular mile markers and time checks.

Are there any steep hills on the course? If you haven't run it before, ask someone who has, or an official. Check the programme to see if it includes a course description.

Leaving a tracksuit during the race can be a problem, and not simply for reasons of security. If you are accompanied by someone to the race, of course, they can look after it. This is probably the most acceptable plan, as long as they know you will need it as soon as you finish and they don't go charging off round the course with it, or lock it in the boot of their car and disappear with the key.

At races where the start and finish are at different points, the organizers usually provide a numbered plastic bag in which you can put your gear, and they will take it to the finish, where you reclaim the bag by showing your race number.

But one of the disadvantages of a race as big as the London or New York City Marathons, where so many thousands of athletes have to gather at the start early in the morning, is that tracksuits which have to be taken to the finish must be handed in at least 30 minutes before the start. This means that for half an hour or more, the runners could be stripped off waiting to run, and in cold, windy conditions, that is no joke. So in such circumstances, the well-prepared runner will take along an old sweater and trousers to keep over his running gear until a few minutes from the start. Then, he discards the old clothes forever (at New York, special containers are provided by the organizers, and any useable clothing is washed and passed on to charity). At the finish he simply picks up his tracksuit, as at any other race.

Again, reuniting an exhausted runner with his tracksuit becomes a bigger problem as marathons expand. With thousands of runners, can a friend or relative easily find the specific body needed to fit the tracksuit they hold anyway? In such cases, the numbered bag system would seem ideal, as long as there is someone to organize the bags numerically at the reclaim area during the race. In London, a fleet of lettered buses ferries the gear to the finish. But I have been at marathons where the mass search for bags among thousands stacked indiscriminately on a huge floor has been reminiscent of the January sales rush, and is totally impractical.

Usually the best plan is to have some kind of 'fail-safe' system, involving a second, or even third, set of clothing stored at a guaranteed point if your original kit goes temporarily missing for whatever reason. At the end of a marathon, particularly on a bad day, you simply cannot take a chance on having to wander around shivering in a search for your tracksuit.

After the Race

You will not need advice on the very first thing you want to do when you cross the finishing line. Between them, your mind and body will have been telling you for some miles that you want to (a) take these wretched shoes off; (b) lie down on some cool grass; (c) get another drink; (d) be sick; or (e) jump up and down like a dervish in celebration at having completed the course.

The initial reactions are, most popularly, 'It's over!' closely followed by 'Never again!' – although the desire will probably return sooner rather than later.

But first you want to get this one out of the way. After your initial reaction – whether it is (a) to (e) or something quite different – check your feet for any blisters or toenail damage which might require first-aid treatment, and seek out the St John Ambulance if necessary.

If you get any attacks of cramp, they can be relieved by stretching the affected muscle fully; persistent cramp may need massage. Those frequently affected could try taking salt tablets before and after the race.

Unfortunately, it is rarely possible to have a warm bath at the finish of a marathon, but showers, even lukewarm, can still be very refreshing.

You will almost certainly want to drink more liquid at the finish, and there is usually another refreshment table near by. You may not want to eat anything solid for some hours afterwards, as your appetite diminishes and your thirst increases during the race. But some hours later your stomach will certainly tell you that it is ready for a good meal.

Try to walk round for a while after you have first recovered, to keep the circulation moving, which in turn may help to shift the fatigue debris from your muscles and lead to less stiffness next day.

The official times from the race will normally be posted up near the dressing room as soon as they are available, so don't worry the timekeepers unnecessarily by peering over their shoulders while they are still trying to record other runners home. You may distract them, and someone may be missed altogether. Usually full result sheets are sent out in the week or two after the race, together with any time certificates to which you may be entitled.

Before you leave for home, make sure you have all your belongings. Offering a brief word of thanks to any of the race officials you may come across after the race, whether it's the linch-pin organizer of the whole race or a marker in a plastic orange waistcoat, will never go amiss. Even raising your hand in acknowledgement to a marker during the race will show him that you at least appreciate him giving up four hours of Grandstand to endure wind and rain on this exposed, isolated corner. He may even have rather been doing what you're doing.

On the day after the race, and the day after that, you will almost certainly be feeling some degree of leg stiffness, even to the extent of finding it easier to walk up and down the stairs backwards, to relieve pain in the thighs and hamstrings. But jogging even half a mile or a mile very gently each day, followed by a hot bath, will help ease the stiffness. It may take as long as a fortnight before you are back in full training again, but most people find that within that time they are already planning their next marathon.

It is best to wait at least three months before tackling another, to ensure you have recovered fully and can start building up afresh for the next, rather than simply repairing the damage from the last one. The first marathon is always a question of 'Can I get round?'; after that, it is a question of 'How can I get round faster?'

10

FIRST STEPS TO
26 MILES 385 YARDS:
Training Schedules

The better marathon runner you become, the more other considerations, like competition and performance, will eventually become relevant to you. Sometimes a top-class marathon runner drops out of a race, not because he is incapable of finishing the course at a slower rate, but simply because competitively it has not gone well. Or perhaps he realizes that the final time is going to be relatively poor, and he does not want to push himself into the most traumatic part of the race to suffer unnecessarily, and possibly delay his return to the fray another day.

Of course, there are also runners who refuse to quit, whatever the circumstances, however badly the race has gone, and who finish in shoes stained with blood from raw blisters, or with agonizing cramp, or limping with a muscle strain, when perhaps it would have been wiser to stop altogether.

That decision has always been very much a personal one, except in the case of imminent physical collapse. The Amateur Athletic Association Rules state: 'A competitor must at once retire from the race if ordered to do so by a member of the medical staff officially appointed.' Fortunately, this situation arises very rarely.

But for those of more modest ambition who wish to complete a marathon, stopping to walk when you feel the need (which does not automatically disqualify you, as some people think) is a wise move. In fact, you could theoretically walk the whole way if you wanted to, but that would seem a rather pointless, selfish exercise in what is after all a running event, and you would be taking a great chance on anybody still being at the finish line waiting for you.

So let us examine in the following pages, stage by stage, what you need to do and what you need to know in preparing for your first or your fiftieth marathon. Let us look at some training schedules which might suit you, whether or not you are already a runner, and let us hear as well from some of the runners who have already followed this type of schedule: their experiences, their successes – and their failures. We can learn from them all.

In undertaking any training programme for the marathon, whether at beginner or advanced level, the single most important consideration is achieving regularity in training, on a graduated scale, to provide the necessary stress for adaptation and improvement. There are events, particularly the shorter middle-distance track events, which rely on a fair measure of that type of training (very fast, getting into an oxygen 'debt', and holding it) for their success. If you never rehearse the physical conditions produced by such a race, you cannot expect to be able to cope with them on the day.

And so it is with the marathon, in a more relaxed way, as you seek stamina, economy and efficiency in your running, built upon hundreds and hundreds of training miles.

The purpose of having any sort of training programme then, whether it is taken from this book or one you devise yourself, is to allow you to follow a graduated path from *now* (when perhaps you can jog for only five minutes) to *then* (possibly eight months from now, when you hope to be able to run a marathon).

The training schedule is the map for your journey. When you are driving along a road, you cannot necessarily see your destination, but you know the map will get you there if you follow its directions. You may have to stop briefly to mend a puncture, or to get some petrol. But by and large if you keep going in the same direction, you'll reach the horizon.

All the training schedules in this book, whether for the new or experienced, are balanced. They are balanced from day to day, as well as week to week, because if you go out on a Saturday morning and complete the longest continuous run of your life, you are not likely to want to get up on Sunday morning and be faced with the prospect of having to go even further. Instead, you will need a shorter run, to consolidate, to work any stiffness out of your legs, and to be able to gloat over having achieved yesterday's run. Only later in the week do you run long again.

t to improve your performances in running you have to run, whether you are Sebastian
e training to defend his Olympic 1500m title on hills (above), or a group of primary
1ool Mums training for the Sunday Times National Fun Run (below).

n hot days, staying in the shade as long s possible (above) helps reduce later roblems, while taking a drink during the ace (right) also wards off dehydration.

Getting the drink at speed (above) requires some rehearsal before your first race. But if you are not in a hurry, you can take your time (below) and ensure you drink enough.

onges, too, are essential to keep cool (above), but some race problems can't be
edicted. Tim Hutchings (below left) tries to get rid of stitch in the World Cross Country
ampionships, while Ann Ford (below right) suffers blister problems after a road race.

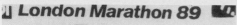

The 1987 World champion Douglas Wakiihuru wins the 1989 London Marathon (left), while the 1988 Olympic champion Rosa Mota (below) is on her way to a 1987 World title win in Rome.

Opposite: The varied challenges open to the runner today can be as tough as the Snowdonia Marathon (above) or as gentle as a fancy dress fun run (below).

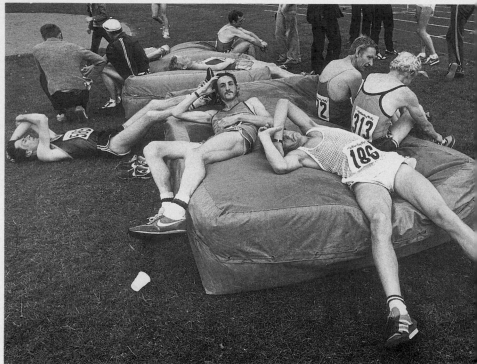

These days welcome encouragement to runners comes from everywhere (above), and the exhaustion (below) is only temporary. Tomorrow, they will all be thinking about the next race.

The recurring rule of thumb for getting fitter is: Hard work plus rest equals success. Hard work, plus hard work, minus rest, equals injury.

The training schedules are divided into two sections. The first section, contained in this chapter, is meant primarily for joggers and newcomers to running, who want to build up towards a marathon from virtually no background or previous experience. The second section, in the next chapter, is aimed at those who are already fairly fit, perhaps club runners covering 40 miles a week or so, who would like to use their background and develop it towards a reasonable marathon. And this second section goes on to recommend the type of training schedule a top-class international marathon runner of the nineties might use.

A primary difference between these two sections is that the first deals in 'running minutes' while the second is confined to miles of running. Don't mix them up, or you may find yourself out on a Sunday morning 90-mile run!

The reason for the difference (which has intriguing possibilities if misused) is that from practical experience joggers and new runners seem to prefer being set a specific time to run regardless of distance, because it is a unit with which they are familiar and which they can control. But more experienced runners will have a greater familiarity with miles, and in fact 'miles per week' is the currency club runners use, like motorists discussing their relative 'miles per gallon'.

We may be making a rod for our own backs by using two separate systems, especially as the jogger will eventually become a club runner. But by that time he or she should have more working knowledge of pace and distance.

There is another difference. The 'joggers/new runners' schedules graduate from the first day to the last (the marathon itself) with no hint of any other competitive or non-competitive events being included. This is because some potential marathoners have eyes only for the day when they will be able to run that 26 miles 385 yards, and they are content to go out running every day with no thought or desire for any other, shorter type of running event, even if one is right on their doorstep.

For instance, I was advising one quite fit young man in his preparation for the London Marathon, and I kept suggesting various low-key running events in which he could take part as a 'mental break', and to see how he was faring. At first, he made excuses for each date I suggested, but finally he admitted that he really didn't want to take part in any other running events. All he wanted to do was to train for the marathon. And he was not, it transpired, alone in this attitude.

So these schedules show no intermediate events, not even the *Sunday Times* National Fun Run! But I nevertheless suggest that the potential marathoners do keep their eyes open for road races and fun runs in their area; anything that will give them even a little taste of competitive experience.

The schedules for the most experienced runners do indicate points at which a road race of 10–20 miles might be beneficially introduced to break up the grind of training. It still has to be accepted that if the marathon is the prime goal, then training cannot be eased down too much before the big day, and that some races will have to be undertaken (or missed out) in a state of slight residual fatigue. Occasionally, to make up the quota of miles for the week, it may even be necessary to train on the morning of one of these races, or afterwards.

But this has previously been an effective way of long distance preparation: to 'train through' lesser races.

Don't let anyone tell you that a distance runner is someone who shakes off germs like water off a duck's back, and is a constantly lively soul, bubbling with health and effervescence. No, a distance runner in training is someone who is perpetually tired, usually moving sluggishly from one comfortable perch to another. His approach is normally heralded by the sound of someone sniffing.

You run a long way, you get tired, you barely recover, and then you run a long way again. Consequently, you are more susceptible to any bugs floating around than the average person, and you are always one step away from an excruciating pain in your lower left leg, or a sharp twinge in your hamstring.

Distance runners getting together before a race to compare their latest injury symptoms can be like a gaggle of gossips. Everyone pretends to listen, but really they are just dying to get in with their own three ha'pence worth.

Sometimes as a distance runner you have just a little too much time to think to yourself, 'Is my left foot hurting today? Yes . . . yes, I think it is! And the right knee? . . . Yes, that too.' By the time you get home you're barely fit enough in your own mind to crawl upstairs and get somebody to call an ambulance. There are only three normal states of health for a serious distance runner: injured, recovering from injury, or deciding which injury you'd like to have next. Such is the paradox!

The Beginner's 52-Week Build-Up Programme

If I had to pick a figure, I would say that one year is the minimum amount of time a normal, healthy, unfit person should reasonably allow to prepare from scratch to run the marathon distance. And in that year he or she would have to run regularly six days a week at a comfortable pace for increasingly long periods of time, as indicated in running-minutes on the chart, which has been specially prepared for this book.

Having said that, I will doubtless be inundated with details of the hundreds of people who did so on much less. All I can say is: 'I know. But what I wrote was that one year is the minimum amount a normal, healthy, unfit person *should reasonably allow*.' A little later I'm even going to suggest how it could be achieved in less than half that time when you're really desperate, and we'll hear about people who did. But I still recommend that one year minimum.

What the bare columns of figures on pages 150–1 cannot tell you, as your eyes scan over the increasing denominations of running-minutes, is that running for 40 minutes after 14 weeks will not seem eight times harder than running for five minutes now. It will take eight times longer, certainly, but as your cardiovascular fitness increases, so the longer runs may eventually seem actually easier than your first ones, as your lungs, heart and muscles respond to the slight stress to which you are subjecting them, and in turn become stronger and more efficient.

In that initial 5-minute session, we are not looking for 1¼ miles; instead, we are simply seeking 5 minutes of steady running, close to the pace at which you eventually hope to run the marathon. An average pace of 10 minutes per mile, for instance, will give you a final time of 4 hours 22 minutes 13 seconds; a 7½-minute mile pace would give you 3 hours 16 minutes 39 seconds and a 5-minute mile pace would end up as 2 hours 11 minutes 6 seconds. But that last figure would certainly be too ambitious!

It is as well to reserve one day as a rest day, so that you have a regular recovery space at the end of the week before tackling the weekend's running, which will normally entail a relatively high proportion of the week's total.

From Week 27 to Week 42, the chart shows two separate runs on the Saturday, as a subtle method of layering the overall increase. In fact, in marathon terms, one single run of 60 minutes could be said to be more beneficial than two of 30. But that is to overlook the mental lift of not having to run quite so far each time, and perhaps even faster, which could well outweigh any shortfall in conditioning. There are plenty of other long runs in the week, so enjoy the brevity. It changes again in Week 43, so why hurry?

The week is shown in its chart form from Sunday to Saturday, and its framework is built around the supposition that the runner has Saturday and Sunday as weekend. For those who haven't, or who work shifts or have midweek days off, amend the days of the week at the top of the columns to suit you. But try to keep the progression of runs themselves intact.

It would be miraculous if you went through the whole year without missing a single scheduled session as a result of illness or injury. If you do have to interrupt the schedule, when you have recovered it is best to pick it up gradually at a point some days before you left off; don't try to pick it up where you otherwise should have been. You may then have to adjust the final weeks, but remember to taper right down before the race itself, as shown in Weeks 51 and 52.

Schedule No. 1 The Beginner's 52-Week Build-Up Programme

N B Values are in 'running-minutes'

	Sun	Mon	Tues	Wed	Thur	Fri	Sat
Week 1	5	5	8	5	8	5	8
Week 2	10	5	10	5	10	5	10
Week 3	12	8	10	8	12	5	12
Week 4	15	8	10	8	12	5	12
Week 5	18	8	12	8	12	8	15
Week 6	20	8	12	10	12	8	15
Week 7	20	10	12	10	15	Rest	15
Week 8	25	10	15	10	15	Rest	15
Week 9	25	10	15	10	15	Rest	20
Week 10	30	10	20	15	15	Rest	20
Week 11	30	15	20	15	15	Rest	20
Week 12	35	15	20	20	15	Rest	20
Week 13	35	20	20	20	20	Rest	25
Week 14	40	20	20	25	20	Rest	25
Week 15	40	20	25	25	20	Rest	25
Week 16	45	20	25	30	25	Rest	25
Week 17	45	25	25	30	25	Rest	30
Week 18	50	25	25	30	25	Rest	30
Week 19	50	25	25	30	25	Rest	30
Week 20	55	25	20	35	25	Rest	30
Week 21	55	30	20	35	30	Rest	30
Week 22	60	30	20	35	30	Rest	30

First Steps to 26 miles 385 yards

	Sun	Mon	Tues	Wed	Thur	Fri	Sat
Week 23	60	30	20	40	30	Rest	30
Week 24	60	30	25	40	30	Rest	30
Week 25	60	30	25	45	30	Rest	30
Week 26	65	30	25	45	30	Rest	30
Week 27	65	35	30	50	40	Rest	2×20
Week 28	70	35	30	50	40	Rest	2×20
Week 29	70	35	35	50	50	Rest	2×20
Week 30	75	35	35	50	50	Rest	2×20
Week 31	75	40	45	60	40	Rest	2×20
Week 32	80	40	45	60	40	Rest	2×20
Week 33	80	40	45	60	40	Rest	2×25
Week 34	85	40	45	60	40	Rest	2×25
Week 35	85	40	50	45	60	Rest	2×25
Week 36	90	40	50	45	60	Rest	2×25
Week 37	90	40	50	45	60	Rest	2×30
Week 38	95	40	50	45	60	Rest	2×30
Week 39	95	40	55	45	60	Rest	2×30
Week 40	100	45	55	45	60	Rest	2×30
Week 41	100	45	55	45	70	Rest	2×30
Week 42	110	45	55	45	70	Rest	2×30
Week 43	110	45	60	45	70	Rest	60
Week 44	110	45	60	45	70	Rest	60
Week 45	120	45	60	45	75	Rest	60
Week 46	120	40	60	45	75	Rest	60
Week 47	130	40	70	45	80	Rest	60
Week 48	140	40	70	45	80	Rest	60
Week 49	140	40	75	40	70	Rest	60
Week 50	150	30	60	30	70	Rest	60
Week 51	120	20	40	30	60	Rest	40
Week 52	80	Rest	30	20	Rest	5	The Race

The Beginner's Sunday Times *21-Week Crash Programme*

When the date of the first London Marathon (29 March 1981) was announced in late October 1980, I spent some time working out a training schedule which would fit into the 21 weeks then remaining between those dates, and which might enable a potential participant to scramble together enough fitness to get round the course.

Then that schedule was published in the *Sunday Times* with the same advice as I'm going to offer now: Forget it, and give yourself a year to prepare properly for the marathon.

But there would probably be, I knew, a considerable number of people who would not wait a year, and whose spirit would tell them to get in there and run next March. There would probably be people who would be reasonably fit to begin with anyway, and there would certainly be those who would totally underestimate the sheer distance involved in a marathon. There were, it transpired, all three categories and many more.

But it seemed reasonable that they should at least have the opportunity of following a graduated programme which had tried to make use of the time available as well as possible, even though it would still be like climbing the stairs three at a time.

From the letters I received before and after the London Marathon, it appeared to work, and later in this chapter some of the runners tell their own stories. Their experiences may help to illustrate not just that the 21-week chart itself can work, but, more important, that it is possible to run the marathon distance, given patience and dedication. That also applies, of course, to the 52-week chart which I would prefer you to try. But only you know how important it is for you to run it with less preparation.

You can, incidentally, always elongate the 21-week chart quite simply to suit a period of time lasting anywhere between the 21- and 52-week schedules. All you do is subtract 21 from the total number of weeks you have available – say 26, which would leave you 5. Then count back 5 weeks from Week 20 (skip Week 21 for the moment), which will take you back to Week 16, and mark it.

Start following the schedule normally, but when you reach Week 16, simply repeat each week's programme before moving on, as follows:

Weeks: 1.2.3.4.5.6.7.8.9.10.11.12.13.14.15.
   16.*16*.17.*17*.18.*18*.19.*19*.20.*20*.21.
Total: 26 weeks.

Schedule No. 2 The Beginner's Sunday Times 21-Week Crash Programme

NB Values are in 'running-minutes'

	Sun	Mon	Tues	Wed	Thur	Fri	Sat
Week 1	10	10	15	10	15	Rest	20
Week 2	25	15	20	15	20	Rest	30
Week 3	35	20	25	20	30	Rest	35
Week 4	40	25	30	20	35	Rest	40
Week 5	45	30	35	20	40	Rest	45
Week 6	50	30	40	25	40	Rest	50
Week 7	55	35	45	25	50	Rest	50
Week 8	60	35	50	25	50	Rest	60
Week 9	70	40	55	30	55	Rest	60
Week 10	80	45	60	30	60	Rest	60
Week 11	90	45	60	35	70	Rest	60
Week 12	100	45	70	35	80	Rest	60
Week 13	105	50	70	40	80	Rest	60
Week 14	110	50	80	40	80	Rest	60
Week 15	120	55	80	40	80	60	Rest
Week 16	130	60	80	40	80	60	Rest
Week 17	140	60	80	40	80	60	Rest
Week 18	140	60	90	45	80	60	Rest
Week 19	150	60	80	45	70	60	Rest
Week 20	105	45	70	30	60	Rest	Rest
Week 21	75	15	45	Rest	15	Rest	The Race

If your total number of weeks is higher than 40, then repeat the later weeks three times. But always end by doing Week 21 (the taper-down week) just once. And remember that the longer you spend in overall, regular preparation, the greater will be your chances of succeeding.

Some further tips on the crash programme:
* Allow yourself an extra hour's sleep at night. Training for distance running is tiring, and its long-term success depends on a good recovery rate.

* The occasional day off, if you feel you really need it, will do no harm. Otherwise the rest day could be used to replace any session you have had to miss earlier in the week.
* Don't run for three hours after a meal.
* If you have to miss a section, perhaps through illness, gradually pick up where you left off, not where you should have been on the schedule.
* Keep at it. Otherwise the distance will usually win in the end.

In the weeks following the publication of that 21-week 'crash' schedule, we were left in no doubt that a good number of readers (and even *Sunday Times* staff) were following the chart carefully. To be honest, the situation filled me with some degree of apprehension, because it meant that in effect I was encouraging in practical terms what I really believed to be inadvisable – the preparation for a marathon by non-runners in little more than five months.

That apprehension did not totally disappear until a short while after the London Marathon, when the accounts of the progress some of the beginner runners had made in training, which had begun to arrive, were subsequently completed by their experiences of the race itself.

I have picked a cross section of these for inclusion here because each story has its own moral for the beginner, its own inspirational example, and its own warning. Each runner made his own decision to prepare for the London Marathon with little more than a grid of numbers for training guidance. None of them knew any of the others, and at the time I knew none of them either. But their stories exemplify one of the great attractions of the marathon: that in Scotland, or Sussex, or Hertfordshire, or Cornwall, or anywhere, a runner on his or her own can prepare in isolation and can, with dedication, determination and luck, succeed.

Andy Puddicombe, twenty-four, from Gosport, Hants, had left college four months earlier and was still unemployed when he decided to use some of the unwanted time on his hands to train for the London Marathon. He had done very little running since leaving school eight years earlier, apart from a couple of miles twice a week training for a local football team.

> The marathon had always been a vague ambition, and the thing which excited me most about the chart was that it made it appear actually feasible. I couldn't wait to start! My immediate plan was to begin in Week 5, figuring that I could manage that easily with all the spare time on my hands. But by the end of the week I was shattered, and went straight back to Day 1 of Week 1 next day.

I kept a diary as I went along, and wrote that I was sometimes running too fast in the early weeks on the 20-minute runs and consequently I was more tired after those than after the 40–45 minute runs. In general I was able to complete each week without undue difficulty, and always had a feeling of exultation when I broke new ground, even though it was only five minutes. Week 6 was a bad one, the muscles in my legs were hurting, and at one point I feared that I had a stress fracture. But I was able to run through it, so it couldn't have been that serious, and in fact Weeks 7–10 were about the best of the whole schedule.

In Week 11 I completed the 1½ hours, which proved about the hardest run of all. I was very tired in the last 30 minutes, and quite pessimistic about ever finishing a marathon. It was also the last time I ran an 'out and back' course. I found it quite depressing being so far from home, and I always ran laps of never more than six miles round from then on.

In Weeks 12–15 I was beginning to find the rest day as important as the other six, and I experienced another great feeling of achievement when I ran non-stop for two hours.

Week 16 was something of a watershed in that I had now got a job, and this was my first week of training as well as doing a 40-hour week. It had obviously been a great help being able to choose when to run; also it worked both ways – running helped the drudgery of being unemployed. But it is also probably true that the extra discipline was useful. In the crucial Weeks 16–18 I was so determined not to let work interfere that I probably did slightly more than the schedule.

I got through the 2 hours 10 minutes and 2 hours 20 minutes barriers, but owing partly to a rather hectic social life at the time I became a bit ragged in Weeks 18–20. I had three attempts at the 2½ hours run, never actually giving up on the first two failures, but simply electing halfway round to do a shorter run and postpone the 2½ hour effort. Discipline was definitely waning, as I figured I had already done the hard part. But psychologically I desperately wanted to run 2½ hours before the big day.

With shame I can remember the morning of Sunday, 15 March, exactly a fortnight before the London Marathon, as I stood at the back door, dressed and ready to go out but knowing that it would be quite futile owing to the worst hangover I had suffered for six months. Luckily, that experience quite shook me from my recent lethargy, and I duly completed the 2½ hours run the following day. Thus, Week 20 was a little up and down, but Week 21 was exactly to the schedule.

I always ran alone, but two friends were also training for the race, one copying the schedule, and while we were never rivals it certainly helped having someone with whom to compare notes. I rarely ran in the morning, and was somewhat worried about the 9 a.m. start, but I'm sure it made no difference, as I was up by 6 a.m. on race day.

I never really worried about distances in training, always running to the specified time, but in fact I was nearly always on course for a marathon of 3¼ to 3½ hours. My ill-discipline towards the end prompted me to start with the 3¾ hour starters, but in fact I completed it in 3 hours 20 minutes 8 seconds, placing 2349th. What really pleased me was that my halfway time was 1 hour 37 minutes, so I only slowed up by 6 minutes in the second half. Both my friends, while finishing 5 and 9 minutes faster than me, slowed up by 15–20 minutes in the second half. Both walked at some stage, whereas I ran completely non-stop. Certainly I felt it was important not to go too fast at the start, when it would have been easy to be carried away by the crowd. I was shattered at the end, but within a day I was wondering when and where to run my next one, and was determined to get inside three hours.

Ken Laidler, forty-seven, from Tring, Herts, had taken part in no serious athletics since he left school, although he cycled and played rugby until the age of thirty-eight. Then he stopped, and put on weight. In January 1980 he scaled 10 stone 7lbs for his height of 5ft 6½ins. So he started jogging, and was down to 10 stone 3lbs by October 1980, when he started following the 21-week schedule with a view to running the London Marathon. By the day of the race itself, five months later, he had trimmed down to 9 stone 3lbs, and had lost three inches from his waist.

The marathon itself was, he says, a highly emotional experience. 'It took the best part of a week following the race to be able to discuss it rationally and without bringing a lump to my throat. It does seem stupid, a grown man of forty-seven talking this way, but it's true.'

Through his jogging, he was already in advance of Week 1, and had progressed well until just before Christmas.

I was running everything at approximately 8-minute miling pace, and was virtually able to set my watch to it. In most cases, it was a floating sensation. As most of my running had to be in the evenings, and I live in a very small country town, I was unfortunate in that most of my runs took me into dark, badly-lit areas. The pavements were either rough or non-existent, and so I had to run on roadsides which were rough or on the side of steep cambers. This, I am sure, caused a serious knee injury which also affected my two training partners, Bernie and Roy, at the same time. The left knee used to lock.

I went to a physio without much success. I rested it. Little help. Walked and jogged slowly. No effect. And having lost the best part of three weeks' training, I decided that I had to just get out and run through it if I was to make the start. If it didn't work then, except for the pain, I would lose nothing.

One of my training partners, Bernie, decided to do the same, but Roy decided against it, and quit. We had to take it easy at first but after about three weeks we ran through it. Every now and again we were given a sharp reminder, but we improved our training conditions by travelling the 7 miles to Aylesbury, and taking advantage of the well-lit streets there. The surfaces were generally better and certainly a lot flatter.

Training was going well again and we were pushing into the unknown each weekend. Now I was beginning to feel stress. Not during the runs themselves, but afterwards. I took longer to recover and felt a little nausea. This only started when I reached distances of 15 miles. I'm sure it was mild dehydration, and we overcame the problem by placing beakers of sugared orange juice and blackcurrant in the hedge along the training circuit so that we were able to take fluid at about 7 and 12 miles, and it worked. No more stress.

However, I found the need every three weeks or so for an extra day's rest. This was obviously fatigue, but I usually found that I then ran my next training session at a faster pace without effort. We got up to 19¾ miles three weeks before the marathon, and were really enjoying our training. It was then time to start tapering down.

I had lost weight (over a stone) and was just a little worried that it was too much, but with six weeks to go it levelled off and even increased slightly during the last two weeks. I was eating well, and luckily my wife Rosalyn (who had thought me mad) entered into the spirit of the thing and cooked me all the right foods. I hadn't had Spotted Dick for years!

The last week before the marathon I had a scare. My daughter had flu. My son had just recovered from it and I had the symptoms of sore throat and headache, but I didn't tell anyone. I just stopped training. All the written advice, including the official medical sheet received with the acceptance, advised against running if you had flu. All that work! I had to be sensible and consider my family, but in the end it had to be my decision. By Saturday I felt better, and decided to give it a go, bearing in mind that I would stop if I should feel any adverse effects.

Well, we started. Gosh, it was fantastic! It took 10 minutes for the first mile as I just had to run with the crowd at Greenwich, but then I got into my 8-minute miles. My rhythm was good, but I had a small blister after only two miles. I was very surprised, but it was no problem and I soon forgot it. I'd started with my training partner Bernie, but we were separated at 8 miles, and did not see each other again. I was running like a bird, just floating, and by 12 miles there were some people around me who were beginning to suffer and didn't want to talk.

Where was that bloody bridge? Someone must have hidden it! I was feeling impatient to get to Tower Bridge, the halfway point, because I knew my wife and close friends would be there, and I was looking forward to seeing them. But we finally reached the Bridge, and they weren't there. I was very disappointed and felt a little low. Then we crossed it and turned right, and there they were: a quick hello and a wave and I was away again, lifted mightily by their presence.

I reached 15 miles on schedule in 2 hours 6 minutes but realized that fatigue was setting in. By 17 miles, and the Isle of Dogs, I was looking for each mile marker earlier and earlier, and slowing slightly. Then it happened. It seemed as though someone drilled a hole through my hips, put in a long bolt and screwed it up. I hadn't experienced anything like it before. I saw the 18 miles marker. Hell! Another 8 to go. I felt I'd never make it. I tried to run but was reduced to little more than a shuffle. It really hurt, but I had to carry on. There were no underground stations before 20 miles.

Anyway, I had to keep going until we passed the Tower again so that my wife would know I was okay. The pain in the hip was bad though. We passed by Tower Bridge again, crossing those awful cobbles. Now I experienced another phenomenon. I call it Marathon Knee. It wasn't overly painful, but it just didn't seem to function. It was difficult to describe. It was floppy, and tended to give way each step. I had no control. It was like a kind of paralysis.

I was still okay in the upper body, but I had to walk and shuffle for a mile. I saw my wife again and felt happier for a moment. But there were still 3 long miles to go. I closed my eyes. Then I heard a shout: '3–9–2–5! 3–9–2–5!' My number. I thought it must be one of my friends and I opened my eyes. But it was a total stranger, clapping his hands in time as he called out again '3–9–2–5!', and urging me to keep going. Others took up the chant, and for a brief moment so did the crowd. Tears came to my eyes, and I thanked them and kept going. There was no way I could let them down after that. Three more miles of purgatory.

At Big Ben, the blind man passed me. It was his mate I really admired. What a responsibility! I saw Rosalyn again in Birdcage Walk. I was nearly there. And then I finished. Someone gave me a medal. But no-one I knew was there to share my triumph. I fought back the tears.

I couldn't find the bus with my clothes in. I was getting a little annoyed, but it was only fatigue. Eventually I found the right bus, sat down and felt a little deflated. It was all over. I took off my sodden vest and put on my sweat top. It was impossible to put on my tracksuit trousers. My legs wouldn't move. I just sat there. Where was everyone? My wife? My friends? After five minutes or so they battled through the crowds to reach me. Two men lifted me off the bus. Rosalyn hugged me, and I cried a little. They all hugged me and shook me by the hand. The triumph was complete.

Geoff Hayles, a thirty-six-year-old dental surgeon from Brighton, married with two daughters, developed his marathon interest through the Brighton Hash House Harriers, a social running group which covers 4–8 miles every Monday night.

I played rugby, soccer and swam at school, and after qualifying I played some golf and squash. Three years ago I started jogging occasionally in an attempt to improve my fitness for squash, and a year later joined the Hash House Harriers. But their training runs often clashed with Round Table meetings, and I only went about twenty times in two years. But in spite of the limited outings, I enjoyed running with this jovial group and heard some of the keener ones discussing 10-mile races, half-marathons and marathons. In October 1980 I took part in the Round Table National Sporting Weekend 3½-mile cross country race, and finished 34th out of 83, and shortly afterwards the London Marathon was announced, the schedule appeared in the *Sunday Times*, and I began following it.

Being not averse to a pint or two in good company over the two weeks of the festive season, 1980–81, my body suffered the worst physical assault it has had to endure in its thirty-six years to date. Crying out for sleep, comfort and soothing medicines, the aching head and limbs were forced into action and joggled around the streets and paths of Brighton. And that was near the start of the schedule! This for me was the critical phase, and having survived that I felt confident of keeping the schedule up for a while at least.

It was consoling and encouraging to re-read the advice offered with it at difficult times, and the only part I ignored was when I fell behind schedule (a couple of weekends away from home) and I put in extra time to catch up. That was difficult – 2½ and 3 hours behind at different times, but I felt that if I did every minute of the schedule, my confidence would be that much more. And with my running background, I needed all the confidence I could get!

I found I liked the simplicity of the schedule, and I preferred it being based on time rather than distance. There is a world of difference between knowing you've got to go out and run 10 miles in a certain time, and knowing you can jog along for 20 minutes as slowly as you like. In the latter case, often there is a pleasant surprise at the end, at the distance actually covered.

The low point was always putting the tracksuit on, the high point was soaking in a hot bath afterwards. The ecstasy of heat soaking into aching muscles makes it almost worthwhile on its own.

In February I entered the Woking Athletic Club 10-mile road race to see how I was faring, and finished 475th out of 630 finishers in 65 minutes 38 seconds. In the London Marathon I was around the 3000th mark in 3½ hours, and my wife, Jacky, was so impressed with the London event that she asked for a tracksuit as a present on our next wedding anniversary.

Peter McGough, thirty-one, from Nottingham, had some background of running from 1975, but for the sake of fitness rather than competition. He virtually ceased physical activity between July 1978 and June 1980, as his seventeen-month-old son Michael died of liver disease. During this tragic period, in which the Michael McGough Research Fund for Liver Disease in Children was established, his weight ballooned to 200lb. He started running again in June 1980, covering 4 miles a day plus circuit-training, and by October 1980 his weight had dropped to 175lb. The announcement of the London Marathon at that time spurred him to begin the training schedule with a view to raising money for the Research Fund by sponsorship in the marathon.

First of all I copied the routine into a diary to chart my future progress and performance against it. I did not keep pace session for session with the routine, but rather used it as a barometer of the amount of training and peaks I would need to achieve in the pre-marathon period. I felt that as long as I could consistently 'hit' the big Sunday runs, I would be okay.

This is where the routine had its biggest impact on me. I saw that it was not necessary to run ridiculously high mileages in preparation, but what was important was to attain a condition whereby the legs could be kept moving for 2½ hours plus. For a first-timer it also imposed a sense of discipline and commitment to an event which commands respect.

Weeks 1–4: These were okay, as it was not a significant increase on my then current training. I was still maintaining circuit training, but my plan was to decrease this activity as my running times were upped. As things worked out, I circuit-trained right up to marathon week.

Weeks 5–8: Found it difficult to slow down from my 6 minutes-per-mile pace, and therefore was running too fast, with a high knee lift. Joints began to ache.

Weeks 9–11: The worst period. I over-indulged in food at Christmas and I also caught a virus which I couldn't shake off. I began to have doubts as to whether my entry would be accepted among the 21,000 applications when I realized I had not put a stamp on my final self-addressed acceptance envelope. So it was hard to find motivation for going out on long training runs for an event I might not get into. Net result – no running of any sort. My weight returned to 200lb.

Weeks 12–13: Recommenced training in Week 12, but at Week 4 targets. I planned to step up in fortnightly increments to get back to actual schedule around Week 18. Motivation still low; sessions missed.

Weeks 14–20: New motivation was received through the letter box: my acceptance form arrived, thanks to an anonymous soul at the GLC who had franked it. Knee and ankle joints began to suffer. I had to shelve plans to go on a crash diet (to reduce weight impact) as my energy levels became very low. I evolved a more economic style of running. I started hitting the schedule targets again in Week 18, and went above thereafter in an effort to catch up some of the previously missed mileage. My major Sunday runs: Week 18: 17 miles in 2 hours 19 minutes; Week 19: 20 miles in 2 hours 53 mins; Week 20: 24 miles in 3 hours 11 minutes. I went beyond the 2½ hour-mark because psychologically I needed to know that I could get nearer the 26 miles.

Week 21: I did not ease down all that gradually, running in total 35 miles ceasing three days before the race. Weight 180lb.

I found that when running for over an hour or so, I almost went into a 'high', my senses became sharper and more acute, my clarity of thought remarkable. I experienced a tremendous, almost spiritual high during the Marathon too. I went steadily for 18 miles, then finished the last 8 miles 385 yards in under 55 minutes, actually sprinting the last 200 yards. My time was 3 hours 39 minutes 38 seconds, and I finished, full of running, 3658th.

(Peter McGough's run also raised £2000 for the Research Fund.)

David Wilson, thirty-seven, a veterinary surgeon from Dorchester, Dorset, also had marathon dreams. He tells a different story.

Despite the chart, I failed. My training came to an abrupt halt in December on a Monday run which had started off as a normal session, after having had a very good run on the Sunday. I quickly realized that my calf muscles were in trouble, and returned home. I think there was widespread tearing of the muscle fibres but mainly around the medial aspect of the proximal end of the tibia. I had also been in trouble with knee-ache in the hours after running but had tried to ignore this.

(A few days earlier the author had written to him in reply to a training inquiry, and speculated that if he became injured he might have to be put down.)

During all this crash programme, I was never free from aches and pains and would spend the rest of the working day, walking and climbing gates, with great difficulty. Basically my heart and lungs were very good (resting pulse down to 48) but the legs could not keep up – too much, too quickly, too old! – and I refused to listen to warning signs.

After the muscle breakdown I rested, apart from a bit of swimming and a week's walking in the Lake District over the New Year. When my London Marathon entry application form came, it inspired me to have one last try and I had a good relaxed 25-minute run, which was most enjoyable. But then within 24 hours I had knee-ache again which lasted for another week, and resigned myself to having another go next year.

But this is not a tale of woe. It is the start of a new interest, and I am running 25–30 minutes three times weekly (with a constant temptation to go further). I had no running experience before, although I played football until I was twenty-seven. Then for the last ten years, nothing.

My job in a mixed vet practice often means a long day from 8.30 a.m. to 5 p.m. around the farms and stables, and then alternate evenings another 2–3 hours standing during evening surgery. I am sure that this was responsible for my legs having very little recovery time between runs. But the mental effect of a run in the evening away from the telephone was the big bonus. That, and dreaming about the ultimate challenge still to come.

Bill Crotty, a senior sales superintendent for British Telecom, from Uckfield, East Sussex, was just a few months short of his fiftieth birthday when he ran in the 1981 London Marathon. A dabbler at sports after leaving school, he had stopped altogether when he married in 1956, and admitted to having led a very sedentary life for twenty-five years. At the back of his mind, though, was a vague dream about possibly running a marathon one day, inspired by reading accounts of the New York Marathon. He was, to say the least, an unlikely candidate.

When firm plans for the London Marathon were announced, I was still dreaming of taking part, but the training chart and its accompanying article got me started. I felt it was now or never, and I wanted to be in the first real London Marathon. With the chart, which I cut out, I felt I had a starting point and a guide to get me there.

On Monday 27 October, the day after the chart appeared, I bought my first ever pair of training shoes from Debenhams in Brighton, who had a sale on! They were recommended for road training and racing and turned out to be a super buy because they were so comfortable. I also bought a tracksuit, sweatshirt and waterproof jacket with hood. Thus equipped, I arrived home to impart the good news to my wife that I was about to commence training for the London Marathon. Being a reasonably sane sort of person, she naturally thought I had finally flipped. I changed, and set off on my first training run of Week 1, Day 1: 10 minutes. 5 minutes out and 5 back again. . .

But I couldn't run for 5 minutes! I couldn't believe it. I was exhausted and had to stop for a few minutes' rest. I might add that this was at a very gentle pace, and all my 'running' since then has been at a very gentle pace too. This was a great shock to me, and I decided two things: (1) That I would only take part in the marathon if I was physically fit, and free from any sort of injury; and (2) I would only start if I felt I had a reasonable chance of finishing the course.

I also decided to make it a solo effort. I work in Brighton, which has a first-class athletics club, but I have always felt that athletes tend to look down their noses at people not as good/fit as themselves, and don't really want to know old-timers like me. In any case, I leave home at about 7.30 each morning and return about 5.40 in the evening, and didn't fancy going back into Brighton again last night.

I progressed to some semblance of fitness remarkably quickly following the chart. I had difficulty actually getting out of bed and negotiating the stairs each morning but by the time I got to the office I had usually loosened up again. I trained alone, and because of the dark evenings I had to stay in Uckfield where there is street lighting, pavements or footpaths.

Possibly the worst times were at the start of a run on a frosty, dark evening straight after coming home from work. As I left home with, say, an hour's run in front of me, I wished that I were just finishing. Passing familiar landmarks time after time, night after night, didn't help.

On Christmas Day I went for a 5-mile run, which took about 55 minutes. During this, I turned over my left ankle. It hurt a bit at the time and I almost fell over, but I thought no more of it until the next day when I couldn't run for the pain across the top of my foot. In all, that kept me off the road for ten long days. It was a miserable experience, and I seemed to feel my 'fitness', such as it was, slipping away and with it my chances of taking part in the London Marathon. However, I tried to pick up the chart again, but I couldn't. This depressed me even more.

On Sunday 18 January, I decided to try a run along part of the new Lewes by-pass. I measured out, by car, a convenient distance of 5.2 miles (2.6 there, and 2.6 back again). I then ran, and couldn't believe my eyes when I saw my time of just under 45 minutes. Allowing for a bit of error all around, this was 5 × 9 minute miles – fabulous running for me, I can tell you, and a real boost.

I felt great, and decided that Cliff Temple and his chart were too tough for me! It seemed to me to be too much to expect myself to do. I thought the chart was all right for people who had done some running, no matter how minimal, before. I had given it a good try but I couldn't cope with it, and that was all there was to that. Instead, I decided to carry on running regularly and try to build up a good mileage. I stuck to the idea of running six days a week and I also tried to do reasonably high weekly mileages because I believed the warning about the distance beating me otherwise.

Then, would you believe it, on Wednesday 28 January, I turned over my right ankle (the left foot was still a bit dodgy so I may have been favouring it and brought this second injury on myself). I knew that I, of all people, could not afford another ten days off the road. I even began to hope my entry would not be accepted. I went to a physiotherapist, who told me it was nothing really, just a minor injury to my 'triangular' ligament. He couldn't feel the pain I felt, of course. He was marvellous, and I was back running again (minus a few quid) on Monday 2 February.

On Sunday, 8 February, I did my Lewes by-pass 5 miles again, in wind and rain. It was tough but I enjoyed it and despite awful conditions ran it in 45 minutes again. It was another confidence booster, but I couldn't help thinking that 5 miles is a lot different from 26-plus, and I wasn't going to make it. A week later I completed 10 miles on the good old Lewes by-pass (what would I have done without it?) in 1 hour 40 minutes. 10 × 10 minute miles – a major achievement for me. I was on top of the world.

By now the evenings were a little lighter, so I was able to run along badly surfaced footpaths on the A22 to the next village and back for about 7 miles total. I also mapped out a 10-mile circuit, with two 5-mile laps shaped like a figure eight, at Crawley.

I completed my longest training run, 15 miles, at Crawley on 12 March in just under 2 hours 40 minutes, or about 10½-minute miles. I felt reasonable at the end of it but very apprehensive about carrying on for another 11 miles; in fact, I had grave doubts that I could do it. But I felt I'd come this far so I might as well continue.

I took a week's leave beginning Monday 16 March, to wind up my training with a hard week of between 50–60 miles. I then planned to have a quiet week leading up to the big day. It didn't work out like that, perhaps because I switched to morning runs. On Monday I just could not get into the right frame of mind. It took all my self-control to force me to keep going for a 50-minute 5-mile run. Tuesday and Wednesday were only marginally better with a 75-minute 7½-mile spin each day. However, the Wednesday run left me with a sore Achilles tendon – something I had never experienced before and at this late stage somewhat frightening. I didn't run at all on Thursday as a precautionary measure and only did a very easy 4 miles on Friday. Another day off on Saturday and I ended the week on a better note with a 140-minute run of 13½ miles on Sunday.

I felt no more ill-effects from the tendon, but after that easy Friday run I finished with the skin under and between the toes of my left foot cracked and painful to walk on. (I covered them in Vaseline before the Sunday run which did the trick.) I had hoped for so much during that week and finished with a miserable 37½ miles plus a bit of foot trouble. My morale was at an all-time low now. I really felt bad because it seemed to me that things had gone wrong so late that I didn't have time to put them right again.

As you will have gathered I am no runner. All I wanted was to finish in 5 hours (as I had put on my entry form). I had planned to start off the marathon at about 11-minute mile pace and reckoned this would give me enough time in hand in the second half to reach my target time. Since I had reached a reasonable level of fitness my speed had not increased. Although it can be argued that from not being able to run for five minutes to being able to run 15 miles in under 2¾ hours is an infinite improvement,

I turned out 10-minute miles all the time. In fact, they became so regular that I got to the stage where I felt I could confidently go out anywhere and run for an hour and it would be a distance of 6 miles! However, I could not improve on that. There are two ways to tackle a marathon, one is to run around and the other is to jog around, which is what I wanted, but this last week undermined my confidence to such an extent that I didn't believe I was capable of doing even that.

I stuck to my plans for an easy last week, going for my final winding-up run on Tuesday 24 March. I went out straight from work on a miserable grey misty day. It had been like this all day so I just went out in my tracksuit, up the A27 from Brighton to Lewes (via pavement and footpath). After a while it began to drizzle and by the time I reached Lewes it was raining properly. As I turned to run back to Brighton it began to pour, and I was running into the wind. I finished soaked to the skin and cold but I felt great (funny game this running!) and the 12½ miles had been covered in 2 hours 5 minutes. Incredible. Everything was together again, the Vaseline had worked and once again in awful conditions I never once felt like giving up.

The next day I awoke with a painful back, I thought. Actually it was the left shoulder. At lunchtime I bought a pair of shorts, running socks and vest for the big day. I had never owned these before and left the purchase of them so late because I didn't want to buy them and then not run. On Thursday 26 March I had a short run to try out the shorts and vest. Every time my left foot hit the ground the shoulder hurt, and I felt very conspicuous in shorts and vest! I was in fact full of trepidation about running the marathon in shorts and vest. I believed I would get cold, as I had always run in my tracksuit. Anyhow that was my training, for better or for worse, wrapped up.

My wife and I stayed at one of the Trust House Forte hotels on the Saturday night and shared a taxi to Greenwich with another runner on Sunday morning. We didn't attend the famous pasta party, and I just ate normally all the way through my training. We both thought the organization for the start and all the way through was magnificent.

At the start I felt the usual butterflies in my tummy but the shoulder was OK as was everything else – plenty of Vaseline on my feet and a thin green woolly over my vest to keep me warm. A couple of thirty-two-year-old men from another part of my office had also entered. On the Friday before the race I told one of them I was in it and he found me as we lined up to start. I didn't really want to run with him as he is seventeen years younger than me, big, strong and fit (football and cricket non-stop for about seventeen years now). The first 6 miles he stayed back with me and consequently I went far too fast for my plan (one hour). It happened again with the next 7 miles too, covered in about 70 minutes. 15 miles came up in 2½ hours. 15 × 10 minute miles! Much too quick for me and I was beginning to worry a little at the fast pace (for me). I ran for a while with a girl who said she hoped to finish in about 3½ hours. She was worried about the bleakness of the Isle of Dogs portion, and said the furthest she had run in training was 14 miles. I lost sight of her when on two occasions I slowed for drinks but she kept on going. I looked for her name among the finishers but I couldn't find it. I hope she made it.

I took a drink at almost every feeding station. I missed the 17-mile sign and by 18 was suffering and couldn't read my watch (I ran without my specs and what with the rain and perspiration I had difficulty reading the dial). Just after 18 miles I couldn't run any more, so I walked for a while. Once again I had no thoughts of giving up. I felt that after five months of training and having made it to 18 miles I was home and dry even if it took me the rest of the day. I enjoyed the champagne provided by the Wapping Wine Store and thought the marina at St Katharine's Dock looked great.

I walked for a while, then ran for a while. Breaking into a jog again after walking was murder but once I made the effort I managed to keep going for a fair bit. I hated the cobbles at the Tower, but from there onwards it was roses all the way. At about the 24 miles mark I began to feel intoxicated as I knew there was nothing on earth that could stop me from finishing. All the way around the spectators had been wonderful. From the beginning they had encouraged us. I couldn't have retired in front of them even if I'd wanted to. They clapped and cheered all the way. I did the same to them. I told hundreds that they were 'winners' too to stand out in the rain for hours to watch a bunch of rag, tag and bobtails like us, and they were.

When I turned into Birdcage Walk the crowd lifted me with a great roar. I was able to respond and ran up past the Palace feeling 10 feet tall. I was cheered all the way and my wife (who had begun to think I was on a bus somewhere) says she couldn't believe the way I finished. She said it quite brought a lump to her throat and a tear to her eye.

I suppose the icing on the cake was to hear the announcer at the finish booming out: 'And here comes Bill Crotty from Uckfield, in East Sussex, finishing his first-ever marathon, in under 5 hours.'

I could hardly believe this was happening to me. My official time was 4 hours 46 minutes 53 seconds. Steve Ovett never felt better than me! I finished 6243rd of those timed by computer (out of 6255). Another 163 finished behind me, and 637 retired. It was the best day of my life. I was on cloud nine. At last I'd done something almost unique, and I still keep the medal with me everywhere I go, like a big kid.

Of course it will wear off, or some of it, but I feel I have something in common with world class athletes, and Olympic gold medallists. I've run a marathon! I didn't beat many people; I didn't expect to, and I didn't set out to. But I did beat 26 miles 385 yards. Nobody can take that away from me.

11

FURTHER ALONG THE ROAD

The 24-Week Marathon Build-Up Programme for the Active Club Athlete

Another type of runner, distinct from those who have little or no running background, is the club athlete who has already been active for some time, competes regularly in shorter road races, and has long been toying with the idea of running a marathon without actually taking the plunge. He or she has the advantage of a reasonable running background, knowledge of the sport and personal abilities and limitations, and an experience of racing. But so far he or she might not have managed to sustain training at a level high enough to feel ready to tackle a marathon (even though such a runner is probably much fitter than many of those who have already run the distance).

For many years I was in this category myself. As a schoolboy runner devoid of speed, I could hardly wait to be old enough to run a marathon and firmly intended to find one as soon as possible after my twenty-first birthday (as the age limit then was). When I reached twenty-one, I decided to get somewhat fitter first, and stuck to 10-milers. Year after year, as my fitness rose and fell, it never quite reached the point where I was satisfied with it. I ran the Finchley 20-mile road race in 1974 in 2 hours 3 minutes, but the last 5 miles were hard. I needed to get fitter for the extra 6, I decided. Instead, I became less fit. It was another four years – ten years later than I'd planned – before I finally lined up for that first marathon at the age of thirty-one. And then I wished I'd done so long before.

So the next training schedule is designed for the 'almost' marathon runner: the athlete who hovers around 30–40 miles a week of mainly steady running, turns out for the club most weekends, and finishes down in the pack somewhere. Not a prize-winner. Not a star. Perhaps even rather directionless in approach. But with a bit of a push, a potential sub-3-hour marathon runner. Don't waste time like I did. This is for you.

If you have read the beginners' charts on pages 150–3, the first difference you will notice with this one is that the sessions are given mainly in miles rather than 'running-minutes'. Most club runners have a reasonable idea of distance, and probably have their own regular training routes of different lengths anyway.

But the overall pattern is the same: the long run on Sunday, gradually increasing in length over the training period to acclimatize the body to simply running for that length of time. Then the rest of the week is divided between medium sessions, with the second-longest run of the week normally coming on the Wednesday. Club races also play their part, with a gradual increase in competition distance as fitness builds up.

To provide more training variety, and to allow for a faster training pace on some days, two shorter sessions are suggested, or else a period of *fartlek* (see page 16) in which the runner surges, sprints and jogs as he feels, rather than on a pre-set pattern. Again, this provides a mental relief as well as a change of pace, although it must never be forgotten that the marathon itself requires a steady, economic effort and the sudden bursts of speed are in the main best kept for training.

A weekly run including hills is also part of the schedule. This can either be carried out on a particularly hilly course, where the gradients are a natural part of the run, or else as a deliberate session of running up a steep hill, then jogging back down, and repeating six to eight times during the middle of a run. The point always to remember with any interval hill work, though, is to run right over the top of the hill for a short distance before you stop and turn. It is a good habit to develop, for otherwise your body starts looking for an automatic rest after a climb during a race.

Again, the schedule allows for one rest day a week, although when the mileage gets to its heaviest this is not always possible.

So make particular efforts at that time to get proper sleep and relaxation, to keep late-night socializing to a reasonable minimum, to offset the possible cumulative effects of fatigue and to try to reduce the likelihood of injury.

Incidentally, I make no concession to the female runner in this schedule. Her pace may be slower, but the marathon she runs is exactly the same distance as the men's, so the quantity of training is exactly the same.

Schedule No. 3
The 24-Week Marathon Build-Up Programme for the Active Club Athlete

Week	Approx Weekly Mileage Total	Sun	Mon	Tues	Wed	Thur	Fri	Sat
1	40	10 miles	6 miles fartlek	4 miles	8 miles	5 miles	Rest	7 miles
2	45	11 miles	7 miles fartlek	5 miles	8 miles	7 miles	Rest	7 miles
3	50	12 miles	8 miles	5 miles fast	9 miles	6 miles	Rest	*Race* 10 miles
4	55	12 miles	8 miles	6 miles fast	9 miles	8 miles	Rest	2×6 miles
5	60	12 miles	8 miles	8 miles fast	9 miles	8 miles	5 miles	*Race* 10 miles
6	60	14 miles	8 miles	6 miles fast	10 miles	2×6 miles	Rest	10 miles
7	65	14 miles	2×5 miles	8 miles fast	10 miles	2×6 miles	Rest	11 miles
8	55	15 miles	8 miles	6 miles fast	10 miles	6 miles	Rest	*Race* 10 miles
9	65	15 miles	2×5 miles	8 miles fast	12 miles	8 miles	Rest	12 miles
10	70	16 miles	2×5 miles	10 miles incl. hills	12 miles	10 miles fartlek	Rest	12 miles
11	65	16 miles	2×5 miles	10 miles incl. hills	12 miles	1 hour fartlek	Rest	*Race* 10 miles
12	75	17 miles	2×5 miles	10 miles incl. hills	12 miles	2×6 miles	Rest	8 miles + 6 miles
13	65	17 miles	8 miles	10 miles incl. hills	12 miles	1 hour fartlek	Rest	*Race* 10-12 miles
14	80	18 miles	8 miles	10 miles incl. hills	14 miles	1 hour fartlek	2×5 miles	12 miles
15	70	18 miles	2×5 miles	10 miles incl. hills	12 miles	1 hour fartlek	Rest	*Race* 10-13 miles
16	85	20 miles	2×5 miles	10 miles incl. hills	14 miles	1 hour fartlek	9 miles	8 miles + 6 miles

Week	Approx Weekly Mileage Total	Sun	Mon	Tues	Wed	Thur	Fri	Sat
17	80	20 miles	2×6 miles	10 miles incl. hills	14 miles	1 hour fartlek	6 miles	10 miles
18	75	18 miles	2×5 miles	10 miles incl. hills	12 miles	1 hour fartlek	4 miles	*Race 12-15 miles*
19	90	12 miles	2×6 miles	10 miles incl. hills	15 miles	1 hour fartlek	7 miles + 4 miles	22 miles
20	60	10 miles + 8 miles	5 miles	8 miles incl. hills	12 miles	1 hour fartlek	4 miles + 5 miles	Rest
21	70	*Race* 20 miles	8 miles	10 miles incl. hills	14 miles	1 hour fartlek	2×5 miles	Rest
22	80	22-24 miles	5 miles	10 miles incl. hills	14 miles	1 hour fartlek	2×5 miles	10 miles
23	50-60	15 miles	5 miles	8 miles incl. hills	10 miles	6 miles	Rest	6 miles
24	50	10 miles	Rest	6 miles incl. hills	6 miles	Rest	2 miles jog	*The Race*

The Ambitious International Runner

So we come to the élite marathon runner, the serious competitor, whose aim is not simply to complete the distance, but to do so faster than anyone else, even if it means doing so at well under 5-minute-mile pace for every single mile.

Whereas a good club-level runner may run 15–20 miles on a Sunday, the serious runner is someone who covers that distance every single day of the week. Not always in one session, but as part of a regular routine which will mean training twice or even three times a day. And while a club runner may fit his training around his work, often the very ambitious runner will prefer, or need, to fit his work around his training.

What exactly constitutes the right training for an ambitious runner? Every athlete has his or her own answer, and there is the intriguing possibility that the perfect method simply may not yet have been discovered. But, far more likely, the perfect method to suit everyone simply could not exist. What each runner has to discover, therefore, is a personal ideal method through trial, error and more trial.

So the search for that correct balance of hard, easy, fast, slow training continues the world over. Ron Hill, the former European and Commonwealth champion, and one of the marathon's most successful experimentalists and innovators, suggests that we may be coming close to the optimum performance in the event. 'People talk about the possibility of a 2-hour marathon, but I think 2 hours 5 minutes would be a more realistic limit,' he says. 'When it is reached, it will be done by a 10,000 metres runner who is motivated towards the marathon. When I ran my fastest time of 2 hours 9 minutes 28 seconds, I went through 10 miles in 47:45, and the next 10 miles in under 50 minutes.

'But unless doctors find a method, or evolution results in bigger people with longer legs, we'll never get down to 2 hours. I think it's impossible simply because I don't believe the human body is capable of carrying that much energy store in available glycogen or fat.'

Approaches to training do change. A 1920 newspaper reported that four US runners had completed their preparation for the Olympic marathon in Antwerp by running round the whole course in 2 hours 46 minutes 55 seconds just eleven days before the race itself.

Yet at the Games, the best-placed of them, Joe Organ, was 7th in only 2:41.30, with Carl Linder 11th in 2:44.21 and Charles Mellor 12th in 2:45.30, and it seems likely that they had already left too much of their form on the road. These days no one would dream of running the whole course eleven days before a marathon in a time so close to their best, and still expect to be fresh for the race itself. (Incidentally, my favourite 1920 Olympian must be the other American, Arthur Roth, who started that training run with them, broke a shoelace after 20 miles, and while hurrying to catch up was knocked out when a careless Belgian peasant opened a door in his face. Now I can identify with that. And he didn't finish the Olympic race either.)

The training chart on page 173 shows a typical 16-week schedule for an athlete who is already training at a high level, and has an important marathon coming up. There are dozens of possible variations on such a chart, but I prefer to keep basically to the principle of hard/easy weeks in the belief that recovery afforded by a relatively low-mileage week is even more essential at this level than during a much more modest programme.

Too often, it seems, the ambitious athlete fears that to drop, even briefly, below a certain quantity of training will mean impending disaster. But I feel the opposite is true: *not* to drop below a certain level, and give the body a chance to recover and repair before the next hard week, is tempting fate in terms of injury. The motto: hard work plus rest equals success.

For not only is such a volume of running extremely hard, but relaxation in between is equally important. Too much stress at work, too much travelling, or overtime, or irregular hours, or the actual physical demands of the job, may not necessarily ruin the really determined runner's training progress. But they certainly won't help either.

Yes, I know that it is easy for me to say, 'Give up your job because it involves a stressful 80-minute rush-hour rail journey every day,' or 'Don't do two hours' overtime because a 10-mile run will have greater benefit for your marathon training,' while conveniently overlooking that you may have a mortgage and bills to pay, mouths to feed, and a career to sustain. Rationally, it may be quite ludicrous even to think of putting your livelihood and your family's comfort in jeopardy, simply so that you can go out and run 10 miles in the hope that eventually you may be able to run it faster than the next man.

The theory of amateur sport is admirable: you have a job and a domestic situation, and in your spare time you can engage in some physical recreation like running to keep fit, and for a little friendly competition and socializing in off-duty hours. For a lot of people that is exactly how it is, and how it should be, and the saddest part is that many others do not even take *that* amount of physical exercise.

But the theory is not always so practical when we are talking about people who want very much (for whatever reason) to become one of the finest exponents of long distance running in the entire world. Bearing in mind the intense competition, it is plain that to reach such a level is going to take more than a casual half-hour here and there.

As you get nearer and nearer to that goal, so running encroaches on every working, domestic and social activity to some degree, and whether or not you succeed may depend a very great deal on how understanding and supportive are your immediate family and friends. If your disappearance out of the front door on a training run is habitually followed very shortly afterwards by a torrent of abuse, a vase of flowers, the clock, and Fluffy the cat, and you are met on your return by your burnt dinner at head height, then the chances are that you are probably not receiving sufficient sympathetic backing from home in your endeavour.

A survey of competitors in the 1980 New York City Marathon showed, in common with other obsessive people, a divorce rate 3½ times higher than for non-runners with similar backgrounds. 'The key difference between a person who becomes an addict and one who uses running sensibly, is moderation,' says Dr Michael Sacks, Associate Professor at Cornell Medical School. 'But many marathon runners train by doing 70–100 miles a week. A married addict will start to pay less attention to his spouse. Some totally change their lifestyle to accommodate what is supposed to be a leisure-time activity. They change their diet, their clothes, their friends, their attitude to their careers and, in some cases, even their spouse.' That was an American survey, and by no means automatically applicable in the UK. But don't say you haven't been warned!

As far as a career goes, there is no doubt that many leading athletes (and not only marathon runners) have in the past turned down possible promotion or even a better job because it would leave them less time for training. Or they simply never had the chance for promotion in the first place because they rarely worked overtime, or were so frequently away from work on overseas athletics trips, often without pay.

Every individual has to weigh up the various considerations and decide whether he is willing to put in an attempt to reach international class as an athlete ahead of his career. It is not an easy question, bearing in mind that there are no guarantees that concentration on marathon running will produce the results, or the income necessary to replace a full-time job.

It may eventually be possible for a top marathon runner to pick up as much from prize money, appearance money and advertising as the world's top golfers and tennis players do now. But even potential pro golfers and tennis players have to make a decision at some point as to whether, and when, they should turn full-time professional, and any amount of determination is not necessarily going to turn every sub-2:20 marathon runner into a millionaire within a month.

Above all, the consideration of how much you want running to dictate your life should really include as a high priority the very relevant question: 'Am I, or could I be, good enough?'

You really need to recognize a burning feeling inside you that it *is* only the restriction of work, or whatever, which is holding you back. There must be some signs of your ability to become a good runner, for it might be totally irresponsible to risk jeopardizing a career in an endeavour to become a great athlete when the basic ability is plainly not there in the first place. But then again, that ability is less essential in the marathon than in, say, the sprints, where you need to have been born with a considerable amount of natural speed.

Schedule No. 4
The Ambitious International Runner (16-Week Build-Up)

Week	Approx Mileage Total		Sun	Mon	Tues	Wed	Thur	Fri	Sat
1	80	a.m.	18 miles	5 miles	7 miles	7 miles	7 miles	7 miles	5 miles
		p.m.	–	8 miles fast	6×1 mile, 5 min jog between	8 miles	8×600m on track, 200m jog	–	Low key 5 miles race
2	90	a.m.	20 miles	5 miles	5 miles	5 miles	5 miles	8 miles	5 miles
		p.m.	–	8 miles fast	7 miles	12 miles	6×1000m on track, 200m jog	–	Low key race?
3	100	a.m.	20 miles	6 miles	5 miles	7 miles	5 miles	10 miles	5 miles
		p.m.	–	8 miles fast	9 miles	12 miles	6×800m on track, 200m jog	–	8 miles
4	95	a.m.	20 miles	5 miles	7 miles	–	7 miles	7 miles	10 miles
		p.m.	–	8 miles fast	6×1 mile, 5 min jog	12 miles	8×600m on track, 200m jog	–	Low key race?
5	110	a.m.	20 miles	5 miles	7 miles	5 miles	7 miles	5 miles	12 miles
		p.m.	5 miles	9 miles fast	6×1 mile, 5 min jog	12 miles	6×1000m on track, 200m jog	–	6 miles
6	90	a.m.	20 miles	5 miles	5 miles	5 miles	5 miles	5 miles	–
		p.m.	–	7 miles fast	6×1 mile, 5 min jog	12 miles	8×800m on track, 200m jog	–	10 miles road race
7	120	a.m.	22 miles	7 miles	5 miles	7 miles	7 miles	10 miles	5 miles
		p.m.	4 miles	10 miles fast	6×1 mile, 5 min jog	12 miles	8×600m on track, 200m jog	–	half-marathon race
8	100	a.m.	20 miles	5 miles	7 miles	5 miles	7 miles	5 miles	10 miles
		p.m.	5 miles	7 miles fast	6×1 mile, 5 min jog	12 miles	8×800m on track, 200m jog	–	–
9	120	a.m.	22 miles	7 miles	5 miles	7 miles	5 miles	7 miles	10 miles
		p.m.	5 miles	10 miles fast	6×1 mile, 5 min jog	15 miles	6×1000m on track, 200m jog	5 miles	5 miles

Week	Approx Mileage Total		Sun	Mon	Tues	Wed	Thur	Fri	Sat
10	100	a.m.	24 miles	5 miles	5 miles	7 miles	5 miles	7 miles	–
		p.m.	–	6 miles fast	6×1 mile, 5 min jog	15 miles	8×800m on track, 200m jog	–	10 miles race
11	130	a.m.	24 miles	7 miles	7 miles	7 miles	7 miles	7 miles	12 miles
		p.m.	5 miles	10 miles fast	8×1 mile, 5 min jog	15 miles	8×600m on track, 200m jog	–	6 miles
12	100	a.m.	22 miles	5 miles	5 miles	5 miles	5 miles	3 miles	–
		p.m.	–	5 miles fast	6×1 mile, 5 min jog	12 miles	6×1000m on track, 200m jog	–	20 miles road race
13	140	a.m.	15 miles	8 miles 5 miles	8 miles	5 miles	8 miles 5 miles	7 miles 5 miles	10 miles
		p.m.	5 miles	10 miles	10 miles	15 miles	10 miles	8 miles	6 miles
14	100	a.m.	22 miles	–	5 miles	5 miles	7 miles	5 miles	–
		p.m.	–	7 miles fast	6×1 mile, 5 min jog	15 miles	8×800m on track, 200m jog	–	10 miles road race
15	70	a.m.	20 miles	5 miles	5 miles	–	5 miles	5 miles	–
		p.m.	–	7 miles fast	–	12 miles	6×1000m on track, 200m jog	–	5 miles road race
16	75	a.m.	15 miles	–	5 miles	–	2 miles jog	2 miles jog	*The Race*
		p.m.	–	7 miles fast	6×600m, 5 min jog	10 miles	–	–	

12

WHAT'S THE WEATHER LIKE?

Adapting to the Conditions

Two people looked out of their windows on the same summer morning and saw clear blue skies and a bright sun. One said: 'What a marvellous day!' The other groaned to himself, and sat down to think about the problems it would cause. Which one was the marathon runner?

Two people looked out of the window and saw a grey, cheerless day, with a light rain spattering the window panes. One groaned to himself, and cancelled his plans for that morning. The other said nothing, but felt a surge of adrenalin in the face of such weather conditions. Which one was the marathon runner?

When all the training has been done, every last preparation made, the one factor over which you have no control is the climate, which in Britain seems to become more and more unpredictable. In the past couple of years I've watched midwinter cross country races in warm sunshine, and competed on the track in May in snow! In an event lasting as long as the marathon, conditions may even change radically between start and finish; but generally you can tell how it is likely to affect the race.

Heat

Of all the different conditions you meet, heat is the most difficult with which to deal, because you cannot escape from it, like wearing extra layers in the cold or sheltering behind someone else in the wind. You can only try to minimize its effects.

As the body produces heat through hard exercise, the internal (core) temperature rises and nearly three-quarters of the total energy generated by exercise may be released simply as heat rather than actually powering the muscles. To avoid heat storage, and a subsequent rise in temperature, cooling the body obviously becomes of major importance. But on a hot day this process is hampered, especially if there is high humidity (which hinders the evaporation of sweat), or a light following wind which, unlike a headwind, offers no relief of convection to the runner.

Convection is one of the three mechanisms on which the runner relies to help him lose excess heat, and is simply the cooling of the skin by the air. Simple heat radiation is another mechanism, while the third is sweating, which is not a method of heat loss in itself. Rather, the fluid released on to the skin by the sweat glands evaporates, thus lowering the skin temperature. But if the air is humid, the sweat does not evaporate so easily, and its efficiency as a heat loss agent diminishes, while the athlete becomes more dehydrated from the sweat loss.

Dehydration in turn raises the body temperature, and the athlete may find himself in a vicious circle, as the flow of blood to the skin surface (which transports the heat from the muscles) is reduced and diverted as reinforcement *to* the muscles themselves. This vicious circle, known as the hyperthermic spiral, will continue until heat stroke unless the runner reduces the amount of heat being produced by easing off the pace, or stopping altogether.

Therefore, the runner needs to take certain precautions before and during any long race in hot weather. Running kit should be light in texture and colour, allowing maximum skin contact with the air. Mesh or string vests are ideal, and even women's models with mesh panels are available now too.

Plenty of fluid should be drunk before the race, and taken at every opportunity during it, without waiting to feel thirsty. Runners can lose between 1 and 2 litres of sweat per hour, and as much of it as possible must be quickly replaced because a fluid loss of more than 3 per cent of the total body weight brings on the first stages of dehydration. Cold water is rapidly absorbed, but adding large amounts of glucose to it, as some runners do, actually reduces the speed of absorption and thus its effectiveness in preventing dehydration. Solids taken during a run (other than in ultra-long-distance events) should also be avoided because they can delay the absorption of liquids too, and use up valuable energy in being absorbed themselves. They cannot quickly provide any additional calories anyway.

The rules of road racing state that in events over 5km refreshment

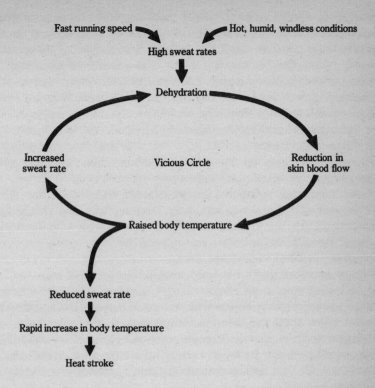

stations 'may' be provided; in races over 10km refreshments 'should' be provided; and in marathons they 'must' be provided, together with the provision of water and sponges. A refreshment station in this instance does not mean somewhere you can buy a cup of tea and piece of cake. That comes after the race. During the event it consists instead of a roadside table on which plastic cups of water, orange squash, lemon squash, cold sweet tea and even de-fizzed Coke may be provided for the runners.

Apart from the obvious revitalizing value, they are there for the more serious reason that on a hot day dehydration could occur in a long race as the body squeezes out its fluid through sweating in an effort to cool the skin surface. Taking drinks during the race helps to replace the liquid lost, and the hotter the day the earlier drinks should be taken – even before you feel the need.

Anyone who saw the classic marathon scenes in Kon Ichikawa's documentary film of the 1964 Olympic Games, *Tokyo Olympiad*, will remember how easy the great Ethiopian runner, the late Abebe Bikila, made taking a drink during a marathon seem.

The vivid scenes showed Bikila heading down a long, straight motorway-like road with the Olympic flame at the stadium in the distance as his goal. He came to a refreshment station, grabbed a cup of water, drank the contents and threw it down without disturbing the pattern of his effortless running. I always used to think it was as easy as that until I first tried it! Instead of the Bikila smoothness, I found orange squash sloshing from side to side in the cup as I ran, spilling over the sides and sticking my fingers together for the rest of the race. And, when I went to try to drink it, it was swirling about so much that most of it went either up my nose or down my chin, with just a few drops going in my mouth, as I desperately tried to keep running.

It was reassuring to find that it even happens to the stars too. When Bill Rodgers, the American marathon runner, first won the Boston Marathon in 1975, he stopped – completely – several times in the closing stages of the race to take drinks, even though he was running just inside the course record for this classic event.

'I know everyone thinks I'm crazy to stop, but I think it helps me,' he said. 'If I don't stop, I can't drink – it just splashes.' His point was that it was more important to ensure that he took in some of the liquid rather than just a few drops and then risk dehydrating in the final miles.

Taking a drink on the run requires some getting used to, and before a first marathon it may be worth setting up a table with plastic cups of water in a quiet spot and to run circuits past it, rehearsing picking up and drinking on the run.

When you have got hold of your cup, don't start to drink immediately. Let the cup and liquid get into your running rhythm first. You can keep your hand partially over the top of the open cup to reduce spillage, and indeed while you drink.

Another method of overcoming the spillage problems in smaller marathons, where competitors can hand in their own drinks beforehand to be put out at specific refreshment stations around the course, is the use of small plastic bottles with a squirting top. With these it is possible to squeeze the liquid in a jet into your mouth and thus remove the need to suck in a drink while trying to maintain your breathing rhythm.

Bottles for this purpose are sold in specialist running shops, although a number of runners have successfully used the type of hair spray bottles which can be bought (empty!) at many chemists, enlarging the hole through which the jet comes if necessary.

The pre-filled bottles have to be marked with your race number so that officials at the various refreshment stations can identify them and hand them to you, or at least put them in a prominent position on the table as you approach; trying to find your own drink among dozens of different bottles in the closing stages of a long race on a hot day can be a challenge in itself.

At one such marathon a complex system was in operation whereby every runner who had handed in personal drinks beforehand had a yellow circle on their race number. Officials with walkie-talkie radios were positioned 100 yards down the road from the refreshment table, and as the runners passed them they relayed the numbers of all approaching competitors with yellow circles ahead to the table officials who then put the corresponding drinks to the front.

After you have finished with the plastic bottles or cups, you simply drop them on the pavement or in the gutter, from where they will be collected up. The bottles are sometimes returned to the finish, although you must expect to lose most of these relatively inexpensive items at each race.

The concept of personal drinks is a good one for a reasonably compact field, but for the mass marathons, like London and New York, impossible to organize. In these big events, some runners do arrange for friends in the crowd to hand them personal drinks at prearranged points on the course, and in New York, Boston, and many other US races, spectators spontaneously offer drinks to runners along much of the route. Children, particularly, are delighted if a runner accepts the cup they are holding out, and this brief Samaritan act between two people who will meet each other for no more than a fleeting second adds to the community spirit of the whole race.

Others set up fine sprays with garden hoses to cool down runners on hot days, or special frames, like doorways, with a spray on top through which the runners can decide whether or not to run. In Boston there is not always the choice at some of the narrower parts, but the spray is normally welcome and refreshing to the runners. Only occasionally, like the time a well-meaning bystander threw a bucket of icy water over an unsuspecting runner, immediately causing both of his thighs to cramp up, has such help been positively unwelcome.

Strictly speaking, the passing of drinks and other aid must be considered as contravening the rules, as the IAAF Rules are the same in essence as those in Britain, while adding: 'A competitor who takes refreshments at a place other than the refreshment stations renders himself liable to disqualification.'

Sponging points, situated between the refreshment stations, are where officials establish a line of buckets of water into which they dip a host of sponges and hold them out to competitors as they pass (the sponges, not the buckets). If you take one (a sponge, not a bucket) it can be quite refreshing to wipe your face, neck and shoulders with, but in general it is not too good an idea to try to drink water from such a sponge unless you are in great need of the liquid. The sponges, like the cups, are often dropped in the gutter when they have served their purpose, and usually they are collected up again by hordes of enthusiastic youngsters who rush them back to the buckets. By the time a few dozen dropped sponges have been dipped into the water, it begins to get somewhat gritty and dirty, and there is not always time or opportunity for the officials to change it. A cold sponge can be reviving, but the water it contains is often less than palatable, and if there is a lot of grit around it can be like wiping your face with a Brillo pad.

The warm-up before a race on a hot day should be minimal and undertaken without a tracksuit. Some runners stay completely in the shade before such a race, and keep their racing vest somewhere cool until a couple of minutes before the start, then discard their warm-up vest and change into the cooler one. Every little helps in keeping body temperature down on such a day.

Make due allowance for the temperature in assessing the pace to run. If in doubt, err on the side of caution in the early stages, and make the most of every sponging point on the course, for a few extra seconds spent there may save you minutes later on – or could even make the difference between finishing the race or not. Sponge well over the head, shoulders and thighs; the latter produce a large proportion of heat because of the hard work performed by the muscle groups situated there.

If, despite all precautions, you do begin to feel the effects of heat, which may include shivering, or a confusion of thoughts similar to drunkenness, you should slow down considerably, and if that does not improve matters, stop altogether. Lie down in the shade, with the feet raised if possible. A good intake of liquid and sponging down should aid recovery, although in more serious cases, such as nausea, sickness, dizziness, headaches and disorientation, medical help will probably be needed.

Cold

For a heat-producing activity like running, a cold day is less of a problem than a hot one. Apart from sensible dressing for the weather in training, with layers of T-shirts, tracksuits and other kit according to personal preference, a woollen hat (for a third of body heat is lost through the head) and gloves or mittens may be favoured by some runners during races as well as training. Both can be discarded if you feel you are over-heating. An alternative to ordinary gloves is the fingerless variety, which help to keep your hands at a moderate temperature.

Although cold muscles perform less efficiently than warm muscles, the well-protected heart actually works more easily in cold weather, because it does not have to pump blood continually to the skin surface for cooling, as it does in hot weather. Additionally, fewer calories per mile are burned. Dr Frank Consolazio of the Letterman Army Institute of Research in California, reviewing medical literature on calories used in heat and cold, found that there is an increase of only between 2 and 5 per cent in energy-utilization in extremely cold weather, which can be attributed entirely to the effect of having to wear extra layers of clothing. In cold weather, energy requirements are otherwise dependent simply on bodyweight and intensity of exercise. But in exceptionally hot weather there is an estimated increase in energy requirements of 0.5 per cent for every one degree increase in temperature between 30° and 40° Centigrade, because of this need to pump blood to the skin surface for cooling.

The wind chill factor is also a consideration in the bitterest climates. This is the estimated decrease in temperature according to the strength of the prevailing wind. For example, a 10 m.p.h. wind blowing at 32 degrees Fahrenheit (freezing point) will cool the face twice as quickly as still air at the same temperature, while the same wind on a day when the thermometer shows zero will produce a wind-chill factor of minus 24 degrees.

The table below, produced by J. Karr Taylor, a Montana doctor with a great deal of experience of running in very low temperatures, indicates the effect of the wind in lowering temperature.

Wind direction is critical because a side wind has only a fraction of

WIND CHILL TABLE

Estimated wind speed (m.p.h.)	Actual thermometer reading (°F)						
	50	40	30	20	10	0	−10
	Equivalent temperature (°F)						
calm	50	40	30	20	10	0	−10
5	48	37	27	16	6	−5	−15
10	40	28	16	4	−9	−24	−33
15	36	22	9	−5	−18	−32	−45
20	32	18	4	−10	−25	−39	−53
25	30	16	0	−15	−29	−44	−59
30	28	13	−2	−18	−33	−48	−63
35	27	11	−4	−20	−35	−51	−67
40	26	10	−6	−21	−37	−53	−69

the impact of a headwind. The trailing wind is important only if you have to return into it. It is worth noting, too, that to run into the wind at, say, 5 m.p.h. increases the wind chill appreciably.

A rain-suit jacket, even on a dry day, worn over other layers will help to take the worst of the wind off you. When training on a cold, windy day, try to set out into the wind and return with it behind you, rather than the other way round. If you start with the wind behind you, you will sweat early on, then have to run into the wind which will evaporate the sweat and make you even colder.

On the day of the race, when limbs may be exposed to the elements, some runners like to rub olive oil, or even the type of warming massage creams used for soft tissue injuries, on to the areas of skin to be exposed as a way of trying to retain body heat.

Snow

Running in soft, fresh snow can be an exhilarating experience and provides the legs with some cushioning and resistance at the same time. What is less fun for the runner is the time when the snow starts to melt by day and then freezes over again at night, turning roads and pavements into a giant ice rink. If possible, you should try to find somewhere which has escaped the snow through being covered. Some shopping precincts, subways or station approaches may fit the bill; anything with some form of roof which gives you a non-slippery surface on which to run. I have used the stands of Folkestone cricket ground, running up and down between the rows of seats, which was less boring than you might imagine, given the alternative of skidding around the local roads.

But if you do have to run on snow and ice, try to stick to known routes, because otherwise your ankles may discover unknown pot-holes and steps which have been covered by the snow. And, if you should approach a group of children who all suddenly stand back to watch you coming, beware! You are probably about to set foot on their sliding patch, and you may cover the next 20 yards a good deal faster than you expect!

Rain

Running in the rain can help to cool the body on a mild day, and be positively refreshing in washing away dust, salt and sweat. On other occasions, when it lashes down, it can be a curse, especially for those of us who wear glasses. The use of a long-peaked waterproof cap can often keep the worst of it from covering your spectacles (and there may be a fortune for anyone who invents a micro-chip windscreen-wiper for glasses).

Vaseline in the friction areas can be especially important on a wet day, and the nylon kit which can be so uncomfortable in hot conditions is more practical through its minimal absorbency, especially when the rain stops, as it dries off so quickly.

Wind

There are few more frustrating experiences if you want to run a particular time in a race than being caught in a vicious wind which forces you practically to run on the spot. I still remember my helpless annoyance when I competed in my first 10-miler, at Tonbridge in 1968, desperately keen to break the hour, and being brought almost to a standstill by the winds at one point. There was simply no-one who could be handily blamed! In such circumstances there is little you can do, except try to relax into the wind, almost leaning on it, and try to avoid tensing up, which will restrict your running action.

On a circuit course, you will naturally also benefit from the wind following you at some point (and at Tonbridge, which has two 5-mile laps, I eased the frustration when I was blown up a longish climb, and finished in 57.26). But they do not exactly balance out. When you run into a wind you are increasing the velocity at which it hits you. When you run *with* the wind, you are reducing the amount it helps you, although there is a bonus in as much as the wind allows your muscles to relax more, and work with greater efficiency.

On an A-to-B course, though, a headwind can be a disaster. It can also be a fickle friend, as runners in New Orleans know well. At the 1979 Mardi Gras Marathon there, a local police strike caused a last-minute change of course to include a 24-mile long, flat, straight causeway over Lake Pontchartrain, which provided a strong following breeze. The winner, John Dimick of the USA, improved his best time by over 4 minutes to 2 hours 11 minutes 53 seconds, while the women's winner, Gayle Olinek, improved hers by a full quarter of an hour to a Commonwealth 'record' of 2 hours 38 minutes 12 seconds.

The organizers subsequently realized that their makeshift course could actually attract a lot of runners wanting such favourable conditions for setting a personal best time, so they adopted it as their normal route. In 1980, Ron Tabb of the US duly set a personal best, winning in 2 hours 11 minutes and 1 second, with Olinek improving the women's course record of 2 hours 35 minutes 39 seconds. Its fame spread.

By 1981 there were no less than 2000 starters on the white concrete causeway, all confidently expecting super-fast, wind-assisted times. Alas for them, the gusts changed direction and blew at 35 m.p.h. into their faces all the way, and Doug Kurtis (who had run 2:14.16 the previous year) staggered home to win in 2:33.59, while the women's winner did just under 3:10. 'It felt like I was running uphill the whole way,' said Kurtis, and while the miserable leaders had battled the wind up front, one even threatened to throw another over the edge of the causeway if he stepped on his heels again. Now that *is* frustration.

13

FOOD FOR THOUGHT

Many thousands of words have been written in recent years about the dietary needs of the athlete, while the level of concern among athletes themselves ranges from the youngster who, on race days anyway, seems to exist on a combination of crisps, lemonade and Mars bars, to the more cautious international who arrives at the airport with small packets of different substances, all carefully weighed and measured, to sustain him through the following days in case the local diet is unsuitable.

You can read in various publications about the absolutely irreplaceable need for meat in the diet, and an impassioned defence of the vegetarian diet for runners. One nutritionist will insist that you keep your body stoked up for activity at all times; another will recite the apparently revolutionary endurance achievements by long distance runners who fasted for 24 hours beforehand.

Eventually your head is spinning with the conflicting lists of Dos and Don'ts, as you are urged to eat haricot beans by the sackful, or avoid them like the plague. The runner may be left even more confused, trying to sort the wheat from the chaff ('Eat chaff in great quantities to increase your leg speed . . .'!).

The best answer I have heard to questions about whether long distance runners need special diets probably came from Brendan Foster. 'I eat exactly the same as my wife,' he said, 'only more of it.'

It has been estimated that an adult distance runner may burn up in excess of 4000 calories a day during hard training and, if he is fit and at his best racing weight, he will not want to lose any more weight. Consequently, he will eat sufficient food to provide the fuel, and a table of sample calorific values appears on page 190, but in the main his eating habits will be a response to the messages from his body.

Obviously, it would be undesirable, as well as excessively boring, to supply all the calories from one type of food, and the aim should be for a varied diet which ensures a good intake of proteins (milk, meat, cheese etc.), vitamins, minerals and carbohydrates. Such a mixed diet will help to maintain health, assist recovery, repair damaged tissues and, in the case of younger athletes, ensure natural growth. As long as a runner is eating well and regularly, dietary problems should be at a minimum.

But one problem which sometimes affects distance runners, particularly females, is iron deficiency anaemia. This often turns out to be the cause of an otherwise unexplainable drop in form of a runner who has been training hard and should be racing well. The symptoms, in addition to poor form, are a constant tiredness even after resting, headaches, occasional giddiness (especially when standing up suddenly) and general lethargy.

This form of anaemia is caused by a lack of iron, which helps transport the oxygen around the blood, and in many cases it can be cured by a course of iron tablets within a couple of weeks of diagnosis. In more serious cases, injections of iron may be needed. Your family doctor can perform a simple blood test to confirm whether or not you are anaemic and, if you are, prescribe the tablets.

The best precaution, of course, is simply to ensure that your diet includes plenty of iron-rich foods, like corned beef, dates and liver. In the case of female runners, anaemia may be caused or aggravated by blood loss during the menstrual periods, and during that time it may be wise to take an iron supplement if your doctor recommends it.

Athletes living on their own, or working or studying away from home, should take a special look at their weekly diet pattern. Does it consist of a wide variety of foods including fresh fruit and vegetables, or is it a constant succession of supermarket tins and fish and chips? One runner was an unwitting victim of anaemia for a long time when first going to university and living in a flat away from home for the first time. He trained hard, but existed on the simplest, most convenient foods to prepare, whose value he judged not nutritionally but simply on the amount of washing up they created, and subsequently his form at the time dropped off badly. Once diagnosed, though, the problem was soon corrected with iron tablets, and he began to pay more careful attention to his diet.

Some runners, particularly girls, are actually motivated chiefly by the weight control effects of running, and even experienced runners may sometimes be faced with having to shed a few surplus pounds after several weeks of injury, or a deliberate lay-off at the end of the season. Such runners tend to go on eating at the same rate during their non-active period as when they are training hard, but as they are not burning up the same amount of calories a surplus develops and is stored in the body as fat. In men this is usually seen on the stomach and around the waist (the 'spare tyre'), while girls tend to put it on around their hips and bottom.

The surplus soon disappears once a reasonable volume of training is undertaken again, and the key to losing weight is simply to ensure that the expenditure of calories (through exercise) is greater each day than the intake. But not by too much, because crash diets can make you feel weak or faint.

If you think a few extra pounds do not matter, just imagine carrying that weight as a bag of potatoes when you run. A distance runner wants the minimum percentage of fat in his body to allow it to work with maximum efficiency and excess weight means having to work harder for the same results.

Joggers are sometimes disappointed if they do not lose at least 2 stone in their first week but in fact they may lose very little weight, if any, at first. But they are burning up calories, lowering the level of fats in their blood, strengthening the cardiovascular system, and in general preparing the body to be able to do the work which will eventually lead to weight loss, as long as they also restrict their intake of calories.

Like a swan crossing a lake, all the action is below the surface at that stage, but they are getting there nonetheless. The motivation could be the knowledge that the fit distance runner, who trains hard six days a week, can usually afford to eat what he or she likes without putting on weight, and that in itself must be a tempting target for those people who cannot pass a biscuit tin without finding their hand inside it.

The question of how much to eat before a race, and when, is always a matter of personal preference, but generally it should be something light, easily digestible, and consumed no less than 3 hours before the race. Because the digestive process is a long one, the food you eat the day before will have more bearing on your performance than that eaten on the day itself. You have to satisfy your natural hunger without lining up for the race with a stomach full of undigested food.

Soccer teams may have steak for lunch before a match, but it will help them through the next game, not this one. There is no time for the body to make use of it. One of the boys I used to coach suffered from a mysterious stitch in some of his most important races. He was a good runner, a county champion at cross country, but he sometimes almost had to come to a halt because of mid-race stitch. Then I discovered that his father had been surreptitiously giving him a Mars bar to eat just before races 'for extra energy'!

Of course, it had just the opposite effect, because when food arrives in the stomach the body sends extra blood to help the digestive process. If you then start taking vigorous exercise as well, with the muscles also calling urgently for extra blood, the body simply cannot cope efficiently with the demands of both.

Trying to run a race with a stomach full of food is uncomfortable anyway, and if a race is important enough you may be too nervous to eat anything for some hours before. Nervousness is a natural feeling before any race, often characterized by frequent yawning (an involuntary method of dragging in extra oxygen), and an increased number of visits to the toilet beforehand. The body is merely 'clearing the decks for action' and to empty the bowels and bladder should be a part of every runner's pre-training or pre-racing routine, particularly when a long distance is involved. Races on cold days are notorious for the higher percentage of runners disappearing into nearby bushes, which may be free but costs a lot of ground in the race, and is often avoidable.

Anorexia Nervosa

Although the so-called slimmer's disease of anorexia nervosa has been identified for more than a century, a definite link with runners and running has only recently been highlighted.

The compulsive desire to lose weight, which mainly, but not exclusively, affects adolescent females becomes an obsession which takes them well below their natural weight and can, in extreme cases become life-threatening and even fatal.

It is usually triggered psychologically, but in the case of some female endurance runners starts with the linking of an initial weight loss with better racing performances. Oxygen uptake can be improved to some extent by the shedding of surplus pounds, but there is no reliable indicator as to when the optimum weight has been reached. A 10-stone female runner who slims down to 8 stone will almost certainly notice an upturn in performance. But if she continues losing weight down to, say, 6 stone, she will become weaker and slower and injuries will take longer to heal. At that point the obsession may be so strong that the very thought of putting on weight seems alien.

The success of ultra-thin female distance runners at international level often leads to females trying to emulate their shape and weight, without giving sufficient regard to the fact that some runners are by nature thin. Indeed, those who are naturally thin but healthy do have an advantage in endurance events in the same way that long–legged athletes have an advantage in high jumping. The physiological problems may continue if the athlete's body fat percentage drops below acceptable levels and her periods cease (amenorrhoea) which can lead in turn to the possibility of adolescent osteoporosis or loss of bone density.

In addition to runners already in the sport who develop anorexia or other eating disorders, such as bulimia nervosa, there is an apparently increasing number of already anorectic females coming into running at modest levels, often non–competitively. This may be because they see distance running as a further means of losing weight, of directing the hyperactivity which is a symptom of anorexia and above all as a camouflage for their continuing weight loss in a sport where female slimness is frequently applauded. Indeed, coaches, parents and close friends of anorectic runners are often completely unaware of the existence of the problem. The anorectic may be ingenious and even devious in finding reasons for not eating in public situations or pretending to do so, and then hiding uneaten food in their pockets and sleeves for later disposal.

Help is needed to assist anorectics to unravel the causes of their problem and to understand the physical harm it may be doing them. Sometimes counselling by a trusted friend and simply talking it through can turn the tide. A surprising number of leading female international runners have suffered from eating disorders at some stage during their career and have successfully overcome them.

Happily, there have also been cases where anorectic youngsters of both sexes, who took up running simply as a means of becoming even thinner, found that the pleasure of running actually helped release the tensions and unhappiness which caused their condition in the first place. They were subsequently able to normalise their eating habits and return to a healthy weight while also enjoying the sport.

Calorie values

The table on page 190, which gives approximate calorie values for some everyday foods, is only a guide. Obviously, varying brands and sizes will make a difference, but it can be seen which foods provide many calories and which provide very few. Many of the foods also supply, in varying quantities, vital proteins, minerals and vitamins too, of course.

Food	Calories
Apple	40–50 per 4 oz apple
Bacon	100 for grilled back rasher (1 oz)
Baked beans	25 per oz
Beer (lager)	100 per half pint
Banana	50 for 4 oz banana
Beef	70 per oz cooked lean meat
Beefburger	140–180 each
Biscuits	100 for 2 small plain or 1 small sweet
Bread	70 per oz, white or brown
Brussels sprouts	negligible
Cereals	80–100 per oz
Buns	170 per 2 oz bun
Butter	226 per oz
Cake	100–150 per oz, without icing or filling
Carrots	6 per oz
Cauliflower	negligible when raw
Celery	negligible
Cheese	120 per oz
Chicken	50–60 per oz cooked
Chips	68 per oz
Chocolate	130–150 per oz
Cider	110 per half pint
Coca-Cola	130 per half pint
Cod	40 per oz fried
Coffee	negligible
Corned beef	60 per oz lean
Cress	negligible
Crisps	100 per small packet
Cucumber	negligible
Dates	70 per oz
Doughnut	200 per 2 oz doughnut
Dumplings	120 per oz
Eggs	80–90 per oz poached or boiled; 160 scrambled
Fish	25–30 per oz if steamed, grilled or poached; frying may double the amount
Fruit juice	40–50 per small glass unsweetened (grapefruit and tomato juice – negligible)
Glucose	120 per oz
Grapefruit	without sugar, negligible
Ham	100 per 1½ oz lean
Honey	80 per oz
Ice cream	100 per 2 oz
Ice lolly	50–60 per lolly
Kit-kat	146 per oz
Liver	35 per oz, grilled, steamed or casseroled
Luncheon meat	95 per oz
Meat	approx. 100 per oz, depending on leanness
Milk	19 per fluid oz

Mineral water	none
Nuts	from 100–180 per oz, apart from chestnuts (40 per oz)
Onions, fried	100 per oz. Negligible otherwise
Orange squash	25 per fluid oz
Puff pastry	120 per oz
Peaches	35–40 per fresh peach
Peanuts	170 per oz
Peanut butter	184 per oz
Peas	14 per oz, fresh or frozen
Pork	90 per oz roasted
Potatoes	20 per oz boiled
Raisins	70 per oz
Rhubarb	without sugar, negligible
Sardines	84 per oz
Sausages	approx. 100 per oz raw
Sausage rolls	112 per oz
Scones	105 per oz
Steak	86 per oz grilled
Strawberries	7 per oz
Syrup	70 per oz
Toast	70 per oz
Trifle	43 per oz
Water	none
Yoghurt	12 per oz plain. 130–200 per carton, fruit
Yorkshire pudding	63 per oz

14

INJURIES

(and other pains)

Any activity which pushes the body to the limit, as distance running does, is bound to produce a breakdown of some sort from time to time. Injury is the runner's nightmare, because it restricts him or her from doing the one thing they want to do: run. Occasionally, even seeking medical advice can produce a somewhat unsympathetic response, 'You run 100 miles a week and you say your leg hurts? Well, stop running 100 miles a week and the pain will probably go away. Next, please.'! However, in fairness to the medical profession, the problems of the sportsman are being recognized more widely and there now exist a number of sports clinics around the country which specialize in treating athletes and their particular ailments.

In the distance runner's case these centre mainly around the lower leg – the knee, shin, Achilles tendon, ankle and foot – and tend to be injuries caused by over-use.

There are now generally acknowledged to be three types of sporting injuries. The *direct* injury, such as a fracture or concussion, which results from some form of physical contact, such as a hard tackle in soccer. The *indirect* injury, which is caused by violent forces not involving physical contact, such as sprains and muscle tears, perhaps caused by treading on a stone or down a hole. And there is the *over-use* injury, which is brought about by excessive repetitive movements in training and competition.

The direct injury is not seen in distance running at all, unless we count road accidents or the very rare collision in a track race which results in a fall; limbs have been broken that way. The indirect injury is more common and equally unpredictable. But the vast majority of running injuries stem from over-use, and it is not hard to understand why. Even a runner covering only 20–30 miles a week would still be taking well over 2 million strides a years, and the runner reaching 100 miles a week would take around 9 million strides a year, on top of other everyday activities, with every step involving some thirty different muscles working together to produce the movement.

Much of that running will probably take place on hard surfaces, like roads, and on every one of the strides a great amount of force bears down on the legs. This has been estimated as being up to three or four times the runner's bodyweight – say 500 pounds or more in a 10-stone runner. Normally the body is able to absorb this huge pressure, but only if everything is in balance. If undue stress is placed on one part of the leg for whatever reason – a blister on one foot, or a worn-down running shoe – then the abnormal force, together with the repetition of the action over a long period, can cause injury.

Sheer repetition in itself, without sufficient recovery in between, can also produce the same over-use symptoms. In the chapter on training methods, the essential formula of hard work plus rest equals success was referred to. In direct contrast, hard work plus insufficient rest can equal injury.

Whenever athletes meet at races they usually spend a good deal of time discussing their injuries with other runners, comparing notes and symptoms. To have had a stress fracture of a metatarsal or chondromalacia patellae is almost like a battle decoration, while someone who has actually had an operation on their Achilles tendon has really reached the heights, especially if they had to go to Sweden for it!

But, while one can joke about it afterwards, there are few more miserable, irritable creatures than the injured athlete. They are like caged tigers with withdrawal symptoms, brimming with all that excess energy and the frustration of not being able to use it for running. But I am convinced from my own experience that the worst part of being injured is not the pain of the injury, nor the frustration of not being able to train or race, nor even the despair of feeling that you are losing fitness with every day that passes. Instead, it is the absolute uncertainty of not knowing *how long* the injury is going to last. A few days or all season? You cannot plan training, racing or even social activities with confidence when all the time you are worrying about the pain in your leg. At such times, runners can be very introspective.

If someone could only look into a crystal ball and say categorically,

'You are not going to be able to run for four days, and then it will improve and you will be able to start training again' or 'The problem will need long term treatment, so you can safely take your holidays now without worrying about missing the Digglesbury 10km road race – you're going to miss it anyway', then the injury would be so much more bearable.

But running injuries are awkward things which can sometimes come on suddenly and disappear just as quickly for no apparent reason. Or they may linger with you, despite every known treatment, for months. You end up, while at work during the day or lying in bed at night, constantly stretching and prodding the injury, testing it to see whether the ailment has upped and left within the last few minutes. It rarely has, and instead, just sends back extra sharp mocking pains.

Even the fittest sportsman in the world walks a very narrow tightrope between being a finely tuned, magnificent physical specimen, and a limping wreck. And whatever your standard as a long distance runner you will not be able to escape without, at the very minimum, the odd ache and pain brought about simply by the constant repetition of the running action on hard, unremitting surfaces like roads.

'Most distance runners will have injury problems, but these are of a limited variety and unspectacular from a medical point of view,' says Dr Ian Adams, Medical Adviser to the British Marathon Runners Club, sounding almost disappointed. 'Stopping running will cure these injuries, which are generally caused by minor abnormalities which are of no significance in the general population, so do not be surprised if the doctor does not welcome you with open arms, and advises rest.

'The great majority of injuries will occur through breaking simple rules of training. Just as many of us, in spite of prodigious training, could not be top-class sprinters, there are others with structural faults which will never withstand 100 miles per week for month after month. We are all different heights and weights, we all have different shaped knees and feet, some made for high mileage whilst others are made for limited mileage. There are injuries which can be directly treated, there are others which can be indirectly treated, and there are some which are untreatable in the context of running 100 miles per week.'

Sooner or later, though, most injuries heal and then you immediately have to curb your own enthusiasm to rush out and run 20 miles a day to make up for lost time. Instead, you just have to face the fact that to be sidelined through injury will inevitably have cost you some degree of fitness, and the longer you have been unable to train, the more fitness you will have lost. A loss of two or three days will probably make little difference, and may even do you good if you are one of those runners who is normally loth to rest (which is why you may be injured in the first place; your body was trying to tell you something). But after three days of inactivity you will start to lose a little condition, so when you start training again you must do so gradually and make due allowance for your time off. Training is like trying to run up a down escalator. If you work hard, you will make progress, but if you have to stop you will be gently taken down again. So don't expect to pick it up exactly where you left off before the injury. And don't push the training beyond a point where the injury starts to hurt again. Stop short, for nature has its own way of letting you know when enough is enough – through pain.

Catching an injury early is half the battle, so take note of your body if it starts to hurt. Try to diagnose what the problem is, and how it could have been caused. Have you made any changes in your training routine recently? Are you suddenly running up hills a lot, or in spikes for the first time this year? Have you suddenly increased your mileage by a large percentage? If the answer is no, then look at your running shoes. Are they worn down at the heels, making you run awkwardly and stretching the Achilles tendons too much? Is the sole of one shoe worn more than the other? If so, you are running out of balance, but why? Do you run on a road with a camber, for instance?

If there is no apparent cause, consider the over-use possibility. Have you been giving yourself enough rest? If not, take it a little easier or even stop training for a couple of days. A few days off now are preferable to several months off later.

Although you can often work out for yourself why a particular injury has been caused, prevention is obviously far better than cure, and the use of stretching and strengthening exercises before a run, as described on page 29, will lessen your chance of injury. When increasing the total weekly training mileage, any step up of more than 10 per cent per week often invites trouble, while putting foam rubber padding in the shoe will help to reduce jarring effects for the high mileage road runner.

Eventually, though, despite everything, you may find yourself on the injury list, and the following section outlines some of the most prevalent injuries and ailments among distance runners, their cause and treatment. It is meant only as a self-help guide, but in some situations it may be enough. With more severe cases, and some other injuries, nothing can replace on-the-spot medical expertise.

Achilles tendon injuries

The Achilles tendon, or heel cord, connects the calf muscle and the heel bone, and is one of the commonest areas of injury among distance runners. The severity may range from the inflammation known as tendinitis to complete rupture, although the latter is rare in distance running, involving as it does a sudden load being thrust upon the tendon, which is far more likely to occur in sprinting or jumping events.

The usual tendinitis, consisting of a thickening of the actual body of the tendon, is very painful and tender when pinched, but nearly always clears up of its own accord eventually after a modification of training to a bearable amount. This form of tendinitis is quite separate from the condition in which pain is felt at the insertion of the tendon into the heel bone. In this case, there is no swelling of the tendon itself, little or none at the site of the pain, and often it does not clear up on its own, perhaps eventually needing an operation.

The cause of the pain is usually traceable either to a sudden change in training routine, whether it be to hill running or sand-dune running (involving extra stretching of the tendon), or to putting on spikes after a winter spent mainly in heavy training flats, or to an increase in interval work, with recovery jogs in spiked shoes with little heel support. Other causes include running in road shoes with worn-down heels, and general overload of training.

One key to prevention is to graduate any change. In hill running, for example, the tendon has to stretch considerably more than it does on the flat to touch the ground even briefly. To run a long session of hills with no similar type of work in recent months is to invite Achilles problems, which are usually discovered not at the time but when the athlete gets out of bed next day and tries to walk; pains above the back of each ankle will tell him that he has overdone it.

A high mileage during winter months will probably have been accomplished in training shoes with a substantial heel to reduce jarring. But the tendon may shorten during that time, as its range of movement is curtailed, and a sudden switch to heavy track work in the spring could produce severe tendinitis if the spikes initially worn on the track did not have a similarly built-up heel.

Many spiked shoes have very little support under the heel, which may help to keep the shoe light in weight, but means that the tendon is repeatedly stretched beyond the limits to which it has become used in road shoes. In this respect, the 'recovery jogs' in between hard runs on the track may be worse than the runs themselves. In running fast, the athlete gets on to his toes more. When he jogs, his heel lands first, again overstretching the tendon and placing a great pressure on it. Thus, more and more athletes are now using 'interval shoes', which have built-up heels like road shoes, but spikes in the sole.

A similar cause, not immediately related to sport, is our everyday shoes – a particular problem with female runners. During the day most people wear shoes with some sort of built-up heel, and in the case of women it may be several inches of heel. The tendon duly adapts to the very limited range of movement required of it during walking. To go out running then in shoes with much less heel means that the tendon is suddenly stretched beyond its 'normal' limit again.

So, in many cases, prevention is possible by removal or avoidance of the cause. Once the cause has been attended to, the pain should disappear, although the volume of training should be reduced until it does. Other activities, like cycling and swimming, can be added or substituted as a means of keeping the cardiovascular system exercised and reducing the amount of conditioning lost through the lesser training. In severe cases, where all other treatment has failed, surgery may be necessary.

Ankle injuries

Ankle injuries tend to be more prevalent in other athletics events, but some distance runners do suffer from them, usually as a result of an outside element, such as tripping over a kerb or a rut. A sprain (a tear or rupture of ligaments) of varying seriousness may result, and the American podiatrist Dr Steven Subotnick in his book *The Running Foot Doctor* divided them into four degrees, described below.

The first-degree sprain is just tender, with little damage done and, after application of ice to the affected area, the ankle might be bandaged. If it is stable, the athlete can resume training almost immediately, as the sprain will clear up in two or three days.

A second-degree sprain involves more damage to the ligaments and causes the runner to limp slightly, but it responds well to application of ice and if it is well bandaged it may be no more serious than a first degree sprain.

The third-degree sprain is a more serious one, which needs careful examination to rule out the possibility of any bone fracture or complete rupture of ligaments. It is impossible to run and difficult to walk, and the ankle needs to be elevated when possible, and treated with ice. Crutches may be needed until the athlete can walk without pain, and even light training must be approached cautiously after the injury appears to have healed.

The most severe sprain, the fourth degree on Subotnick's list, is the one in which ligaments are completely ruptured. Examination is made more difficult 20 minutes after it has happened because swelling takes place and makes it difficult to estimate the damage. Sometimes a plaster cast is needed for 4–6 weeks, and occasionally surgery is performed after the injury has been sustained to repair the ruptured ligaments.

The more severe ankle sprains are, fortunately, rare among distance runners, but often badly worn shoes (the culprit for a whole range of injuries) are the prime factor in ankle injuries. If the runner's foot is continually thrown on to the outside throughout a series of training runs in old shoes, the tendons of the outer ankle will become strained.

Sometimes the ankle is the victim of an imbalance injury, in which the runner throws more weight on to one leg than the other, and the imbalance causes a strain in one ankle only. However, in subconsciously trying to protect that ankle and get back into balance, the runner may over-compensate and end up injuring the knee on the opposite leg, which has to absorb most of the redistributed weight.

Backache

Backache is by no means an ailment exclusive to the elderly. A high percentage of the adult population suffers from some form of intermittent back pain, and the distance runner is no exception. It can be caused by a high intensity of training on the road, with the consequent absorption of a large amount of shock in the small of the back. A switch to softer surfaces, and increased padding in the shoes, or at least a switch to shoes with a more substantial shock-absorbing heel, should alleviate the problem, together with regular mobility exercises. Strong abdominal muscles are also helpful in prevention of back ailments, and exercises like sit-ups and leg raising when lying on the ground can help develop these.

Black toenails

Black toenails are another occupational hazard of long-distance running, and are caused by shoes which do not fit properly, so that the toe is jammed hard against the roof of the shoe on every step. The toe starts to bleed under the nail, and the blood causes a painful build-up of pressure.

Although the nail may then die, to be slowly replaced by a new growth some weeks later, it is meanwhile fairly tender. One recommended method of alleviating the pain is to straighten out a paper clip, heat one end strongly in a flame, and then put the point of the clip on the centre of the nail, which has a gelatin-like consistency, and will melt. Make a small hole in the nail with this, then apply downward pressure to both sides of the nail and the fluid will shoot through the hole created by the hot paper clip. Mop up, clean the area with antiseptic, and cover it with plaster. The nail may remain tender for some days afterwards, and you should avoid running in the shoes which caused the problem.

To prevent it happening again, make two small slits (or even a hole) in the shoe over the point at which the nail was rubbing in the first place to eliminate the pressure. If the shoes are too narrow anyway, consider replacing them, because the chances are that another nail will be similarly affected next time.

Blisters

Every distance runner gets a blister at some time, and the most common causes are shoes that fit badly, or ones that have inner seams which rub against the foot or have not been properly broken in. Beginners and runners stepping up their training mileage or returning from a lay-off are the most likely sufferers, as their skin is softer than on a hard-training runner's foot, but no one is immune. Friction causes the blister, as the outer layer of skin (epidermis) separates from the layer below it (dermis) and the body sends a watery component of the blood, called serum, to fill the space in between and to provide a cushion against the friction.

Sometimes, if the damage is more serious, the blister will fill with blood, and this type should be treated very carefully as infection is a danger if the skin is broken, even minutely.

An ordinary clear blister, however, can be drained quite simply, once the skin has been sterilized with meths, using a needle which has been sterilized (by heating it red-hot in a flame and allowing it to cool) and piercing the outer skin of the blister. This is a virtually painless operation, and you can then squeeze out the clear fluid and mop it up with cotton wool. The operation may need to be repeated two or three times to drain all the fluid, then the area should be cleaned again with a disinfectant and covered with Elastoplast or similar protection for several days. Leave the outer skin in place, as this helps the healing process, and studies by US army doctors showed that in 90 per cent of the cases of drained blisters they examined, the outer skin re-attached within four days.

Draining simple blisters not only reduces pain, it also allows you to continue training. To carry on running with blisters is to risk a sub-conscious, or even conscious, alteration of the running action, perhaps favouring the affected foot and causing a compensatory muscle injury in the leg or foot.

Prevention of blisters is, of course, preferable. Shoes that are too tight or too big are always going to present problems, so care must be taken when buying shoes to ensure they are comfortable.

In these days of nylon uppers, breaking in shoes is much less of a task than it used to be with leather uppers, but nevertheless wearing new shoes around the house for a few days will help to adapt them to your feet.

Running socks should be clean and comfortable. Sweaty socks dry hard and create folds and crinkles which can cause blisters rather than protect your feet against them. Dusting the feet liberally with talcum powder, sprinkling it inside your socks and shoes, will also help to absorb sweat, for wet feet are particularly prone to blisters; soldiers who have marched long distances in wet boots, or hikers, can confirm this. Use of Vaseline over the toes or any other area liable to blistering is a good precaution as it reduces friction almost to a minimum.

Elastoplast, or gauze covered with sticking plaster, can help protect any spots liable to blistering if firmly applied before a race or long training run. If you have consistent problems with a particular pair of shoes, throw them away, and if one pair of shoes which are normally comfortable causes a blister problem (perhaps through being wet) don't wear them again until the blisters have cleared.

Cramp

Cramp is a sudden and sustained spasm of a muscle, and can also be very painful, not to mention unexpected. Medical experts say that it has not yet been fully explained, but an imbalance of electrolyte and fluid (often caused by excessive sweating) is certainly one cause. It can affect the legs during the closing stages of a marathon, and the immediate treatment is to stretch the affected muscle to halt the spasm, stop or walk, and gently massage the area before gingerly starting to jog again.

The Olympic runner Tony Simmons was particularly prone to cramp in marathons, and in the last mile of a televised marathon was almost forced out of the race while well in the lead when a spectator waved to a TV camera, knocking into Simmons and causing both of his legs to seize up temporarily. Fortunately, he got going again and won the race.

The prolonged, unchanging use of a certain muscle group can also increase the likelihood of cramp, and ironically a marathon course with one or two hills in the latter stages, where a slightly different running action is used to tackle the incline, may be less likely to cause cramp than a totally flat, unremitting course with no such contrasts.

Even after the race or a long training session has been survived unscathed, a slight overstretch in bed at night has awakened many a runner from a pleasant dream with a searing leg cramp, causing them to roll around the floor in search of a suitable position for relief (much to the surprise of their spouse). Occasionally, trying to relieve one leg sets off a cramp in the other, and so on. It is not so funny at the time for the affected runner, but it can be quite a spectacle for bystanders.

For the beginner, muscle groups used in unfamiliar style to excess are also liable to cramp. As an example, I was once team-managing a group of British runners at a French marathon, where the organizers had lent me a bicycle to enable me to follow the race more closely. I hadn't ridden a bike for years, and I had to pedal it quite fast to cut across sections of the course, especially after getting lost on unfamiliar roads.

That night the reception for the competitors was rudely interrupted by me jumping up from our table with sudden cramp spasms in the hamstrings and quadriceps from all that cycle riding. Explanatory word went round to the other tables: the runners are all okay, but the team manager has got cramp.

Runner's knee

Runner's knee, or *chondromalacia patellae*, is still something of a mystery in medical circles, but knee problems figure very highly on any list of the distance runner's All Time Most Popular Injuries. Chondromalacia is a softening of the cartilage of the undersurface of the kneecap (patella), which normally moves smoothly over the end of the thigh bone (femur). This softening may be caused by excessive rotation of the knee as the foot hits the ground, possibly due to the athlete being slightly knock-kneed, bow-legged or having a foot imbalance. One American doctor, who is also a runner, suffered from chondromalacia in his left knee and found that, when he ran on the right-hand side of the road, where the camber forced him to run on the inside of his left foot, the pain vanished. From this experience, he and a number of his runner patients used specially designed arch-supports in their shoes, which had a high success rate in clearing up the problem.

The knee is the shock absorber of the body, and the Clapham Junction of the leg, with bones, muscles, tendons and ligaments being anchored at this joint. Torn cartilage and strained ligaments are other causes of knee pain and, if it is persistent, medical help should be sought.

Sciatica

Pain down the back of the leg, particularly in the buttock or hamstring region, is often misdiagnosed as muscular in origin. It may well be referred pain, resembling a dull ache and numbness like toothache, emanating from the sciatic nerve. This condition, quite common among distance runners, is known as sciatica.

The sciatic nerve emerges from the spinal cord between the lumbar vertebrae in the lower back, and travels down the full length of the rear of the leg. Thus, referred pain could extend right down the leg, even though it is more usually felt higher up.

The actual cause of the inflammation will normally be in the lower back itself, which may have absorbed an enormous amount of the shock generated by every footfall in training runs. This may lead to a slightly misplaced or slipped disc, where one of the connective tissue rings separating the row of bony vertebrae which form the spine may have become marginally dislodged and protrude outwards, pressing on the sciatic nerve. In that case, specific medical advice is necessary and an osteopath or chiropractor may prove to be particularly effective.

Sometimes the inflammation may be caused simply by a compression of the lower vertebrae through too much shock being absorbed in the back. In this case a form of gravity inversion treatment, where the sufferer is placed upside down, relieving the stress on the lower back in the process, has sometimes proved beneficial. So has a relaxing massage of the lower back muscles in the lumbar region.

As a precaution against recurrence and also to help alleviate the problem itself a switch to training shoes with greater shock absorption qualities and the selection of softer training surfaces can help.

Shin soreness

Shin soreness, or shin splints, is suffered by some runners during or after prolonged exercise, and consists of a sharp pain and tightness on the outside of the shin. The problem arises because the anterior tibial (shin) muscles, which also support the arch mechanism of the foot, have little room to expand, as they do during sustained exercise. This causes a build-up of pressure within the restraining sheath, which restricts proper circulation of the blood.

Heavy mileage on the road or other hard surfaces, and even inflexible shoes, have been cited as further contributory factors; if a shoe has a hard sole, it does not bend when the foot strikes the ground and an unusually large amount of shock is then absorbed by the shin muscles.

Inflexibility of the ankles and an imbalance of strength between the shin and calf muscles are other possibilities which have been suggested as causes in a somewhat controversial area. In 1970 a *Sunday Times* investigation into the specific shin soreness experienced among race walkers, conducted at the Royal Free Medical School in London, blamed a condition called ischaemia (a lack of oxygen) in the shin muscle, but this appeared to be caused mainly by the strict rules governing the race walking action.

Treatment of shin soreness includes a switch to running on softer surfaces while it persists and the application of ice or cold packs to the muscles on the outside of the shins two or three times a day, for 5–10 minutes at a time. Wearing different training shoes for each session, rotating several pairs to alter foot balance, helps, and any adjustment of the running action so that less strain is placed upon the anterior tibial muscles, by ensuring that the feet do not turn significantly outwards, should reduce the aggravation.

Attention must be paid to the shoes and condition of the feet, for any shoe wear or feet problems, like corns or calluses, can result in a faulty running action which places extra strain on the shin muscles. And, although it may be tempting to bind the legs in an effort to reduce pain, this could actually make the problem worse, and anything which grips tightly around the lower leg, like knee-length socks, should be avoided. If all else fails, rest may be the only answer. To continue to run bravely on despite shin soreness could even produce a stress fracture, and indeed great care must be taken not to confuse the two.

Stress fractures

The stress fracture is another common injury among distance runners, particularly those churning out a large amount of mileage on the road, and usually occurs either in the metatarsal bones in the foot or the tibia or fibula of the lower leg. It is not quite as dramatic as it sounds, for there is no sudden and apparent snap of a bone cracking and usually the runner has no idea that a stress fracture has occurred until they notice a recurrent sharp pain in the foot or lower leg. The latter may at first seem to be shin soreness, sometimes accompanied by local swelling and tenderness. In fact, it is a classic case of an over-use injury, where repetitive stresses across a long bone have produced a minute crack which does not always show up on X-rays.

Obviously, complete rest would allow the bone to mend, but runners hate having to stop completely unless it is unavoidable, and a carefully thought-out exercise programme will allow some activity to continue while still enabling the bone to mend. The essential thing is to cut down immediately on heavy mileage, avoid all competition and to keep off roads and other hard surfaces during this period. Steady running or jogging on soft grass is often possible, as long as it is not carried to extremes, and the measure of how much actual running can be undertaken will be made by signs coming from the injured area itself.

Other aerobic exercises, like swimming and cycling, will help to keep the cardiovascular system ticking over without putting any pressure on to the affected area, and thus help to minimize the inevitable slight loss in running condition while the bone heals.

A period of three to six weeks is usually needed to complete this process, but much will depend on the severity of the fracture and how quickly it was diagnosed; to have continued to train hard on a stress fracture will obviously have aggravated it, perhaps even to the point where complete immobilization and a plaster cast are required. Once the healing process is complete, the return to full training should be gradual, and accomplished in well-padded shoes with particular avoidance of too much road work in the early days.

Stitch

The unpredictable onset of 'stitch' can affect anyone from the beginner to the Olympic athlete, and no one has yet come up with an indisputable theory about the cause or, more important, a quick cure. Stitch is generally accepted as being that sharp pain in the side, or sometimes in the shoulder, during a run, and in its most widely accepted sense it is probably caused by a spasm of the diaphragm. This often gives the runner great difficulty in breathing deeply and almost inevitably leads to a slowing of pace, voluntarily or not. W.G. George, the world record holder for the mile from 1880, wrote on the subject of stitch in his book *Training for Athletics and Kindred Sports*, published in 1902:

'Never stop when this distressing trouble overtakes you. Slow up, even walk, but *never* stop. Immediately it becomes less painful, increase pace, and keep running until it is quite gone. It is probable that the next time the trouble attacks you, it will be less severe, and if the suggested remedy is persisted in, stitch will soon be a thing of the past.'

Which was a roundabout way of saying that he had no solution to offer, and now, nearly eighty years later, we are still little the wiser. But what causes the spasm in the first place? Again, there is no hard and fast answer. Running straight from emptying the bladder seems to cause stitch in some athletes; running *without* emptying the bladder causes it in others!

A poor physical condition is another possible reason, but then that does not apply to Olympic runners who have been struck by the pain. Running too soon after a meal, and thus asking your body to digest food and to perform a vigorous exercise efficiently and simultaneously sometimes produces the same effect, but no experienced athlete would do that anyway. It should, however, be remembered that nervousness or anxiety may slow down the digestive processes, and that where three hours may be sufficient to allow after eating before training, it may need four to reach the same digestive stage before a big race.

Certainly it is extremely frustrating to have to watch rivals in a race pull away from you simply because stitch is slowing you, and not the limitations of your muscles. My own preferred method of getting rid of it, reached merely through personal trial and error, is to run 'tall', lifting the body from the waist, and trying to stretch out any poor form in running style which may be caused through a slight loll to one side or the other. It usually works for me, but I can't guarantee what it will do for you.

Twang-Krukkk! A final word . . .

Impatience is probably the distance runner's worst enemy. Every day of inactivity is multiplied in their mind by X minutes or Y miles of lost running. But the body takes a fair old battering in the course of distance training: leg-jarring pounding, coupled with great fatigue, which almost inevitably, by its very nature, will result in some kind of physical breakdown sooner or later.

The runner is always searching for the magic formula which will allow him to take one more pace further forward than before, but without injury. Then one more, and one more, until – Twang-Krukkk!

When you reach the stage of Twang-Krukkk! your main objective suddenly switches from being able to run faster to simply being able to run again. It is always a frustrating time, when most runners suffer from training withdrawal symptoms and get irritable, introspective and unsociable. Unless it is to talk about their injury, of course. 'Good evening, your Majesty. Did you hear about my cracked metatarsal? Just hold my shoe a minute, and I'll show you. . . .'

Appendix 1 – Pace Chart

1 Mile Pace	5 Miles	10 km (6.2M)	15 km (9.3M)	10 Miles	20 km (12.4M)	half-marathon (13.1M)	15 Miles	25 km (15.5M)	30 km (18.6M)	20 Miles	40 km (24.8M)	Full Marathon
4.45	23:45	29:27	44:11	47:30	58:54	1:02:16	1:11:15	1:13:38	1:28:21	1:35:00	1:57:48	2:04:33
4.50	24:10			48:20			1:12:30			1:36:40		2:07:44
5.00	25:00	31:00	46:30	50:00	1:02:00	1:05:33	1:15:00	1:17:30	1:33:00	1:40:00	2:04:00	2:11:06
5.10	25:50			51:40			1:17:30			1:43:20		2:15:28
5.15	26:15	32:33	48:50	52:30	1:05:06	1:08:50	1:18:45	1:21:23	1:37:39	1:45:00	2:10:12	2:17:40
5.20	26:40			53:20			1:20:00			1:46:50		2:19:50
5.30	27:30	34:06	51:09	55:00	1:08:12	1:12:07	1:22:30	1:25:15	1:42:18	1:50:00	2:16:24	2:24:12
5.40	28:20			56:40			1:25:00			1:53:20		2:28:34
5.45	28:45	35:39	53.29	57:30	1:11:18	1:15:23	1:26:15	1:29:08	1:46:57	1:55:00	2:22:36	2:30:46
5.50	29:10			58:20			1:27:30			1:56:40		2:32:56
6.00	30:00	37:12	55:48	1:00:00	1:14:24	1:18:39	1:30:00	1:33:00	1:51:36	2:00:00	2:28:48	2:37:19
6.10	30:50			1:01:40			1:32:30			2:03:20		2:41:41
6.15	31:15	38:45	58:08	1:02:30	1:17:30	1:21:56	1:33:45	1:36:53	1:55:45	2:05:00	2:35:00	2:43:53
6.20	31:40			1:03:20			1:35:00			2:06:40		2:46:03
6.30	32:30	40:18	1:00:27	1:05:00	1:20:36	1:25:13	1:37:30	1:40:45	2:00:44	2:10:00	2:41:12	2:50:25
6.40	33.20			1:06:40			1:40:00			2:13:20		2:54:47
6.45	33:45	41:51	1:02:47	1:07:30	1:23:42	1:28:29	1:41:15	1:44:38	2:05:33	2:15:00	2:47:24	2:56:59
6.50	34:10			1:08:20			1:42:30			2:16:40		2:59:09
7.00	35:00	43:24	1:05:06	1:10:00	1:26:50	1:31:46	1:45:00	1:48:30	2:10:12	2:20:00	2:53:40	3:03:33
7.10	35:50			1:11:40			1:47:30			2:23:20		3:07:55
7.15	36:15	44:57	1:07:26	1:12:30	1:29:54	1:35:03	1:48:45	1:52:23	2:14:51	2:25:00	2:59:48	3:10:06
7.20	36:40			1:13:20			1:50:00			2:26:40		3:12:17
7.30	37:30	46:30	1:09:45	1:15:00	1:33:00	1:38:19	1:52:30	1:56:15	2:19:20	2:30:00	3:06:00	3:16:39
7.40	38:20			1:16:40			1:55:00			2:33:20		3:21:01
7.45	38:45	48:03	1:12:05	1:17:30	1:36:06	1:41:36	1:56:15	2:00:08	2:24:09	2:35:00	3:12:12	3:23:13
7.50	39:10			1:18:20			1:57:30			2:36:40		3:25:23
8.00	40:00	49:36	1:14:24	1:20:00	1:39:12	1:44:53	2:00:00	2:04:00	2:28:48	2:40:00	3:18:24	3:29:45
8.10	40:50			1:21:40			2:02:30			2:43:20		3:34:07
8.15	41:15	51:09	1:16:44	1:22:30	1:42:12	1:48:10	2:03:45	2:07:53	2:33:27	2:45:00	3:24:24	3:36:20
8.20	41:40			1:23:20			2:05:00			2:46:40		3:38:29
8.30	42:30	52:42	1:19:03	1:25:00	1:45:24	1:51:26	2:07:30	2:11:45	2:38:06	2:50:00	3:30:48	3:42:51
8.40	43:20			1:26:40			2:10:00			2:53:20		3:47:13
8.45	43:45	54:15	1:21:23	1:27:30	1:48:30	1:54:43	2:11:15	2:15:38	2:42:45	2:55:00	3:37:00	3:49:26
8.50	44:10			1:28:20			2:12:30			2:56:40		3:51:35
9.00	45:00	55:48	1:23:42	1:30:00	1:51:36	1:57:59	2:15:00	2:19:30	2:47:24	3:00:00	3:43:12	3:56:00
9.10	45:50			1:31:40			2:17:30			3:03:20		4:00:22
9.15	46:15	57:21	1:26:02	1:32:30	1:54:42	2:01:16	2:18:45	2:23:23	2:52:03	3:05:00	3:49:24	4:02:32
9.20	46:40			1:33:20			2:20:00			3:06:40		4:04:44
9.30	47:30	58:54	1:28:21	1:35:00	1:57:48	2:04:33	2:22:30	2:27:15	2:56:42	3:10:00	3:55:36	4:09:06
9.40	48:20			1:36:40			2:25:00			3:13:20		4:13:28
9.45	48:45	1:00:27	1:30:41	1:37:30	2:00:54	2:07:49	2:26:15	2:31:08	3:01:21	3:15:00	4:01:48	4:15:33
9.50	49:10			1:38:20			2:27:30			3:16:40		4:17:50
10.00	50:00	1:02:00	1:33:00	1:40:00	2:04:00	2:11:06	2:30:00	2:35:00	3:06:00	3:20:00	4:08:00	4:22:13

Appendix 2

Extract from International Amateur Athletic Federation Rules

RULE 165
Road Races
1. The standard distances for men and women shall be 15km, 20km, Half-Marathon, 25km, 30km and Marathon (42.195km).
2. The races shall be run on made-up roads. However, when traffic or similar circumstances make it unsuitable, the course, duly marked, may be on a bicycle or footpath alongside the road, but not on soft ground such as grass verges or the like. The start and finish may be within an athletic arena.
Note: It is desirable to have a course with a single turning point, or, alternatively, a single circuit.
3. In events on roads the course shall be measured along the shortest possible route that a competitor could follow within the section of the road permitted for use in the race.
  The length of the course must not be less than the official distance for the event.
4. A competitor must retire at once from the race if ordered to do so by a member of the medical staff officially appointed and clearly identified by an armband.
5. The distance in kilometres on the route shall be displayed to all competitors.
6. Sponging/Drinking and Refreshment Stations.
  (a) Sponging/Drinking Stations – For all events of 10km or more, sponging/drinking stations may be provided at suitable intervals.
  (b) Refreshment Stations – For all events longer than 20km, refreshment stations shall be provided at approximately 5km and, thereafter, at approximately every 5km.
  In addition, sponging/drinking stations, where water only shall be supplied, shall be placed midway between the refreshment stations. Refreshments, which may be provided either by the organiser or the athlete, shall be made available at the stations nominated by the competitors. They shall be placed so that they are easily accessible to, or may be put in the hands of the competitors. A competitor who takes refreshment at a place other than the refreshment stations renders himself liable to disqualification.

NB. An extract from the IAAF Rules relating to cross-country running appears on page 54. The full IAAF Rules are contained in its annual handbook, obtainable from the IAAF at its headquarters, 3 Hans Crescent, Knightsbridge, London SW1X 0LN, England (Tel. London (01) 581–8771).

The Handbook of the AAA, which follows broadly the same rules as the IAAF for road and cross country for domestic competition, is obtainable from its offices at Edgbaston House, 3 Duchess Place, Hagley Road, Edgbaston, Birmingham B16 8NM, England (Tel. Birmingham (021) 456–4050).

Appendix 3 – Marathon: Records and Winners

The marathon is steeped in history, and this section records the names of the men and women who created that history, and who pushed back the frontiers of what was thought possible for the human body in terms of running endurance.

In chronological order, here are the world and UK 'best performances' (in view of the differing terrain of the courses, no official records are ratified for the marathon), the medallists in Olympic, World, European and Commonwealth Games marathons.

(N B: In accordance with current international ruling, times originally recorded to a tenth of a second have been rounded up to the nearest full second.)

World's Best Progression – Men

2:55.19	John Hayes (USA)	Windsor–Shepherd's Bush	24 July 1908
2:52.46	Robert Fowler (USA)	Yonkers, New York	1 Jan. 1909
2:46.53	James Clark (USA)	New York	12 Feb. 1909
2:46.05	Albert Raines (USA)	New York	8 May 1909
2:42.31	Fred Barrett (Gt Britain)	Windsor–Stamford Bridge	26 May 1909
2:38.17	Harry Green (Gt Britain)	Shepherd's Bush	12 May 1913
2:36.07	Alexis Ahlgren (Sweden)	Windsor–Stamford Bridge	31 May 1913
2:32.36	Hannes Kolehmainen (Finland)	Antwerp	22 Aug. 1920
2:29.02	Albert Michelsen (USA)	Port Chester	12 Oct. 1925
2:27.49	Fusashige Suzuki (Japan)	Tokyo	31 March 1935
2:26.44	Yasuo Ikenaka (Japan)	Tokyo	3 April 1935
2:26.42	Kitei Son (Japan)	Tokyo	3 Nov. 1935
2:25.39	Yun Bok Suh (Korea)	Boston	19 April 1947
2:20.43	Jim Peters (Gt Britain)	Windsor–Chiswick	14 June 1952
2:18.41	Jim Peters (Gt Britain)	Windsor–Chiswick	13 June 1953
2:18.35	Jim Peters (Gt Britain)	Turku	4 Oct. 1953
2:17.40	Jim Peters (Gt Britain)	Windsor–Chiswick	26 June 1954
2:15.17	Sergei Popov (USSR)	Stockholm	24 Aug. 1958
2:15.17	Abebe Bikila (Ethiopia)	Rome	10 Sep. 1960
2:15.16	Toru Terasawa (Japan)	Beppu	17 Feb. 1963
2:14.28	Buddy Edelen (USA)	Windsor–Chiswick	15 June 1963
2:13.55	Basil Heatley (Gt Britain)	Windsor–Chiswick	13 June 1964
2:12.12	Abebe Bikila (Ethiopia)	Tokyo	21 Oct. 1964
2:12.00	Morio Shigematsu (Japan)	Windsor–Chiswick	12 June 1965
2:09.37	Derek Clayton (Australia)	Fukuoka	3 Dec. 1967
2:08.34	Derek Clayton (Australia)	Antwerp	30 May 1969
2:08.18	Robert de Castella (Australia)	Fukuoka	6 Dec. 1981
2:08.05	Steve Jones (Gt Britain)	Chicago	21 Oct. 1984
2:07.12	Carlos Lopes (Portugal)	Rotterdam	20 April 1985
2:06.50	Belayneh Dinsamo (Ethiopia)	Rotterdam	17 April 1988

Appendix

World's Best Progression – Women

3:37.07	Merry Lepper (USA)	Culver City	14 Dec. 1963
3:27.45	Dale Greig (Gt Britain)	Ryde, Isle of Wight	23 May 1964
3:19.33	Millie Sampson (New Zealand)	Auckland	21 July 1964
3:15.22	Maureen Wilton (Canada)	Toronto	8 May 1967
3:07.26	Anni Pede-Erdkamp (West Germany)	Waldniel	16 Sep. 1967
3:02.53	Caroline Walker (USA)	Seaside, Oregon	28 Feb. 1970
3:01.42	Beth Bonner (USA)	Philadelphia	9 May 1971
3:00.35	Sara Berman (USA)	Brockton, Massachusetts	30 May 1971
2:55.22	Beth Bonner (USA)	New York	19 Sep. 1971
2:49.40	Cheryl Bridges (USA)	Culver City	5 Dec. 1971
2:46.36	Miki Gorman (USA)	Culver City	2 Dec. 1973
2:46.24	Chantal Langlace (France)	Neuf Brisach	27 Oct. 1974
2:43.54	Jackie Hansen (USA)	Culver City	1 Dec. 1974
2:42.24	Liane Winter (West Germany)	Boston	19 April 1975
2:40.16	Christa Vahlensieck (West Germany)	Dulmen	3 May 1975
2:38.19	Jackie Hansen (USA)	Eugene	12 Oct. 1975
2:35.16	Chantal Langlace (France)	San Sebastian	1 May 1977
2:34.48	Christa Vahlensieck (West Germany)	West Berlin	10 Sep. 1977
2:32.30	Grete Waitz (Norway)	New York	22 Oct. 1978
2:27.33	Grete Waitz (Norway)	New York	21 Oct. 1979
2:25.42	Grete Waitz (Norway)	New York	26 Oct. 1980
2:25.29	Grete Waitz (Norway)	London	17 April 1983
2:22.43	Joan Benoit (USA)	Boston	18 April 1983
2:21.06	Ingrid Kristiansen (Norway)	London	21 April 1985

UK Best Progression – Men

2:42.31	Fred Barrett	Windsor–Stamford Bridge	26 May 1909
2:38.17	Harry Green	Shepherd's Bush (track!)	12 May 1913
2:37.41	Arthur Mills	Windsor–Stamford Bridge	17 July 1920
2:35.59	Sam Ferris	Windsor–Stamford Bridge	30 May 1925
2:35.27	Sam Ferris	Liverpool	28 Sep. 1927
2:34.34	Harry Payne	Windsor–Stamford Bridge	6 July 1928
2:33.00	Sam Ferris	Liverpool	26 Sep. 1928
2:30.58	Harry Payne	Windsor–Stamford Bridge	5 July 1929
2:29.28	Jim Peters	Windsor–Chiswick	16 June 1951
2:20.43	Jim Peters	Windsor–Chiswick	14 June 1952
2:18.41	Jim Peters	Windsor–Chiswick	13 June 1953
2:18.35	Jim Peters	Turku	4 Oct. 1953
2:17.40	Jim Peters	Windsor–Chiswick	26 June 1954
2:14.43	Brian Kilby	Port Talbot	6 July 1963
2:13.55	Basil Heatley	Windsor–Chiswick	13 June 1964
2:13.45	Alastair Wood	Inverness–Forres	9 July 1966
2:12.17	Bill Adcocks	Karl Marx Stadt	19 May 1968
2:10.48	Bill Adcocks	Fukuoka	8 Dec. 1968
2:10.30	Ron Hill	Boston	20 April 1970
2:09.28	Ron Hill	Edinburgh	23 July 1970
2:09.12	Ian Thompson	Christchurch, New Zealand	31 Jan. 1974
2:09.08	Geoff Smith	New York	23 Oct. 1983
2:08.05	Steve Jones	Chicago	21 Oct. 1984
2:07.13	Steve Jones	Chicago	20 Oct. 1985

UK Best Progression – Women

3:27.45	Dale Greig	Ryde, Isle of Wight	23 May 1964
3:11.54	Anne Clarke	Guildford	19 Oct. 1975
3:07.47	Margaret Thompson	Korso, Finland	26 Oct. 1975
2:50.55	Christine Readdy	Feltham	16 April 1976
2:50.54	Rosemary Cox	Rugby	3 Sep. 1978
2:41.37	Joyce Smith	Sandbach	17 June 1979
2:41.03	Gillian Adams	Eugene	9 Sep. 1979
2:36.27	Joyce Smith	Waldniel, West Germany	22 Sep. 1979
2:33.32	Joyce Smith	Sandbach	22 June 1980
2:30.27	Joyce Smith	Tokyo	16 Nov. 1980
2:29.57	Joyce Smith	London	29 March 1981
2:29.43	Joyce Smith	London	9 May 1982
2:28.54	Priscilla Welch	Los Angeles	5 Aug. 1984
2:28.06	Sarah Rowell	London	21 April 1985
2:28.04	Veronique Marot	Chicago	20 Oct. 1985
2:26.51	Priscilla Welch	London	10 May 1987
2:25.56	Veronique Marot	London	23 April 1989

Olympic Marathon Medallists – men

	1	2	3
1896 Athens (40 km)	Spiridon Louis (Gre) 2:58.50	Harilaos Vasilakos (Gre) 3:06.03	Gyula Kellner (Hun) 3:06.35
1900 Paris (40.26 km)	Michel Theato (Fra) 2:59.45	Emile Champion (Fra) 3:04.17	Ernst Fast (Swe) 3:37.14
1904 St Louis (40 km)	Tom Hicks (USA) 3:28.53	Albert Corey (USA) 3:34.52	Arthur Newton (USA) 3:47.33
1908 London	Johnny Hayes (USA) 2:55.19	Charles Hefferon (USA) 2.56.06	Joseph Forshaw (USA) 2:57.11
1912 Stockholm (40.20 km)	Kenneth McArthur (SAf) 2:36.55	Chris Gitsham (SAf) 2:37.52	Gaston Strobina (USA) 2:38.43
1920 Antwerp (42.75 km)	Hannes Kolehmainen (Fin) 2:32.36	Juri Lossmann (Est) 2:32.49	Valerio Arri (Ita) 2:36.33
1924 Paris	Albin Stenroos (Fin) 2:41.23	Romeo Bertini (Ita) 2:47.20	Clarence DeMar (USA) 2:48.14
1928 Amsterdam	Boughera El Ouafi (Fra) 2:32.58	Manuel Plaza (Chile) 2:33.23	Martti Marttelin (Fin) 2:35.02
1932 Los Angeles	Juan Carlos Zabala (Arg) 2:31.36	Sam Ferris (GB) 2:31.55	Armas Toivonen (Fin) 2:32.12
1936 Berlin	Kitei Son (Jap) 2:29.20	Ernie Harper (GB) 2:31.24	Shoryu Nan (Jap) 2:31.42
1948 London	Delfo Cabrera (Arg) 2:34.52	Tom Richards (GB) 2:35.08	Etienne Gailly (Bel) 2:35.34
1952 Helsinki	Emil Zatopek (Cze) 2:23.04	Reinaldo Gorno (Arg) 2:25.35	Gustaf Jansson (Swe) 2:26.07
1956 Melbourne	Alain Mimoun (Fra) 2:25.00	Franjo Mihalic (Yug) 2:26.32	Veikko Karvonen (Fin) 2:27.47
1960 Rome	Abebe Bikila (Eth) 2:15.17	Rhadi ben Abdesselem (Mor) 2:15.42	Barry Magee (NZ) 2:17.19

Appendix

1964 Tokyo	1 Abebe Bikila (Eth) 2:12.12	2 Basil Heatley (GB) 2.16.20	3 Kokichi Tsuburaya (Jap) 2:16.23
1968 Mexico City	1 Mamo Wolde (Eth) 2:20.27	2 Kenji Kimihara (Jap) 2:23.31	3 Mike Ryan (NZ) 2:23.45
1972 Munich	1 Frank Shorter (USA) 2:12.20	2 Karel Lismont (Bel) 2:14.32	3 Mamo Wolde (Eth) 2:15.09
1976 Montreal	1 Waldemar Cierpinski (EG) 2:09.55	2 Frank Shorter (USA) 2:10.46	3 Karel Lismont (Bel) 2:11.13
1980 Moscow	1 Waldemar Cierpinski (EG) 2:11.03	2 Gerard Nijboer (Hol) 2:11.20	3 Setymkul Dzhumanazarov (USSR) 2:11.35
1984 Los Angeles	1 Carlos Lopes (Por) 2:09.21	2 John Treacy (Ire) 2:09.56	3 Charlie Spedding (GB) 2:09.58
1988 Seoul	1 Gelindo Bordin (Ita) 2:10.32	2 Douglas Wakiihuru (Ken) 2:10.47	3 Ahmed Salah (Dji) 2:10.59
1992 Barcelona	1	2	3

Women

1984 Los Angeles	1 Joan Benoit (USA) 2:24.52	2 Grete Waitz (Nor) 2:26.18	3 Rosa Mota (Por) 2:26.57
1988 Seoul	1 Rosa Mota (Por) 2:25.40	2 Lisa Martin (Aus) 2:25.53	3 Katrin Dörre (EG) 2:26.21
1992 Barcelona	1	2	3

World Championship Medallists – men

1983 Helsinki	1 Robert de Castella (Aus) 2:10.03	2 Kebede Balcha (Eth) 2:10.27	3 Waldemar Cierpinski (EG) 2:10.37
1987 Rome	1 Douglas Wakiihuru (Ken) 2:11.48	2 Ahmed Salah (Dji) 2:12.30	3 Gelindo Bordin (Ita) 2:12.40
1991 Tokyo	1	2	3

Women

1983 Helsinki	1 Grete Waitz (Nor) 2:28.09	2 Marianne Dickerson (USA) 2:31.09	3 Raisa Smekhnova (USSR) 2:31.13
1987 Rome	1 Rosa Mota (Por) 2:25.17	2 Zoya Ivanova (USSR) 2:32.38	3 Jocelyne Villeton (Fra) 2:32.53
1991 Tokyo	1	2	3

Marathon, Cross Country and Road Running

European Championship Medallists – men

1934 Turin	1 Armas Toivonen (Fin) 2:52.29	2 Thore Enochsson (Swe) 2:54.36	3 Aurelio Genghini (Ita) 2:55.04
1938 Paris	1 Vaino Muinonen (Fin) 2:37.29	2 Squire Yarrow (GB) 2:39.03	3 Henry Palme (Swe) 2:42.14
1946 Oslo	1 Mikko Hietanen (Fin) 2:24.55	2 Vaino Muionen (Fin) 2:26.08	3 Yakov Punko (USSR) 2:26.21
1950 Brussels	1 Jack Holden (GB) 2:32.14	2 Veikko Karvonen (Fin) 2:32.46	3 Feodosiy Vanin (USSR) 2.33.47
1954 Berne	1 Veikko Karvonen (Fin) 2:24.52	2 Boris Grishayev (USSR) 2:24.56	3 Ivan Filin (USSR) 2:25.27
1958 Stockholm	1 Sergei Popov (USSR) 2:15.17	2 Ivan Filin (USSR) 2:20.51	3 Fred Norris (GB) 2:21.15
1962 Belgrade	1 Brian Kilby (GB) 2:23.19	2 Aurele Vandendriessche (Bel) 2:24.02	3 Viktor Baikov (USSR) 2:24.20
1966 Budapest	1 Jim Hogan (GB) 2:20.05	2 Aurele Vandendriessche (Bel) 2:21.44	3 Gyula Toth (Hun) 2:22.02
1969 Athens	1 Ron Hill (GB) 2:16.48	2 Gaston Roelants (Bel) 2:17.23	3 Jim Alder (GB) 2:19.06
1971 Helsinki	1 Karel Lismont (Bel) 2:13.09	2 Trevor Wright (GB) 2:14.00	3 Ron Hill (GB) 2:14.35
1974 Rome	1 Ian Thompson (GB) 2:13.19	2 Eckhard Lesse (EG) 2:14.58	3 Gaston Roelants (Bel) 2:16.30
1978 Prague	1 Leonid Moseyev (USSR) 2:11.58	2 Nikolay Penzin (USSR) 2:11.59	3 Karel Lismont (Bel) 2:12.08
1982 Athens	1 Gerard Nijboer (Hol) 2:15.17	2 Armand Parmentier (Bel) 2:15.40	3 Karel Lismont (Bel) 2:16.07
1986 Stuttgart	1 Gelindo Bordin (Ita) 2:10.54	2 Orlando Pizzolato (Ita) 2:10.57	3 Herbert Steffny (WG) 2:11.30
1990 Split	1 Gelindo Bordin (Ita) 2:14.02	2 Pier-Giovanni Poli (Ita) 2:14.55	3 Dominique Chauvelier (Fra) 2:15.20
1994 Helsinki	1	2	3

Women

1982 Athens	1 Rosa Mota (Por) 2:36.04	2 Laura Fogli (Ita) 2:36.29	3 Ingrid Kristiansen (Nor) 2:36.39
1986 Stuttgart	1 Rosa Mota (Por) 2:28.38	2 Laura Fogli (Ita) 2:32.52	3 Yekaterina Khramenkova (USSR) 2:34.18
1990 Split	1 Rosa Mota (Por) 2:31.27	2 Valentina Yegerova (USSR) 2:31.32	3 Maria Lelut (Fra) 2:35.51
1994 Helsinki	1	2	3

Commonwealth Games Medallists – men

1930 Hamilton, Can	1 Dunky Wright (Sco) 2:43.43	2 Sam Ferris (Eng) (880 yd down)	3 John Miles (Can) (300 yd down)
1934 London	1 Harold Webster (Can) 2:40.36	2 Donald McNab Robertson (Sco) 2:45.08	3 Dunky Wright (Sco) 2:56.20
1938 Sydney	1 Johannes Coleman (SAf) 2:30.50	2 Bert Norris (Eng) 2:37.57	3 Henry Gibson (SAf) 2:38.20

212

1950 Auckland	1 Jack Holden (Eng) 2:32.57	2	Sydney Luyt (SAf) 2:37.03	3	Jack Clarke (NZ) 2:39.27
1954 Vancouver	1 Joe McGhee (Sco) 2:39.36	2	Jackie Mekler (SAf) 2:40.57	3	Johannes Barnard (SAf) 2:22.58
1958 Cardiff	1 Dave Power (Aus) 2:22.46	2	Johannes Barnard (SAf) 2:22.58	3	Peter Wilkinson (Eng) 2:24.42
1962 Perth, Aus	1 Brian Kilby (Eng) 2:21.17	2	Dave Power (Aus) 2:22.16	3	Rodney Bonella (Aus) 2:24.07
1966 Kingston, Jam	1 Jim Alder (Sco) 2:22.08	2	Bill Adcocks (Eng) 2:22.13	3	Mike Ryan (NZ) 2:27.59
1970 Edinburgh	1 Ron Hill (Eng) 2:09.28	2	Jim Alder (Sco) 2:12.04	3	Don Faircloth (Eng) 2:12.19
1974 Christchurch, NZ	1 Ian Thompson (Eng) 2:09.12	2	Jack Foster (NZ) 2:11.19	3	Richard Mabuza (Swaz) 2:12.55
1978 Edmonton, Can	1 Gidamis Shahanga (Tan) 2:15.40	2	Jerome Drayton (Can) 2:16.14	3	Paul Bannon (Can) 2:16.52
1982 Brisbane	1 Robert de Castella (Aus) 2:09.18	2	Juma Ikanga (Tan) 2:09.30	3	Mike Gratton (Eng) 2:12.06
1986 Edinburgh	1 Robert de Castella (Aus) 2:10.15	2	Dave Edge (Can) 2:11.08	3	Steve Moneghetti (Aus) 2:11.18
1990 Auckland	1 Douglas Wakiihuri (Ken) 2:10.27	2	Steve Moneghetti (Aus) 2:10.34	3	Simon Naali (Tan) 2:10.38
1994 Victoria, Can	1	2		3	

Women

1986 Edinburgh	1 Lisa Martin (Aus) 2:26.07	2	Lorraine Moller (NZ) 2:28.17	3	Odette Lapierre (Can) 2:31.48
1990 Auckland	1 Lisa Martin (Aus) 2:25.28	2	Tani Ruckle (Aus) 2:33.15	3	Angela Pain (Eng) 2:36.35
1994 Victoria, Can					

Appendix 4 – Cross Country

World Cross Country Champions

Year	Venue	Winner and Nationality	Team Champions
Senior Men			
1903	(Glasgow)	Alf Shrubb (Eng)	England
1904	(St Helens)	Alf Shrubb (Eng)	England
1905	(Dublin)	Albert Aldridge (Eng)	England
1906	(Caerleon)	Charles Straw (Eng)	England
1907	(Glasgow)	Alfred Underwood (Eng)	England
1908	(Paris)	Arthur Robertson (Eng)	England
1909	(Derby)	Edward Wood (Eng)	England
1910	(Belfast)	Edward Wood (Eng)	England
1911	(Caerleon)	Jean Bouin (Fra)	England
1912	(Edinburgh)	Jean Bouin (Fra)	England
1913	(Paris)	Jean Bouin (Fra)	England

1914	(Chesham)	Arthur Nichols (Eng)	England
1915–19 Not held			
1920	(Belfast)	James Wilson (Sco)	England
1921	(Newport)	Walter Freeman (Eng)	England
1922	(Glasgow)	Joseph Guillemot (Fra)	France
1923	(Paris)	Charles Blewitt (Eng)	France
1924	(Gosforth)	William Cotterell (Eng)	England
1925	(Dublin)	Jack Webster (Eng)	England
1926	(Brussels)	Ernest Harper (Eng)	France
1927	(Caerleon)	Lewis Payne (Eng)	France
1928	(Ayr)	Harold Eckersley (Eng)	France
1929	(Paris)	William Cotterell (Eng)	France
1930	(Leamington)	Tom Evenson (Eng)	England
1931	(Dublin)	Tim Smythe (Ire)	England
1932	(Brussels)	Tom Evenson (Eng)	England
1933	(Caerleon)	Jack Holden (Eng)	England
1934	(Ayr)	Jack Holden (Eng)	England
1935	(Paris)	Jack Holden (Eng)	England
1936	(Blackpool)	William Eaton (Eng)	England
1937	(Brussels)	James Flockhart (Scot)	England
1938	(Belfast)	Jack Emery (Eng)	England
1939	(Cardiff)	Jack Holden (Eng)	England
1940–45 Not Held			
1946	(Ayr)	Raphael Pujazon (Fra)	France
1947	(Paris)	Raphael Pujazon (Fra)	France
1948	(Reading)	John Doms (Bel)	Belgium
1949	(Dublin)	Alain Mimoun (Fra)	France
1950	(Brussels)	Lucien Theys (Bel)	France
1951	(Caerleon)	Geoff Saunders (Eng)	England
1952	(Hamilton)	Alain Mimoun (Fra)	France
1953	(Paris)	Franjo Mihalic (Yug)	England
1954	(Birmingham)	Alain Mimoun (Fra)	England
1955	(San Sebastian)	Frank Sando (Eng)	England
1956	(Belfast)	Alain Mimoun (Fra)	France
1957	(Waregem)	Frank Sando (Eng)	Belgium
1958	(Cardiff)	Stan Eldon (Eng)	England
1959	(Lisbon)	Fred Norris (Eng)	England
1960	(Glasgow)	Rhadi ben Abdesselem (Mor)	England
1961	(Nantes)	Basil Heatley (Eng)	Belgium
1962	(Sheffield)	Gaston Roelants (Bel)	England
1963	(San Sebastian)	Roy Fowler (Eng)	Belgium
1964	(Dublin)	Francisco Arizmendi (Spa)	England
1965	(Ostend)	Jean Fayolle (Fra)	England
1966	(Rabat)	Assou El Ghazi (Mor)	England
1967	(Barry)	Gaston Roelants (Bel)	England
1968	(Tunis)	Mohammed Gammoudi (Tun)	England
1969	(Clydebank)	Gaston Roelants (Bel)	England
1970	(Vichy)	Mike Tagg (Eng)	England
1971	(San Sebastian)	Dave Bedford (Eng)	England
1972	(Cambridge)	Gaston Roelants (Bel)	England
1973	(Waregem)	Pekka Paivarinta (Fin)	Belgium
1974	(Monza)	Erik de Beck (Bel)	Belgium
1975	(Rabat)	Ian Stewart (Sco)	New Zealand
1976	(Chepstow)	Carlos Lopes (Por)	England
1977	(Dusseldorf)	Leon Schots (Bel)	Belgium

1978	(Glasgow)	John Treacy (Ire)	France
1979	(Limerick)	John Treacy (Ire)	England
1980	(Paris)	Craig Virgin (USA)	England
1981	(Madrid)	Craig Virgin (USA)	Ethiopia
1982	(Rome)	Mohamed Kedir (Eth)	Ethiopia
1983	(Gateshead)	Bekele Debele (Eth)	Ethiopia
1984	(New York)	Carlos Lopes (Por)	Ethiopia
1985	(Lisbon)	Carlos Lopes (Por)	Ethiopia
1986	(Neuchatel)	John Ngugi (Ken)	Kenya
1987	(Warsaw)	John Ngugi (Ken)	Kenya
1988	(Auckland)	John Ngugi (Ken)	Kenya
1989	(Stavanger)	John Ngugi (Ken)	Kenya
1990	(Aix-les-Bains)	Khalid Skah (Mor)	Kenya
1991	(Antwerp)	Khalid Skah (Mor)	Kenya
1992	(Boston, Mass)		

Junior Men

(Under IAAF Rules, Junior Men are those who remain under twenty years of age throughout the calendar year of competition)

1961	(Nantes)	Colin Robinson (Eng)	England
1962	(Sheffield)	Abdesselem Bouchta (Mor)	England
1963	(San Sebastian)*	Declared null and void	
1964	(Dublin)	Ian McCafferty (Sco)	England
1965	(Ostend)	Johnny Dumon (Bel)	Belgium
1966	(Rabat)	Mike Tagg (Eng)	England
1967	(Barry)	Eddie Knox (Sco)	England
1968	(Tunis)	John Bednarski (Eng)	England
1969	(Clydebank)	Dave Bedford (Eng)	England
1970	(Vichy)	John Hartnett (Ire)	England
1971	(San Sebastian)	Nick Rose (Eng)	England
1972	(Cambridge)	Aldo Tomasini (Ita)	Italy
1973	(Waregem)	Jim Brown (Sco)	Spain
1974	(Monza)	Rich Kimball (USA)	USA
1975	(Rabat)	Bobby Thomas (USA)	USA
1976	(Chepstow)	Eric Hulst (USA)	USA
1977	(Dusseldorf)	Thom Hunt (USA)	USA
1978	(Glasgow)	Mick Morton (Eng)	England
1979	(Limerick)	Eddy de Pauw (Bel)	Spain
1980	(Paris)	Jorge Garcia (Spa)	USSR
1981	(Madrid)	Mohamed Chouri (Tun)	USA
1982	(Rome)	Zurubachew Gelaw (Eth)	Ethiopia
1983	(Gateshead)	Fesseha Abebe (Eth)	Ethiopia
1984	(New York)	Pedro Casacuberta (Spa)	Ethiopia
1985	(Lisbon)	Kimeli Kipkemboi (Ken)	Ethiopia
1986	(Neuchatel)	Melese Feysia (Eth)	Ethiopia
1987	(Warsaw)	Wilfred Kirochi (Ken)	Ethiopia
1988	(Auckland)	Wilfred Kirochi (Ken)	Kenya
1989	(Stavanger)	Addis Abebe (Eth)	Kenya
1990	(Aix-les Bains)	Kibiego Kororia (Ken)	Kenya
1991	(Antwerp)	Andrew Tambu (Tan)	Kenya
1992	(Boston, Mass)		

Marathon, Cross Country and Road Running

Women

1967	(Barry)	Doris Brown (USA)	England
1968	(Blackburn)	Doris Brown (USA)	USA
1969	(Clydebank)	Doris Brown (USA)	USA
1970	(Vichy)*	Paola Pigni (Ita)	Holland
	(Frederick, Md)*	Doris Brown (USA)	England
1971	(San Sebastian)	Doris Brown (USA)	England
1972	(Cambridge)	Joyce Smith (Eng)	England
1973	(Waregem)	Paola Cacchi (Ita)	England
1974	(Monza)	Paola Cacchi (Ita)	England
1975	(Rabat)	Julie Brown (USA)	USA
1976	(Chepstow)	Carmen Valero (Spa)	USSR
1977	(Dusseldorf)	Carmen Valero (Spa)	USSR
1978	(Glasgow)	Grete Waitz (Nor)	Rumania
1979	(Limerick)	Grete Waitz (Nor)	USA
1980	(Paris)	Grete Waitz (Nor)	USSR
1981	(Madrid)	Grete Waitz (Nor)	USSR
1982	(Rome)	Maricica Puica (Rum)	USSR
1983	(Gateshead)	Grete Waitz (Nor)	USA
1984	(New York)	Maricica Puica (Rum)	USA
1985	(Lisbon)	Zola Budd (Eng)	USA
1986	(Neuchatel)	Zola Budd (Eng)	England
1987	(Warsaw)	Annette Sergent (Fra)	USA
1988	(Auckland)	Ingrid Kristiansen (Nor)	USSR
1989	(Stavenger)	Annette Sergent (Fra)	USSR
1990	(Aix-les-Bains)	Lynn Jennings (USA)	USSR
1991	(Antwerp)	Lynn Jennings (USA)	Kenya
1992	(Boston, Mass)		

(*In 1970, before the event came under IAAF patronage, two separate races were held, both of which have claims to be considered as the 'International' of that year).

Junior Women

(*Under IAAF Rules, Junior Women are those who remain under twenty years of age throughout the calendar year of competition*).

1989	(Stavanger)	Malin Everloef (Swe)	Kenya
1990	(Aix-les-Bains)	Liu Shixiang (Chn)	Kenya
1991	(Antwerp)	Lydia Cheromei (Ken)	Kenya
1992	(Boston, Mass)		

English Men's Senior National Cross Country Champions

Year Venue	Winner and club	Team winners
1876 (Epping)	Race declared void	
1877 (Roehampton)	Percy Stenning (Thames H and H)	Thames H and H
1878 (Roehampton)	Percy Stenning (Thames H and H)	Spartan H
1879 (Roehampton)	Percy Stenning (Thames H and H)	Thames H and H
1880 (Roehampton)	Percy Stenning (Thames H and H)	Birchfield H
1881 (Roehampton)	George Dunning (Clapton B)	Moseley H
1882 (Roehampton)	Walter George (Moseley H)	Moseley H
1883 (Roehampton)	George Dunning (Clapton B)	Moseley H
1884 (Four Oaks, Sutton Coldfield)	Walter George (Moseley H)	Moseley H
1885 (Manchester)	William Snook (Birchfield H)	Liverpool H
1886 (Croydon)	J 'Flyer' Hickman (Coventry Godiva H)	Birchfield H

216

1887 (Four Oaks, Sutton Coldfield)	J 'Flyer' Hickman (Coventry Godiva H)	Birchfield H
1888 (Manchester)	Edward Parry (Salford H)	Birchfield H
1889 (Kempton)	Edward Parry (Salford H)	Salford H
1890 (Sutton Coldfield)	Edward Parry (Salford H)	Salford H
1891 (Rock Ferry)	James Kibblewhite (Spartan H)	Birchfield H
1892 (Ockham)	Herbert Heath (South London H)	Birchfield H and Essex B (tie)
1893 (Redditch)	Herbert Heath (South London H)	Essex B
1894 (Blackpool)	George Crossland (Salford H)	Salford H
1895 (Wembley)	Steve Cottrill (Thames Valley H)	Birchfield H
1896 (Water Orton)	George Crossland (Manchester H)	Salford H
1897 (Trafford Park)	Syd Robinson (Northampton and CAC)	Salford H and Manchester H (tie)
1898 (Horton, Northants)	Syd Robinson (Northampton and CAC)	Salford H
1899 (Wembley)	Charles Bennett (Finchley H)	Highgate H
1900 (Rotherham)	Charles Bennett (Finchley H)	Finchley H
1901 (Leicester)	Alfred Shrubb (South London H)	Essex B
1902 (Lingfield)	Alfred Shrubb (South London H)	Highgate H
1903 (Haydock)	Alfred Shrubb (South London H)	Birchfield H
1904 (Wolverhampton)	Alfred Shrubb (South London H)	Highgate H
1905 (Lingfield)	Albert Aldridge (Highgate H)	Highgate H
1906 (Haydock)	Charles Straw (Sutton H and AC)	Sutton H
1907 (Colwall Park)	George Pearce (Highgate H)	Birchfield H
1908 (Newbury)	Arthur Robertson (Birchfield H)	Hallamshire H
1909 (Haydock)	James Murphy (Hallamshire H)	Birchfield H
1910 (Derby)	Fred Neaves (Surrey AC)	Hallamshire H
1911 (Taplow)	Fred Hibbins (Thrapston H and AC)	Hallamshire H
1912 (Haydock)	Fred Hibbins (Thrapston H and AC)	Hallamshire H
1913 (Wolverhampton)	Ernest Glover (Hallamshire H)	Birchfield H
1914 (Chesham)	Charlie Ruffell (Highgate H)	Surrey AC
1915–1919 Not held		
1920 (Windsor Great Pk)	Joseph Guillemot (France)* Charles Clibbon (Birchfield H)	Birchfield H
1921 (Doncaster)	Walter Freeman (Birchfield H)	Birchfield H
1922 (Hereford)	Joseph Guillemot (France)* Harold Eckersley (Warrington AC)	Birchfield H
1923 (Beaconsfield)	Charles Blewitt (Birchfield H)	Birchfield H
1924 (Doncaster)	Cpl William Cotterell (R C Signals)	Birchfield H
1925 (Hereford)	Cpl William Cotterell (R C Signals)	Birchfield H
1926 (Wolverton)	Jack Webster (Birchfield H)	Birchfield H
1927 (Crewe)	Ernest Harper (Hallamshire H)	Hallamshire H
1928 (Leamington)	Jack Webster (Birchfield H)	Birchfield H
1929 (Beaconsfield)	Ernest Harper (Hallamshire H)	Birchfield H
1930 (Sheffield)	Wally Howard (Kettering Town H)	Birchfield H
1931 (Kettering)	Jack Potts (Saltwell H)	Birchfield H
1932 (Wolverton)	Alec Burns (Elswick H)	Birchfield H
1933 (Alderley Edge)	Tom Evenson (Salford H)	Birchfield H
1934 (Himley Park)	Sammy Dodd (Wirral AC)	Birchfield H
1935 (Beaconsfield)	Frank Close (Reading AC)	Belgrave H
1936 (Alderley Edge)	Jack Potts (Saltwell H)	Birchfield H
1937 (Stratford-upon-Avon)	Herbert Clark (York H)	Birchfield H
1938 (Reading)	Jack Holden (Tipton H)	Mitcham AC
1939 (Worsley)	Jack Holden (Tipton H)	Belgrave H
1940–45 Not held		
1946 (Leamington Spa)	Jack Holden (Tipton H)	Belgrave H

1947 (Apsley)	Archie Robertson (Reading AC)	Sutton H
1948 (Sheffield)	Sydney Wooderson (Blackheath H)	Belgrave H
1949 (Bromford Bridge, Birmingham)	Frank Aaron (Leeds St Mark's H)	Sutton H
1950 (Aylesbury)	Frank Aaron (Leeds St Mark's H)	Sutton H
1951 (Richmond, Yorks)	Frank Aaron (Leeds St Mark's H)	Sutton H
1952 (Great Barr, Birmingham)	Walter Hesketh (Manchester A & CC)	Victoria Park AAC
1953 (Caversham Park, Reading)	Gordon Pirie (South London H)	Birchfield H
1954 (Arrowe Park, Birkenhead)	Gordon Pirie (South London H)	Bolton United H
1955 (RAF Cardington, Beds)	Gordon Pirie (South London H)	South London H
1956 (Warwick)	Ken Norris (Thames Valley H)	Sheffield United H
1957 (Parliament Hill, London)	Frank Sando (Aylesford PMAC)	South London H
1958 (Arrowe Park, Birkenhead)	Alan Perkins (Ilford AC)	South London H
1959 (Fletton, Peterborough)	Fred Norris (Bolton United H)	Sheffield United H
1960 (Dartmouth Park, West Bromwich)	Basil Heatley (Coventry Godiva H)	Derby and CAC
1961 (Parliament Hill, London)	Basil Heatley (Coventry Godiva H)	Derby and CAC
1962 (Stanley Park, Blackpool)	Gerry North (Blackpool and Flyde & AC)	Derby and CAC
1963 (Coldhams Common Cambridge)	Basil Heatley (Coventry Godiva H)	Coventry GH
1964 (Western Park, Leicester)	Mel Batty (Thurrock H)	Portsmouth AC
1965 (Parliament Hill, London)	Mel Batty (Thurrock H)	Portsmouth AC
1966 (Graves Park, Sheffield)	Ron Hill (Bolton United H)	North Staffs and SHAC
1967 (Agricultural Showground Norwich)	Dick Taylor (Coventry Godiva H)	Portsmouth AC
1968 (Sutton Park, Sutton Coldfield)	Ron Hill (Bolton United H)	Coventry Godiva H
1969 (Parliament Hill, London)	Mike Tagg (Norfolk Gazelles)	Tipton H
1970 (Agricultural Showground, Blackpool)	Trevor Wright (Hallamshire H)	City of Stoke AC
1971 (Agricultural Showground, Norwich)	Dave Bedford (Shaftesbury H)	Shettleston H
1972 (Sutton Park, Sutton Coldfield)	Malcolm Thomas (Thames Valley H)	Tipton H
1973 (Parliament Hill, London)	Rod Dixon (New Zealand)* Dave Bedford (Shaftesbury H)	Gateshead H
1974 (Graves Park, Sheffield)	David Black (Small Heath H)	Derby and CAC
1975 (Stopsley Park, Luton)	Tony Simmons (Luton United H)	Gateshead H
1976 (Western Park, Leicester)	Bernie Ford (Aldershot, Farnham and DAC)	Gateshead H
1977 (Parliament Hill, London)	Brendan Foster (Gateshead H)	Gateshead H
1978 (Roundhay Park, Leeds)	Bernie Ford (Aldershot, Farnham and DAC)	Tipton H
1979 (Stopsley Park, Luton)	Mike McLeod (Elswick H)	Gateshead H
1980 (Western Park, Leicester)	Nick Rose (Bristol AC)	Tipton H
1981 (Parliament Hill, London)	Julian Goater (Shaftesbury H)	Tipton H
1982 (Roundhay Park, Leeds)	Dave Clarke (Hercules-Wimbledon AC)	Tipton H
1983 (Stopsley Park, Luton)	Tim Hutchings (Crawley AC)	Aldershot, F and DAC
1984 (Newark Showground)	Eamonn Martin (Basildon AAC)	Aldershot, F and DAC
1985 (Campbell Park, Milton Keynes)	Dave Lewis (Rossendale H and AC)	Aldershot, F and DAC
1986 (Town Moor, Newcastle)	Tim Hutchings (Crawley AC)	Tipton H
1987 (Stopsley Park, Luton)	Dave Clarke (Hercules-Wimbledon AC)	Gateshead H
1988 (Newark Showground)	Dave Clarke (Hercules-Wimbledon AC)	Birchfield H
1989 (Nonsuch Park, Cheam)	Dave Lewis (Rossendale HAC)	Tipton H
1990 (Roundhay Park, Leeds)	Richard Nerurkar (Bingley)	Valli H
1991 (Stopsley Park, Luton)	Richard Nerurkar (Bingley)	Bingley H

(*denotes actual race winner was a guest, ineligible for title)

English Women's Senior National Cross Country Champions

Year	Venue	Winner and club	Team winners
1927	(Luton)	Anne Williams (Littlehampton AC)	Middlesex LAC
1928	(Chigwell Row)	Lilian Styles (Littlehampton AC)	Middlesex LAC and LOAC tie
1929	( )	Lilian Styles (Littlehampton AC)	Middlesex LAC
1930	( )	Lilian Styles (Littlehampton AC)	Westbury H
1931	(Epsom)	Gladys Lunn (Birchfield HLS)	London Olympiades AC
1932	(Coventry)	Gladys Lunn (Birchfield HLS)	Birchfield HLS
1933	(Warwick)	Lilian Styles (Haywards Heath LAC)	Airedale H
1934	(Kettering)	Lilian Styles (London Olympiades AC)	London Olympiades
1935	(Birmingham)	Nellie Halstead (Bury & RAC)	London Olympiades AC
1936	(Ilford)	Nellie Halstead (Bury & RAC)	Small Heath H
1937	(Perry, Barr, Birmingham)	Lilian Styles (London Olympiades AC)	Birchfield HLS
1938	(Luton)	Evelyne Forster (Civil Service LAC)	Birchfield HLS
1939	(Rugby)	Evelyne Forster (Civil Service LAC)	Birchfield HLS
1940–45 Not held			
1946	(Cheltenham)	P. Sandall (Birchfield HLS)	Birchfield HLS
1947	(Oxford)	R. Wright (St Gregory's, Chelt)	Birchfield HLS
1948	(Sutton Coldfield);	Ivy Kibbler (Birchfield HLS)	Birchfield HLS
1949	(Worsley)	E. Johnson (Airedale H)	Birchfield HLS
1950	(Parliament Hill, London)	Avery Gibson (North Shields)	Birchfield HLS
1951	(Tadcaster)	Phyllis Green (Ilford AC)	Ilford AC
1952	(Birmingham)	Phyllis Green (Ilford AC)	Ilford AC
1953	(Woodgate)	Diane Leather (Birchfield HLS)	Birchfield HLS
1954	(Aylesbury)	Diane Leather (Birchfield HLS)	Birchfield HLS
1955	(Leeds)	Diane Leather (Birchfield HLS)	Ilford AC
1956	(Sutton Coldfield)	Diane Leather (Birchfield HLS)	Ilford AC
1957	(Enfield)	June Bridgland (Southampton AAC)	Ilford AC
1958	(Winton)	Roma Ashby (Coventry Godiva H)	Highgate H
1959	(Great Barr, Birmingham)	Joyce Byatt (Hampstead H)	London Olympiades AC
1960	(Morden)	Joyce Smith (Hampstead H)	Ilford AC
1961	(Sheffield)	Roma Ashby (Coventry Godiva H)	London Olympiades AC
1962	(Wolverhampton)	Roma Ashby (Coventry Godiva H)	London Olympiades AC
1963	(Richmond)	Madeleine Ibbotson (Longwood LAC)	Mitcham AC
1964	(Bury)	Madeleine Ibbotson (Longwood LAC)	Bury and Radcliffe AC
1965	(Birmingham)	Pam Davies (Selsonia LAC)	Maryhill LAC
1966	(Oxhey)	Pam Davies (Selsonia LAC)	Maryhill LAC
1967	(Blackburn)	Pam Davies (Selsonia LAC)	Barnet & DAC
1968	(Coventry)	Pam Davies (Selsonia LAC)	Cambridge H
1969	(Aldershot)	Rita Lincoln (Essex LAC)	Barnet & DAC
1970	(Blackburn)	Rita Lincoln (Essex LAC)	Cambridge H
1971	(Wolverhampton)	Rita Lincoln (Essex LAC)	Coventry Godiva H
1972	(Keep Hill, High Wycombe)	Rita Lincoln (Essex LAC)	Cambridge H
1973	(Rawtenstall)	Joyce Smith (Barnet & DAC)	Cambridge H
1974	(Leicester)	Rita Ridley (Essex LAC)	Barnet and DAC

1975 (Parliament Hill, London)	Deirdre Nagel (Eire)*	
	Christine Tranter (Stretford AC)	Cambridge H
1976 (Blackburn)	Ann Ford (Feltham AC)	London
		Olympiades AC
1977 (Stoke on Trent)	Glynis Penny (Cambridge H)	Sale H
1978 (Hughenden Park, High Wycombe)	Mary Stewart (Birchfield H)	Sale H
1979 (New Town Park, Runcorn)	Kath Binns (Sale H)	Aldershot, F and DAC
1980 (Hagley Park School, Rugeley)	Ruth Smeeth (Aldershot, F DAC)	Birchfield HLS
1981 (University of Essex, Colchester)	Wendy Smith (Boro of Hounslow AC)	Sale H
1982 (Carlisle Racecourse)	Paula Fudge (Boro of Hounslow AC)	Sale H
1983 (Lammas Field, Warwick Racecourse)	Christine Benning (Southampton and EAC)	Sale H
1984 (Knebworth Park, Herts)	Jane Furniss (Sheffield AC)	Aldershot, F and DAC
1985 (Arrowe Park, Birkenhead)	Angela Tooby (Cardiff AAC)	Crawley AC
1986 (Western Park, Leicester)	Carole Bradford (Clevedon AC)	Sale H
1987 (Footscray Meadows, Bexley)	Jane Shields (Sheffield AC)	Sale H
1988 (Roundhay Park, Leeds)	Helen Titterington (Leicester CAC)	Birchfield H
1989 (Birmingham)	Angie Pain (Leeds City AC)	Parkside AC
1990 (Rickmansworth)	Andrea Whitcombe (Parkside)	Parkside AC
1991 (Arrowe Park, Birkenhead)	Andrea Whitcombe (Parkside)	Parkside AC

(*denotes actual race winner was a guest, ineligible for title)
(Benning nee Tranter; Ridley nee Lincoln; J. Smith nee Byatt; W. Sly nee Smith; Shields nee Furniss)

INDEX